THE SINGING FLAME

ERNIE O'MALLEY

THE SINGING FLAME

ANVIL BOOKS LIMITED

First published in Ireland 1978
by Anvil Books Ltd.
90 Lower Baggot Street, Dublin 2

Paperback Edition May 1978

© 1978 by Cormac K. H. O'Malley

Printed in Ireland by
Cahill (1976) Limited.

TO IRELAND THE EVER-LIVING
AND HER DEAD SONS

ABBREVIATIONS

C-in-C	Commander-in-Chief
IRA	Irish Republican Army
IRA STAFF	
CS	Chief of Staff
ACS	Assistant Chief of Staff
QMG	Quartermaster-General
DI	Director of Intelligence
DO	Director of Organization
CID	Criminal Investigation Department
IRB	Irish Republican Brotherhood
MD	Minister for Defence
OC	Officer Commanding
RIC	Royal Irish Constabulary

An outline of reasons for the use of certain capital letters may be useful. Please note that when East Limerick, for instance, is capitalized, this refers to the Brigade (IRA) and not to the geographical location which would be given as east Limerick. Similarly see for South Dublin, north Tipperary and the other brigades and areas.

When specified, the higher military ranks and formations are given capital letters, such as the Brigadier, the Divisional Adjutant, the First Southern Division, the Northern and Eastern Command, but battalions, companies, sections and garrisons, together with their officers, have not usually been capitalized.

A distinction has been made between Headquarters and headquarters, between Staff and staff. While headquarters refers to any localized site, Headquarters always means the GHQ centres of operations. Thus, whereas there is a garrison staff, or staff officers, meaning officers in general attached to those positions, the term Headquarters Staff, or Staff, is used only for the top-ranking members of GHQ.

CONTENTS

INTRODUCTION

ERNEST BERNARD O'MALLEY was born in his parents' house on the main street of Castlebar, Co. Mayo, on 26 May 1898.

He was the second child and second son of Luke and Marion (née Kearney) Malley. Two daughters and seven more sons were to complete the family. About 1906 they moved to Dublin, where his father became a civil servant, and where Ernie attended the O'Connell School and did well enough to win a scholarship to University College Dublin in the autumn of 1915, for the study of medicine.

Early days of his childhood and youth are described in his first book, *On Another Man's Wound,* leading to Easter Week in 1916 when he became caught up in the cause of Irish nationalism for the first time. Then the book tells in detail of his life during the hectic, dangerous years when some of the Irish people took up once again the struggle for national independence from Britain, 'a dream that was dreamed in the heart and that only the heart can hold'—but all these hundreds of years never abandoned and so never wholly lost. He joined the Irish Republican Army as a volunteer in Dublin, but by 1918 he could no longer live at home; his parents were by their background and political outlook hostile to the spirit of the Rising. At the same time he quit the university and his medical studies and became a full-time organizer for the IRA. From 1918–21, as a staff captain attached to General Headquarters, he was active in organizing battalion and company units in some fourteen counties, from Donegal to Limerick, Tipperary to Tyrone, reporting directly to Michael Collins, Director of Intelligence, or to Richard Mulcahy, the Chief of Staff. O'Malley travelled a great deal under difficult conditions during those years.

In the winter of 1920, he was captured while preparing for

an attack on the Auxiliaries in Inistiogue, Co. Kilkenny. His true identity was not learned by the British as he gave the name of Bernard Stewart and their special interrogations failed to make him give the truth. At Inistiogue, and later in Dublin Castle, he was beaten and ill-treated, and then imprisoned in Kilmainham jail, from which he escaped in February 1921. He returned to take command of the newly-formed Second Southern Division, one of the first two divisions set up by the GHQ and second in importance only to the First Southern. From March until the calling of the truce in July that year, he was officer commanding five brigades, a leader who was determined to carry on the war until complete independence was won, or until Ireland was wholly crushed by the might of empire. The man who wrote *On Another Man's Wound* would seek no less.

On Another Man's Wound, its title taken from an old Ulster proverb, 'It is easy to sleep on another man's wound', was, however, only half the story. *The Singing Flame* relates what happened next to the author and his country, and it is right that it should be told in full, for it is a logical continuation of his part in *On Another Man's Wound:* one man's path through wars foreign and domestic for his country, for his Republic.

In the first book the only hint of a sequel comes towards the end, when he is met by Mrs. Tobin of Tincurry, Co. Tipperary, and warned of the dream she had had about him: 'In her dream a house I was in had been surrounded and it wasn't Tincurry. As I came out to fight in the open, I had been wounded many times, and had managed to get in again. . . . But the dream was not to come true for another year and a half.'

In context this must be a mysterious reference to the future, for that book ends two months later and its general readers would hardly be aware of such subsequent events. But here in this new book that blood-soaked dream is enacted out.

When in August 1936 *On Another Man's Wound* was published by Rich & Cowan (of London), it was recognized at once as a classic work on the Irish troubles, and despite the semi-reluctant praise from some old newspaper adversaries who objected to 'disrespectful' remarks about a bishop and some 'crude realism', it has retained its reputation. In *Dublin in the Age of William Butler Yeats and James Joyce,* Richard Kain believed it to be the 'outstanding literary achievement of the Anglo-Irish War, by a field officer, Ernie O'Malley.' More recently, in the most comprehensive work on the history of Irish nationalism over the centuries (by an Englishman), whilst one might quarrel with interpretations, his verdict on O'Malley's book is specially favourable: 'A work of literature, as well as historical interest.' (Robert Kee in *The Green Flag:* bibliography section.) Yet doubtless Ernie O'Malley always realized that the remaining unpublished part of his history could bring out much more divided opinion, dealing as it did with the explosive events of the treaty, the Four Courts and the civil war, all today still largely unrecorded but unforgotten, whereas his first book had shown a united people in common purpose against a common enemy. It had told Ireland's troubles through his own role in action, until the ending of the war of independence, or the Anglo-Irish war, or, in Republican phraseology, the Tan war.

This second part of what was originally planned to make a single volume may not be properly understood without reference to the first; it results immediately from those confused days when he and his divisional staff could not comprehend their GHQ's truce with the British. It is not self-contained, nor intended to be; yet it is not simply a continuation, because the whole scene of action is as it were re-dealt. The British faces fade and are replaced by Irish counterparts. To have read 'part one' would deepen knowledge of his character and his early courage and determination, that persistent allegiance to 'the Republic', thereby making his coming course of action seem all the more inevitable. One would also be aware of the relationships already established with men like Collins, Mulcahy, O'Duffy and de Valera.

Sean O'Faolain, who concluded his long and appreciative review of *On Another Man's Wound* with: 'No critic but must say of it that it has added another name to the permanent list of Irish men of letters', did however criticize some excessive writing which he found in the book concerning the countryside and its flora, which he feared might have been 'compounded in the study'. Others will find the obviously genuine and slowly-taken pleasure in nature as highlighting the tale of violence.

The Singing Flame has little time for what O'Faolain called that 'immense sense of nature'; it is a barer and bleaker picture, since it is harder to exaggerate the beauties of a prison cell, and there Ernie was made to turn more inwardly on himself.

In another long and perceptive review of *On Another Man's Wound*, Padraic Fallon especially praised the later passages and, in particular, singled out the two or three prison chapters: 'The man who was taken prisoner seems to have rounded out his personal identity by a change of name. "Bernard Stewart" is somehow more human than the many aliased O'Malley.' He was being more personal than allowed before because he was a captive. In contrast, more than one-third of *The Singing Flame* is about captivity, and while enduring pain and imprisonment under his own name, O'Malley from his bed remembers much that is not cloaked with dispassion. He had been a lonely man wandering. Now he is more reflective than in the previous book, during the long period of inaction. The 'We' of *On Another Man's Wound* becomes 'I' more often in *The Singing Flame*. He reveals more of himself. It is often more intimate—appropriately so since so much of it takes place in cell or in camp.

It is also intended that it should correct certain errors and misapprehensions that have appeared in the two general histories of Ireland's civil war that are so far published, especially where they refer, briefly, to Ernie O'Malley. Because both of them concentrate in other directions for the first months of conflict, either towards the fighting in the South, or to cover the wider activities of the Government forces, they have mostly ignored the situation in Dublin itself, and consequently they contain very little information about that area under the O'Malley command, not until both give differing and inaccurate accounts of his eventual arrest.

This second O'Malley book should be linked to what he wrote in the 1936 preface: 'My attitude towards the fight is that of a sheltered individual drawn from the secure seclusion of Irish life to responsibility of action.' It is this responsibility which concerns him very much throughout the second volume, for in 1921–22 he held greater responsibility than when he was commanding the Second Southern for the last five months of the Tan war. Now, during this time, he is first the OC of that division; then Director of Organization on the IRA General Headquarters Staff, and a member of the Army Executive; then OC of the Headquarters section in the Four Courts, and later OC of its garrison; then OC of South Eastern Command; and finally for a period of four crucial months the (Acting) Assistant Chief of Staff of the IRA, and OC of the Northern and Eastern Command (Ulster and Leinster), and a member of the five-man Army Council.

It is the fullest personal account to be given until now of the 1921–24 years, and by a very senior officer of the Republicans, one who was at the centre of important events. A previously untold story of such dramas as the Limerick crisis of March 1922; the occupation and surrender of the Four Courts; IRA leaders on the run in Dublin during civil war. It then becomes another of the scarce original sources for the jail experiences of men and women prisoners of the Free State, including many scenes of prison hospitals and prison life.

Moreover, the book demonstrates Ernie O'Malley's share in the shaping of modern Ireland, in as much as his beliefs and actions were directly involved in the causes of the civil war, and then in the course it took. Being OC of the Second Southern, which together with the First had borne the brunt of the fight against the British outside of Dublin—'the men who won the war'—it was his own Second Southern which first broke away from the authority of both General Headquarters *and* Dail Eireann, and acted in independence after the treaty had been approved. This break led to the army crisis in Limerick, a part of his area, that nearly precipitated the war. It was his idea to 'kidnap' General J. J. O'Connell of the National Army, thus creating the 'mini-Sarajevo' of the civil war, as Ernest Blythe of the Provisional Government was to call it. He was indeed that most dangerous of opponents, at once an idealist and a man of action, much more so than were many of his anti-treaty colleagues.

Throughout the three years covered here, July 1921 to July 1924, Ernie O'Malley was twenty-three to twenty-six years old. He noted once 'the youth of our officers'. He himself was a very young man to be in military command, however nominal in practice, of Leinster and Ulster, comprising the half of Ireland. It has been remarked how young were the men of the IRA who fought for and dreamed of 'The Republic', suspicious if not actively hostile towards all politicians, and O'Malley was the youngest of the men of high status on both sides. This was a factor he had grown accustomed to in the Tan days; mentioning his early hesitation in giving orders to men old enough to have been his father—a diffidence that did not last very long as he was a natural leader.

In appearance he is remembered as a long-striding young man, tall and thin, with lean features and steady unflinching gaze, and very noticeable red hair, but a pale complexion. He did not suffer fools gladly.

When he died, in 1957, with five bullets still left in his body, the *Sunday Press* declared: 'His life could itself be a record of the War of Independence in which wounds, imprisonments, hunger strikes, audacious escapes and stern battles were interspersed with years of stern and ardent service.' Ernie O'Malley would not have called it the war of independence, since nations have to win those wars, and like other Republicans he used the words 'Tan war', but his story is incomplete by remembering the Tan years only. *The Singing Flame* tells, perhaps, of an even greater personal contest.

Again it should be recorded that throughout the four years before the opening of this book in mid-1921, as an itinerant IRA officer he had travelled and fought in many areas of Ireland, often in wild or very poor country, to organize, inspire, train and lead into action. From the age of nineteen he knew the hardships of weather, whether on bicycle or on foot, whether winter or summer; the sleeping rough; the unpalatable food; the loneliness of living and working with the country people whom his favoured Dublin upbringing had not prepared him to know; scant privacy, no life of his own, and the strain of little rest and constant peril. During that time he had gathered numerous wounds of his own on which to sleep. He had been shot in the wrist and ankle; afterwards in the thigh. He was twice burnt on face, neck and hands when police barracks were attacked. Once he was hit by bursting grenade fragments and required a secret operation in hospital. When he was finally captured by the Auxiliaries, tougher foes than the Black and Tans, he was maltreated and often threatened with death; his feet were crushed and he was stabbed with bayonets. In Dublin Castle he was so brutally beaten that his friends failed at first to recognize him, and a red-hot poker kept before his eyes had permanently injured his sight.

That British war background should be kept in mind when considering the present story, for much of his subsequent sickness in prison as related in the latter chapters may have been due in part to an eventual collapse after all the privations undergone since 1918. He might say in his first book that he had an Erewonian contempt for disease, and that his body was hardy enough, but the price would be paid one day, especially as it seems that the hardiness he achieved was through his own self-discipline. Apparently he had rheumatic fever as a child, and always had a heart condition.

It is also significant to note how Ernie O'Malley endured all kinds of dangers and troubles associated traditionally with the Republican movement, collectively more than did any others from the army or political ranks. It is true that he was not shot *dead*—the one element missing to make a perfect Republican martyr—but he very nearly died under a hail of Free State bullets, in addition to his other 'honours' which together make up the most comprehensive Irish Republican career of an officer of the period.

His life, then, did surely mirror the whole Irish struggle. No other contemporary went through all his IRA experiences. He was to be the last Republican leader to be released from internment, and although just a matter of hours, it had shown the special value which the Free State always put on him. Always the same story—'outstanding in courage'—said one of his comrades from the wars.

Certainly he was a 'text-book officer' as some of the Cork men complained, but he was a field officer also, and a guerilla fighter, too, which was an unusual combination for the IRA, who were just as 'irregular' in 1919 as when Piaras Beaslai coined the term for them in 1922. O'Malley was not simply an intransigent military man; he was fighting for a better Ireland, socially and politically and economically. When he describes the personal qualities of Liam Mellows on hearing of his death, consciously or not he reflects things of himself as well. Quite probably the Free State feared O'Malley's brand of idealism, courage and spirit of uncompromise at least as much as they feared what were inaccurately labelled as Mellows's Communist policies.

Once he wrote some evocative lines to express that feeling for Ireland, for the Holy Grail of The Republic, and they were selected in 1966 for an anthology of the Easter Rising, although they rightly belong to the civil war period: '. . . a strange love was born that for some was never to die till they lay stiff on the hillside or in quicklime near a barrack wall.'

The Singing Flame will show how the 'notorious rebel', as police reports from Dublin Castle called him in 1921, Ernest Malley, wanted by the British, was to become Earnan O Maille, hunted more bitterly by the Free State forces in 1922.

When Ernie O'Malley began to write down his experiences and memories of the Irish struggle, he was then in New Mexico in the United States, starting to write around 1930, and working on his book at intervals until 1933 in New York. When he returned to Ireland in 1935, and following the publication of his story up until the truce of 1921, he must have intended to complete the second part, for he rewrote some sections of the middle chapters as late as the 1950's. Some of this was partly based on fresh information supplied from the hundreds of interviews he had conducted with veterans of both the wars; but he never assembled the entire work, put it into final shape, or made revisions. I have tried to undertake this task on his behalf.

It has been my wish to produce the definitive version of his civil war memoirs. This has meant the compiling and amalgamating of some drafts, revision and general editorial decisions, but the text is O'Malley's own. It is hoped that the result reads as a fluent and finished story, the one that he wished to tell, and which best continues his first volume.

My own interest began when I first read his name (in 1972)

in Thomas Coffey's book on the Rising, *Agony at Easter:* '. . . later to become an Irish revolutionary hero himself but at this time not yet interested in the nationalist movement', together with some passages from his own book that described the scenes outside the GPO in O'Connell Street. From Calton Younger's *Ireland's Civil War* came a few further glimpses: '. . . O'Malley was to break away from his Unionist background and throw his poet's soul and the steel of him into the struggle for freedom.' Eventually, it was the reading of his own book that caused me to seek for anything else he might have written, especially on the period following the truce. Inquiries were made, research was begun, and in due course his various writings were brought together to make up the content of this book, which he himself entitled, and dedicated to 'Ireland the Ever-Living and to Her Dead Sons'. It is presented especially for those who like myself had regretted that there seemed to be nothing that continued his history from July 1921.

A letter written in recent years by someone who knew him briefly in the civil war period (a man whom Ernie had once liked very much indeed), admired his 'grit and cast-iron courage', but also remembered him in this way: 'He was prepared to win all or lose all, and looked upon compromise as weakness. His estimation of people was similar: they were either the best or the worst. He was rather a lonely type and made very few but very fast friendships. He was not endowed with tact, and I don't think he was much concerned about death.'

I believe there was always more to him than that, but such a man can be more than sometimes seen through the following pages.

Six months before the start of this book, on Christmas Day of 1920, Ernie O'Malley was a prisoner of the British in Dublin Castle, and he made a promise with a garrison officer, an ex-Trinity man who was friendly. ' "Two years from now when the Irish Republic is recognized, we'll meet on Christmas Day and dine." "Remember, that's a bargain," he said, as we shook hands.' So confident a faith, then; so poignant when recalled later in these pages revealing where he was in fact to be at Christmas 1922.

But *On Another Man's Wound* was a story of hope and high endeavour. *The Singing Flame,* that gas-jet flame which flickered and faded in the prison cells, is a study of failure. Much of it is harrowing. There is no happy ending, at least for Republicans. Yet a spirit survived, and at the close he can find some solace in the thought that though he and his companions had lost the war, they had withstood that other fight in jail.

Ernie O'Malley died in 1957. The only books he wrote were about the Irish wars, and it is in those that he should be most remembered.

FRANCES-MARY BLAKE
(1978)

THE ANGLO-IRISH WAR TO JULY 1921

by Ernie O'Malley
OC of the 2nd Southern Division IRA

OUR area was improving daily, the people were becoming more staunch in their allegiance to the Republic, and the British as a government no longer functioned. They were as they had been over a hundred and fifty years ago, a garrison; a garrison which held the cities and towns and made their influence felt in the countryside by force of arms only.

Years ago the country volunteer had been a butt for jokes. Superficial minds could not penetrate beyond his bright-hued cap perched on his head, the way in which he wore his clothes, the peculiarities of his accent and his shyness when in the company of city folk. He might hold himself ungainly, but he had faced disdain and insults and, often enough, parental displeasure; he had fronted public opinion with its major and minor sources of irritation; his sincerity was obvious to all who possessed any themselves. At any rate, his beliefs were worth fighting for, in contrast to those of some who derided him. His capacity for endurance was still unplumbed but he had become more resolute; responsibility had given him a certain air of independence which in some cases might have become aggressive, but he was quiet, his life for the past four or five years had led him to act rather than to talk.

Some areas were weak, that was true, and there the enemy had attempted to cow the spirit by showing their strength and might as brutally as they well knew how. In general, the local IRA companies made or marred the morale of the people. If the officers were keen and daring, if organization was good, if the flying columns had been established, and if the people had become accustomed to seeing our men bearing arms openly, the resistance was stiffened. When the fighting took place, the people entered into the spirit of the fight even if they were not Republican; their emotions were stirred, and the little spark of nationality which is borne by everyone who lives in Ireland was fanned and given expression to in one of many ways.

The enemy controlled the cities and the larger towns but English departments of government did not function as before. Taxes were not collected, their courts were empty; local administration was often managed by Republican county councils which interpreted the orders and decrees issued by Dail Eireann. Dail Eireann was the virtual *de jure* and *de facto* government, and even where the English strength was great, as in Dublin or Cork, they lived a garrison life. Gone was the country of the soft brogue or blarney, the fox-hunting days and the pleasant parties or tennis tournaments. Instead was a hard, steady Ireland, cool, assertive. It had pitted its strength against the Empire and the latter was beginning to waver. The mentality of the island seemed to have changed; the political type with his flow of eloquence and his mouthings, his bland assurances, his ability to 'pull wires', and his gymnastic feats of conscience, seemed to have disappeared. There was no room for oratory. The nation was at war and its intellect had been shriven of dross by suffering. The familiar stage Irishman had disappeared. One met now a young man who did not drink, who had developed a sense of duty and of responsibility, and whose bearing showed it. Simple country boys, simple in that they were not sophisticated, had found they possessed organizing and administrative ability. They had made themselves respected by their own people and, more difficult still, by those of their own class. The enemies anglicization and snobbery, almost synonymous terms, had given way before a national zeal and the development of national consciousness. One was not now judged by one's parents or by the status of one's relatives or of one's position. One was simply judged by one's worth, by one's ability and unselfishness, by grit, determination, and capacity for suffering, and more than anything else by one's courage and readiness for work.

The enemy, on the other hand, had suffered in morale during the past two years, particularly in the past eight months. Their very campaign of terrorism had defeated itself. It had affected the discipline of their police force and of their army. Co-operation between the forces of oppression was anything but happy. The Auxiliaries did as they liked. The Black and Tans followed suit. The old members of the Royal Irish

Constabulary resented the intruders and their tactics. The British Army did not approve, from the point of view of discipline, of unauthorized reprisals. There was dual command: the army and the police force. The civil powers, such as they were, resented the interference of the military and their tendency to abrogate the powers of life and death. The Southern Unionists stood aloof. They did not throw their lot in wholly with the enemy; they could not side with us. They suffered from either side, but they disliked the campaign of terrorism initiated by Dublin Castle. Ireland was no longer a happy hunting ground for fishing or shooting, it did not pay to practice such gentlemanly virtues. Communications were liable to temporary or complete rupture, whether telegraphic, telephonic, postal, rail or motor. The roads were sometimes unpassable and life was not very easy, or indeed very safe.

One evening in July 1921 a despatch rider asked to see me. He was shown into the kitchen of Mrs. Quirke's in Donohill, in south Co. Tipperary. The despatch was from General Headquarters and stated that all hostilities would cease after forty-eight hours by twelve noon on 11 July. Immediately Con Moloney, the Divisional Adjutant, typed orders to the five brigades and arranged for their despatch. Then we sat down to consider the situation. It was the first official intimation we had received and we did not understand it.

Con, Mickey Fitzpatrick and I discussed possible angles and reviewed areas in our own and in other commands, but we failed to arrive at a satisfactory solution. Why had the truce been ordered? We were gaining ground, each day strengthened us and weakened our enemy; then why was it necessary to put a stop to hostilities? We had not time to plan an attack on any of the local posts as we would have wished, and the day of the truce dawned leaving us in a state of uncertainty.

CHAPTER ONE

JULY—OCTOBER 1921

WE thought the truce would last for about two or three weeks, and we issued a series of orders and instructions to cover the change of situation and worked as hard as we could to make the most of the breathing space. Hostilities would soon restart, and we wished to meet our officers and plan operations now that we could move about freely. There was a tendency to relax discipline, especially as the period of the truce became prolonged. Suppressed feeling became articulate, the tension was eased, and men who had been for a long time names only returned to visit their families and friends.

The Irish Republican Army was in danger of becoming popular; recruits came in large numbers. Soon men appeared in uniform who had never shown much anxiety to run special risks when courage was needed. We had to give the officers sufficient work to keep them busy and do our best to prevent them from entering towns and cities where they would become known to enemy intelligence agents.

After three weeks of truce we decided to change divisional headquarters. We had remained in Mrs. Quirke's in Donohill for nearly three months. She had never complained. The numerous despatch riders and visiting officers had been fed there, though occasionally we supplied the food ourselves. I told her that we intended to leave.

'Sure what do you want to do that for?' she said. 'You're always welcome. I'm rough and ready but the house is yours. You're not a bit of bother in the world. I like to see the boys around.'

'We will come back when the war begins,' I said, and she hastened to prepare an egg-flip.

We moved to a small cottage where there was one occupant, a man named Dinny Kelly. It was a red-bricked cottage with a slate roof. There were two rooms on the ground floor, the kitchen and a small bedroom. A steep wooden stairs led to the second storey which contained a room with a low ceiling where Dinny slept. The house was not high and the sloping roof restricted space. We worked in the kitchen at two tables which were piled high with books and papers. Empty wooden boxes, which had once contained explosives, held our files. Maps, fastened by drawing pins, hung on the walls. A large map of Ireland was on the back of the door, with the divisional area outlined in red ink, and underneath it a 1″ map of the surrounding district. Above the table where I worked was a ½″ map of the division. It had been pieced together from four sheets. Brigade and battalion areas were marked in red and green, companies with a red circle, enemy posts in blue. Our belts, with guns in holsters, hung on pegs on the wall, my uniform tunic near them. We cooked in turns at the kitchen fire. The Assistant Quartermaster was the most successful; we thankfully handed over the culinary arrangement to him. The bedroom consisted of mattresses laid on the floor, which were rolled up in the daytime. We slept in blankets, three or four of us in the room.

Eoin O'Duffy, Deputy Chief of Staff, advised me to change to a hotel in Tipperary. 'The place is too small, too uncomfortable, and you will not have proper food. I have advised officers in other areas to go into the towns and cities. You should have a proper headquarters,' he said.

'We have little money,' I said, 'and need it for office expenses.' When I inquired how the bills would be met, he said that I could have credit. 'You can run a bill in the town.' But we remained in the little hut.

The spirit of the people was good in this part of the country. They understood there would be further fighting and were undaunted. We found less difficulty in getting the loan of horses and carts or traps to carry supplies, or for our despatch riders. People who were once indifferent had become friendly, even gracious. 'You're quite welcome,' they said to our demands. The truce had given us additional status in their eyes and somehow they felt sorry that they had remained aloof. The tradition of those who had helped had spread. Some were anxious to join a movement that had now become popular, others began to realize that they had not contributed or had given grudgingly.

Liaison officers were appointed by both armies to see that the truce was kept and to seek redress for such breaches as occurred. In the main the terms of the truce were observed. President de Valera, with members of his Cabinet, had gone to London to meet Lloyd George. The British published proposals for a settlement which de Valera in a reply refused to accept, and in August, at the first meeting of the Second Dail Eireann, his decision was confirmed. The British Premier was acquainted with the decision of the representatives of our people. The English press, even the most liberal elements of it, advocated the acceptance of Lloyd George's proposals, proving that they also, like the British in general, as an Irishman once said, had found Ireland a nation and had left it a question, but the interchange of notes continued.

Our Quartermaster was busy buying military books, getting equipment made, and trying to establish a munition plant. Near Oola in east Limerick he was given outhouses for the factory. Men came from the foundries in Limerick. They had left good positions there, but there was no word of complaint. They were willing to serve in any capacity. Soon piles of scrap-iron were collected and melted down, moulds were made and grenade cases manufactured. Weapons were repaired by the staff at first, then a smith and a boy who had worked in a jeweller's shop looked after the damaged weapons. Empty revolver cases were forwarded, as we hoped to refill them. We found it easier to purchase grenades, bodies and necks, from our Quartermaster-General, but they were expensive and in time we felt we would be able to turn out complete hand-grenades ourselves. Rifle-grenades and improvised Stokes guns were discussed and tried. The Divisional Engineer, Bob de Courcy, and some Limerick officers began to work on a compressed-air gun which they had been planning.

I learned to drive a motor-car. My lessons began at night, the car was a Ford, and it had no lights. I ran into a gate in the darkness, but succeeded in negotiating the winding road near Donohill before I went to bed. I was able to inspect areas over fifty miles away and time was saved. Travelling at night

was a little risky. Trenches and pot-holes on the roads had
not been filled in. We had trouble with the county council
who wished to repair the roads, but we were thinking in terms
of active service. One had to memorize long stretches; a
journey was an undulating spiral, changing from one road to
another, crossing fords, traversing fields. Often our cars had
faulty lights or none at all. That was exciting, driving in the
dark without lights on very bad roads. A journey of forty or
fifty miles became an adventure as exciting as a night advance
before the attack.

One evening after dusk, returning from Kilkenny city with
four officers in a big car, a German Daimler, I ran out of
petrol some miles from Clonmel. It was a commandeered car
and we had to be careful of it in garrison towns.

'We'll halt the next car that comes along,' I said. We
waited in the darkness; I heard the noise of a motor-car, a
high-powered one, I thought, by the sound. As the lights
approached I held up my hand and shouted 'Halt!' The
brakes were jammed on and the car stopped. I could not see it
on account of the headlights. I walked beyond the lights. It
was an open Crossley tender of the Royal Irish Constabulary. They were seated on either side as I approached,
both sides pointing their rifles at me. I reached down, drew
my long-barrelled Parabellum automatic and held it, with
arm bent, in my right hand. The sergeant was seated beside
the driver.

'Can you give me some petrol, please?' I asked.

'What do you want it for?' he asked. He was a big, burly
man and spoke with an English accent, curtly.

'For my car,' I said, pointing to where it stood in the
shadow of the hedge. Two of my officers walked to one side
out of the glare of the headlights; the third had moved silently
some yards to the rear of the tender.

'Whose car is it?' he demanded.

'Mine,' I said. 'It belongs to the Irish Republican Army.'

'Who are you?'

'That does not matter. Can you give me some petrol to
bring us to Clonmel?'

The police talked amongst themselves. The sergeant
hesitated. He wanted to obtain the number of the car, I knew,

but could not make up his mind to order his men to get down.

'All right,' he said, 'I'll give you a tin.'

He handed me a tin and I paid and thanked him. They drove off slowly.

'That was a close thing,' said the Quartermaster, who was standing behind. 'I thought they'd blow into you.'

The truce continued. We did not receive any news from our General Headquarters as to how long it would last. Bob de Courcy had begun a training camp for the engineering officers in the division, and I was looking for a suitable site for a camp which I intended to run; I had no director of training and had to undertake the work myself. Up on the slopes of the Galtees was Galtee castle. It would be far enough from towns to avoid detection; the ground varied in character from wooded country to steep rises, and below in the plain, enclosed territory. I obtained permission from the owner to use the huts of the workmen. The castle was not a mile and a half from the Mitchelstown road, up on the hillside, reached by a winding road, open at first, then bordered by trees, and towards the end a steep ravine running away to the left. The castle was a new building with turrets of the French Renaissance type, strongly built and well furnished.

The huts stood together in a large sloping field; they were in good repair, built of wood, with corrugated roofs. There were fireplaces and stoves, a few tables and chairs. The local commandant promised to obtain long tables, forms, chairs, beds, and to equip the place for sixty officers. In the centre of the group of buildings was a small hut which I intended to use as headquarters. The commandant had to arrange for food supplies and for cooking. 'The Cumann na mBan will be only too glad to cook for the men,' he said, 'and they will want to supply the food, too. One of the girls will be here shortly, if you'll wait.' A girl arrived on a bicycle. He introduced her as the captain of the Cumann na mBan company, a straight-eyed girl with a smiling face. 'We'll be only too pleased to help,' she said. 'The girls can cook in turns, and bake cakes, too. If you're good, we'll wash for you also.'

Each of the five brigades was instructed to send officers from brigade and battalion staffs and to have them thoroughly equipped with rifles, bayonets, small arms, grenades and kit. On the appointed day all the officers arrived, close on seventy, and some in uniform. A camp staff was appointed; the officers were divided into sections and squads and they inspected their quarters. The long rooms overhead had been converted into dormitories and the girls had decorated them with branches and flowers. People in the area had supplied crockery and cooking utensils, the schools had provided forms and blackboards. The commandant, who now became assistant quartermaster, had done his work well. In the centre of the sloping field a flagstaff had been set up, from which floated the tricolour.

I had an American officer, Captain Prout, to help me. Of late he had been attached to the intelligence squad of the Dundrum battalion. We worked hard. The company was first trained for two weeks as volunteers, to make them proficient in the use and application of arms. Officers took squads and sections in turns. By the end of the fortnight they were trained in the elementary work of an infantry soldier. At six o'clock in the mornings the bugle call summoned them on parade. Breakfast, then, and a rest. Inspection of arms, a short route march, and a run across country in full kit, followed. There was a short interval after all classes and field work. At lectures the officers were induced to take notes and copy the blackboard diagrams; lectures were held in the open. Extended order across country, reconnaissance or patrol work. After the midday meal, a rest. Another lecture; then bayonet practice, revolver and grenade training, and musketry with .22 ammunition. That was welcome. We had been so accustomed to save every round of ammunition that the men looked forward to this part of the day's work as a treat. There was great rivalry between the squads to see who would have the highest number of marks and the best grouping on the small targets. An interval of an hour and a half for rest or recreation. The men had their camans and played hurling, or handball, against the gable end of a hut. Tea was at six. A parade in full kit at sunset, the company drawn up two deep in squads, squad commanders in rear, section commanders behind them again. The ceremony was a mixture of Irish, American and English drill. 'The sundown parade,' Prout

called it. The men, with bayonets fixed, were called to attention by their officers, who then gave the order: 'Present arms.'
The rifles were brought to the 'slope', then to the 'present'.
The officers turned and saluted the green, white and orange
flag as it was lowered. Before they went to bed the men were
expected to study for an hour or more, write essays, or read
the books in the library, which was my own. The bugler
sounded 'lights out' at ten o'clock.

In the night-time I dealt with the administrative work of
the division, prepared lectures and helped to type training
notes for the company. The men were not permitted to leave
the camp grounds without a pass but each was given a certain
number of hours' leave a week. Discipline was strict, but
gradually all took a pride in their own efficiency. The rivalry
between the squads developed. All were on their honour not
to drink and to reduce cigarette smoking. All papers around
the camp, dead leaves and weeds had to be taken up; they
had to respect the mountain side as well as their huts. Soon
the surroundings were spotless. During rest intervals men
could be seen picking up odds and ends of paper, decayed
leaves or cigarette butts. The Cumann na mBan girls in their
turns came to cook and wash. Fresh flowers in empty tin cans
would appear on tables; sweet pea, wild roses, bunches of
heather, and carnations. The girls came on foot, on bicycles,
in ponies and traps, some of them in uniform. Always they
brought presents: honey, homemade jam, freshly churned
butter, griddle or large white oven cakes, a flitch of bacon,
packages of cigarettes. Amongst them one day I recognized a
certain girl. She it was who had once stopped me, a year ago,
on the Ballyporeen road and warned me that police were
lying in ambush in the direction I was going. She belonged to
the Mitchelstown Cumann na mBan, outside of the divisional area, but they also helped. The assistant quartermaster
supplied mutton from the mountain sheep, sweet and
wholesome. Butchers from battalion companies had killed
and dressed the meat.

On Sundays we marched to Mass at the chapel, six miles
away, swinging along in the dust of the country roads, singing
Irish marching songs. Places were reserved for us in the choir.
The people stood to watch us as we paraded after Mass, and

passed comments on our appearance. There were weekly
dances which the Cumann na mBan attended. The girls were
interested in the strange officers. Foreign cows, as we said,
have long horns. A local sports was organized and we carried
off some of the prizes. A few days later I heard that one of our
company was a champion weight-thrower, another a fine
long-distance runner; they had assumed different names for
the occasion.

Dermott MacManus, who had been an officer in the British
Army, and was now attached to the training staff at our
General Headquarters, came to inspect and remained a while
with us. There was a special inspection of arms that morning.
One rifle was dirty. I saw the company commander glance
down the barrel after we had passed on to another rank. I
heard his strong whisper. 'Christ, man, there's hair on it.'

We trained the men in administration, organization, scout-
ing, field-sketching, engineering; we rehearsed imaginary
barracks assaults, and ambushes, taught them the use of
explosives and land mines, and how to manoeuvre. One day
on manoeuvres a position up the hill was being attacked;
machine-gun fire was maintained by beating tin cans to make
attackers realize that they could not advance rashly. I was an
umpire, mounted on a horse that seemed to reach the
heavens, he was so high. I came upon one of the defenders in
the angle of a hedged field, sitting down, smoking. 'Why the
deuce don't you open fire?' I demanded.

The officer pointed to his large tin can. 'It's a new make of
machine,' he said, smiling, 'and I think it's jammed. I can't
strip it.'

My motor was used for ambush drill. It had no windscreen,
there was little breakable in it. Men were positioned on the
roadside, unknown to the driver, armed with hard balls of
clay which they threw as the car drove by. The hits of each
squad were registered. Mine operators sat on hillsides and
pressed a switch on a signal from a lookout, as the car
approached. The wire leads were connected with a bell
instead of explosive; an observer hidden close to the road
judged if the mine was properly timed. We practised night
manoeuvres and attempted to advance in the dark without
making unnecessary noise. The weather was fine and all

learned to love the mountains although it was hard work climbing with full kit. In the evenings after the sunset parade we sat outside and watched the mountains above us and the plain spreading out below, the isolated trees receiving the last rays of light silhouetted against small hill tops; the range of the Knockmealdown mountains standing fourteen miles away, blurring slowly; the sky, slowly seeping the colour of the land to decorate itself. The long twilight always gave a touch of fantasy to this country we thought we knew. Hills, mountains, trees, hedges, took unexpected shapes.

After five weeks' training the officers were ready to leave for their areas. Most of them were already weather-beaten; some from the cities had acquired a healthy tan; all were in good health, sorry to leave, yet anxious to return to their own units to undertake the organization of further training camps.

Eoin O'Duffy, Deputy Chief of Staff, inspected the camp and was pleased with the progress. He questioned each officer about the detailed organization of his area, and put them through what we called the third degree. Next day he held a divisional council in the ruins of Tincurry House, in what was once the dining room. The officers automatically picked up all papers and decayed grass as they waited outside for the Deputy Chief. We laughed; respect for ground had become instinctive. After a long discussion on administration, organization, and intelligence, the special services were examined one by one. O'Duffy finally suggested that we ourselves should break the truce, when negotiations were approaching a deadlock, by attacking the British posts without giving the agreed seventy-two hours' warning. Some of the officers were in favour of the project; they felt that the British would probably break the truce in some such fashion. The divisional staff repudiated the suggestion coming as it did from a member of our GHQ. If it was going to be a fight to the finish, let us begin the war honourably, no matter what the enemy intended to do. The officers who had thought only of a local advantage sided with us. After the meeting the officers returned to their brigades.

I was called to Dublin to attend a meeting of senior officers, but many areas were missing: Liam Lynch of the First Southern, Tom Maguire of the Second Western, Billy

Pilkington of the Third, Michael Kilroy of the Fourth Western, Frank Aiken of the Fourth Northern. I wondered why they were absent. Independent brigades were represented, also other areas newly divisionalized. Michael Collins, Director of Intelligence; Richard Mulcahy, Chief of Staff; Eoin O'Duffy, Deputy Chief of Staff, and Emmet Dalton, Director of Training, were present. Officers submitted a verbal report on the condition of their areas, mentioned the amount of arms and ammunition they had, and reported on training. The possibilities of their commands with regard to active service were discussed. Some seemed pessimistic, they had little ammunition and felt they could not maintain themselves for long in case of a resumption of hostilities. We were being questioned in turn.

I interrupted the third speaker. 'Lack of rifles and ammunition is due to the officers in each area,' I said. 'We get little supplies from the Quartermaster-General. Our main source of supply is the enemy. It is not a question of arms or ammunition. I have never yet met a keen, good officer or volunteer who did not by hook or by crook obtain arms and stuff. It's a question, sir, I think,' I said, addressing the Chief of Staff, 'of producing and training officers with sufficient guts, not of moaning about lack of supplies.' I was angry so I sat down.

The officer commanding the Third Southern stood up. I had organized in his area years ago. 'I agree,' he said; 'what arms we possess have been the result of carefully planned operations. We have not been spoon-fed by our Quartermaster-General.'

The discussion lapsed. Seniority amongst officers was elaborated by Mulcahy. The Chief of Staff was to be a general, the Deputy and the Assistant Chiefs, lieutenant-generals, the remainder members of the Staff ranked as commandant-generals. Divisional commandants had ranked as commandant-generals, now they took precedence of other GHQ officers, ranking below the ACS.

Food supplies for areas were discussed. The CS wanted a food survey in order to arrange for an exchange of foodstuffs between different parts as we would probably, he said, have to destroy railroad communications, and we must see that the

civilian population were not starved as a result. Dumps of
food had to be provided for our flying columns, also, and
closer touch had to be maintained between adjoining divisions. We were asked to express our opinions on the
advisability of fighting in uniform. The majority were in
favour of wearing uniforms and of carrying distinctive badges.
In the south during the fighting some of the men in our
columns had worn uniform and were distinguished from the
civilians by their special clothing. Then the discussion went
into a by-channel. The shape of the new uniform cap was
discussed in detail. A soft rim of the Kepi type to distinguish
it from the hard-fixed British rim.

Next day we met the President, Eamon de Valera, and
Cathal Brugha, Minister for Defence in Dail Eireann, in a
room in the Mansion House. They questioned us about the
morale of the people and the possible support in case of a
renewal of hostilities. Civil administration was touched on,
the collection of taxes, the repair of roads, the local and
district courts, and the enforcing of the Belfast boycott and of
Dail decrees. I was called to order by Cathal Brugha for
stating that we had never consulted the feelings of the people.
If so, we would never have fired a shot. If we gave them a
good strong lead, they would follow.

We returned to our areas that day and continued to train
and attempted to equip our commands. We had been led to
expect that the truce would give us a breathing space, would
provide an opportunity for the importation of arms from
abroad; whatever attempts were made to land arms, we knew
nothing of them for we did not receive any. We had received
in our area a few Thompson guns and some small arms. The
much-lauded Thompson was an American weapon, using a
box magazine of twenty rounds and a drum of fifty to one
hundred. We had tested the gun and I had trained a divisional machine-gun officer in its use. It was portable, could be
concealed underneath an overcoat, and was useful for
close-quarters fighting, and for street fighting especially. I
submitted a critical report to the ACS who seemed very
much impressed with the new weapon.

In our little cottage headquarters food supplies were scant.
We did not wish to incur expenses and kept only a small

amount of provisions. We went without food or visited our
friends in the neighbourhood at meal times when we were
particularly hungry. We were always welcome, but we did
not like to abuse their hospitality when we were not on active
service. Each brigade was expected to contribute money from
its funds towards the support of our staff. The money was
used to maintain the munition factory and to purchase arms.
We owed rent which we were unable to pay so I was usually
selected to make the peace with the landlord who often called
in person.

Dinny Kelly, the tenant of the cottage which we called 'the
hut', was sturdily built, with a red weather-beaten face and a
rather thick moustache. He could be about forty years of age.
His command of English was extensive, he was meticulous in
choice of words. He never used a small one when he could
employ a large sonorous word and his selection was accurate.
Often as we sat at the table Con or Mickey Fitz kicked me
when Dinny began to speak. Often we sat listening to him
with tightened lips so that we would not smile. He borrowed
some of my books, Plutarch's *Lives* and the *Decameron*. He
read a few of the stories and winked. 'That's good reading,'
he said. 'There were strange personages in those ancient
times.' He discussed international politics with avidity. His
comments were shrewd and personal. The books he read were
examined round a fire in the night-time. A book when read in
the country was read slowly; it was dissected and the joint
experience of those around the open hearth tested its
accuracy to life and knowledge. Dinny was an authority on
birds, especially singing birds. He compared the rival merits
and demerits of local songsters. He was very proud of his own
male canary. He was a volunteer in the local company,
carried himself with martial air, and attended all parades
assiduously. He was put in charge of a section and bore his
new dignity in a becoming manner. He referred to me always
as 'the officer' and he consulted me on many subjects, but
particularly on points of training. Frequently I stopped from
work to explain extended order with matches, to strip an
automatic, or to draw diagrams of the working of a machine-
gun. Once I inspected the battalion to which his company
belonged. His company carried out drill; then the section

commanders exercised their men. Dinny strode up and down, his face became redder with excitement and with difficulty he refrained from running whenever his voice failed to carry. That night he questioned Con as to what I thought of his handling of the section. Con said he did not know. Next morning I talked of the parade. I told him about his section, which was well trained, I said. He was very pleased because 'the officer' had noticed his men particularly.

CHAPTER TWO

NOVEMBER—DECEMBER 1921

WE needed explosives for the land mines, for attacks on posts and for the munition factory. Our Headquarters was unable to supply us in sufficient quantity. If we were able to purchase the main explosive base we could manufacture 'war flour' and 'Irish cheddar', the official Headquarters explosives and the chemists attached to our staff could then experiment further. Already there had been a few minor explosions in our little laboratory but that was inevitable. No one had been hurt, however.

I went to London with a Limerick officer, Johnny Raleigh, intending to visit the British Disposal Board to purchase material. Surplus war stock was being auctioned off, from aeroplane parts to tin hats—which were being sold as flower pots—entrenching tools as gardening trowels. We inspected the huge sheds and piles of equipment. We bought prismatic compasses, range-finders, prismatic glasses, wireless sets, artillery knee-boots, Sam Browne belts and equipment. A tip to the officials and no questions were asked. A few five pound notes in a chemical factory gave us an entry to order three tons of an explosive base. Beautifully groomed managers accepted the money without blinking. That could not occur in our country, we thought. One could bribe lower down, but important officials would have too much pride to accept a tip.

We stored the explosives and equipment in warehouses in London and arranged for cross-channel transport, giving fancy names to our heavy crates. 'Glass, with care'. We lived simply. I cut expenses to the minimum. Raleigh was of medium height but powerfully built. Afterwards he told me that he practically starved, for we took snatches of food at lunch counters while we thought of ways and means for buying arms and ammunition. We visited greasy shops in the East End and met professional gun-runners. We represented the Ulster Volunteers at times; again we negotiated for the men in Belgium, for the Catalans in Spain. We slipped money into receptive palms and received promises until our money was exhausted. We had been a week in London and I could not remain any longer. Nearly every day the five Irish delegates, Arthur Griffith, Michael Collins, Bob Barton, Gavan Duffy and Duggan, were meeting with the English delegates led by Lloyd George, in Downing Street or in some of the many offices. Crowds of London Irish lined the street near the meeting place to see the men who were now entrusted with the nation's honour. Old and young knelt in the streets to recite the Rosary and to pray for a settlement of the age-long feud.

I visited the Irish delegation in Hans Place and Desmond Fitzgerald, Minister for Publicity, invited us to lunch. My companion, Johnny Raleigh, ate and ate. I watched him in astonishment. Champagne, wines and whiskey were unstinted, but neither of us drank. I thought of my staff in Dinny Kelly's hut, running breakfast and lunch together to economize.

Someone at the table began a story. One day in July, four months ago, an old Irish woman wearing a shawl was observed hovering near the entrance to Lloyd George's house in Downing Street. A towering policeman on duty eyed her suspiciously, as she came there every day. She did not appear to notice him but stood at times to watch the hall door and to scan the windows on the ground floor. The policeman intended to make a report, but she did not act as if she was afraid of being noticed. One day he had made up his mind to report the incident to his sergeant but he was saved the trouble. Lloyd George, who had himself noticed the old lady, came to the door that day, opened it and called to her. She climbed the steps. 'What do you want?' asked the Premier; 'can I do anything for you?' 'Yes,' she replied, 'I would like to see the room where your meetings are held.' He led her inside and showed her the conference room. 'Where do you sit?' she asked. He put his hand on a chair and smiled. She moved away. 'Where will President de Valera sit when he comes?' He pointed out another chair. She crossed to it quickly and caressed it with her hands. 'This very chair?' she asked. 'Yes, that's the chair,' said Lloyd George. She searched in the bosom of her dress and brought out a small corked bottle. The Premier watched her curiously. She took out the cork, sprinkled some of the contents with her fingers on the chair, then on the floor beneath. Then she blessed herself. 'That's Holy Water for the President,' she said. 'May God guide him when he sits here to set old Ireland free.' She walked towards the chair that Lloyd George had indicated was his own. She sprinkled it liberally. The Premier looked surprised at first before he smiled again. 'That's to keep the Devil away,' she said, as she corked the bottle and returned it to her bosom. The diners shouted with laughter. Afterwards I met Michael Collins in one of the rooms.

'What the hell are you doing in London?' he asked.

'Having a break,' I replied.

'That's the way with you bloody fellows,' he said. 'I suppose you think the truce is a holiday. When are you going back?'

'Tonight,' I said.

'That's better. You can take the place of the special messenger tonight and bring back the report to Dev. Mind that some of our now good friends don't steal it from you.'

We talked about the negotiations. 'They will end shortly,' he said. He looked worried, his brows had contracted.

As we walked down Bond Street I looked at Johnny. 'I don't know how you're able to walk,' I said. 'I thought you must have eaten enough for five.' He patted his waistcoat middle buttons with a sigh of complete content. 'By Gosh, I was starved. It's all right for you. I suppose you can live on air, but I hadn't a decent meal since I left Limerick, thanks to you.'

I delivered the bulky envelope to de Valera when I arrived in Dublin. Johnny and I then left by train for Limerick Junction.

Con Moloney, the Adjutant, met me in a car as I walked over from the station. I sat beside him in front. 'There's hell to pay,' he said. 'There's been a raid on the British hutments in Tipperary; about seventy rifles and a machine-gun have been stolen.'

'When did it happen?' I asked.

'About three days ago. The British are raging. Intelligence
officers from our General Headquarters are investigating the
matter in the town. Our lads are blamed for it.' He grinned.
'They don't seem to gather much information.' He levered
hard on the accelerator and the car moved swiftly on the
winding road.

A raid for arms was a breach of the truce. This was a big
raid and in the divisional area. I would be held responsible.
'Did you meet the Headquarters intelligence officers?' I
asked.

'Yes,' said Con; 'two of them came to the hut and inquired
for you, but you were in London. They did not say anything
but drove away in towards the town.'

Well, they had not consulted the Adjutant. They meant to
investigate the matter without informing the division. I did
not hold any inquiry. The Tipperary battalion officers, in
whose area our hut was, used to come to see us frequently.
They did not come near the hut now. I thought they must be
away at a training camp, but they were in the area, I found
out later. They wanted to keep out of my way. That told its
own story.

Three days after my return I received a despatch from
Cathal Brugha and another from Mulcahy.

The army was being reorganized, Brugha stated. He
wished to know if I would accept a commission in this re-
organized army as officer commanding the Second Southern
Division. The commission was enclosed, signed by himself,
the Minister for Defence. What did this mean, I thought?
Why a reorganization? I had heard nothing about it. Perhaps
it meant that Dail Eireann was going to regularize army
appointments, that it would accept full responsibility for our
actions as the army of the Republic. Strange, Mulcahy, the
Chief of Staff, had not mentioned it when last I met him. I
acknowledged the despatch, accepted the commission, and
asked for further particulars about the reorganization. Then I
sent a note to Liam Lynch to ask him if he had also received a
commission and what he thought about it.

The other despatch was brief. All officers of our division
and brigade staffs, with the Tipperary battalion officers, were
to proceed to Dublin at once and report at the Gresham
Hotel.

Con whistled as I read the despatch aloud.

'The plot thickens,' he said. 'As sure as we're here that means an investigation over the rifles. The sleuth hounds from Dublin have not discovered anything. I suppose we'll all get an unmerciful lambasting when we arrive in Dublin. The third degree and a reduction to the ranks.'

We drove to Limerick Junction where we met the boys from Tipperary battalion and brigade officers from Co. Limerick. 'I expect the rifles were paid for,' said Con, as I studied the country from the carriage windows and compared it with my maps. 'You know it's easy to bribe sentries.'

'How do you know?' I asked.

'I'm a bit of a prophet,' he replied.

The Tipperary officers laughed.

'I don't want to hear any prophecies,' I said; 'you can keep them till you reach the Gresham. I suppose I'll have to resign over it,' I said to Brian Shanahan, the Tipperary commandant. 'I should have investigated the seizure of the rifles. It's a serious breach of the truce and you devils know about it, but I don't want to question you now. You might tell me the truth.'

They looked glum and worried.

We were shown into a large ante-room when we reached the hotel. There I met our officers from Tipperary Two and Kilkenny brigades. We sat down and talked. There were over thirty officers present. Eoin O'Duffy called me outside the door. 'The Chief of Staff wishes to see you,' he said, as he opened the door of another room. Seated at a small table were Mulcahy and Collins.

Collins said 'Hello' when I entered. Then: 'Come on over here.' I sat opposite to them. Collins tapped on the table with the blunt end of a pencil as he spoke. 'Had you anything to do with the seizure of the rifles?'

'No,' I replied, 'I was not in Tipperary when it occurred.'

'Did you investigate the matter?'

'No, sir. I was informed that Headquarters intelligence officers were making inquiries in Tipperary. I understood then that the matter rested with General Headquarters.'

'But you did not hold an inquiry?'

Collins did all the questioning.

'No. I thought it unusual for officers to enter my area without reporting to divisional headquarters. It seemed as if they were acting without wishing to consult us.'

'They did call at your headquarters but there was evidently nobody at home,' said Collins. 'All right, Earnan, that will do. I am satisfied that you had nothing to do with the seizure. It's very serious, you know.'

I left and joined the officers in the ante-room. Con was called next and was away some time.

'This will last till Tibb's Eve,' said the Kilkenny Brigadier. 'I don't see what we have to do with it. My headquarters is over sixty miles from Tipperary town.'

Con returned and Mickey Fitz, the Quartermaster, was called outside. 'Well, Con, what penance did you get?' asked Seamus Robinson. We looked like a group waiting for confession. Con's blue eyes twinkled. 'Collins is in a hell of a rage,' he said. 'Watch my poker face.' His muscles tightened and he looked non-committal. One by one the men left the room while we talked, but there was an air of restraint. Some of the men were nervous and ill at ease. The last man returned, closing the door quietly behind him. Suddenly the door was flung open and Michael Collins stalked into the room. We rose as he entered.

He came over to where Brian Shanahan and his officers stood. He planted his legs apart and thrust his head forward. 'Some of you bloody fellows know about this. The rifles did not walk away. Negotiations in London will be held up over a few rifles. The British will say we have broken faith.'

He tossed his hair back from his forehead with a shake of his head. 'Come on, by Christ, and answer the questions I ask.' His voice became threatening. 'We're not going to let you get away with those lousy rifles.'

'We won't be bullied,' said the commandant.

'I'm sorry,' I said interrupting, 'but the officers here are accustomed to being spoken to politely.'

Collins put his hands deep in his trousers' pockets, lifted himself a little on his feet, came back again on his heels, then turned abruptly, walked out and banged the door.

There was silence for a moment. Then we laughed.

'I'm going,' said Brian Shanahan. 'No man is going to talk to me as if I were a dog.' He walked out, followed by his men.

O'Duffy came in. He talked amicably. 'I'm sorry he lost his temper,' he said, referring to Collins, 'but he is very worried and we cannot blame him.' He sat down.

'What about the negotiations? Are they ever going to end?' I asked.

'If they end suddenly, it will be due to the seizure of the rifles. The oath of allegiance seems to be the crux of the matter, but it looks as if our delegation will return shortly. Negotiations will be completed one way or the other, war or peace.'

The following day, in long boots, with two guns, I accompanied the Assistant Chief of Staff, Ginger O'Connell, when he inspected an officers training corps in University College. Large numbers of students appeared on parade outside the main entrance; they were now eager, and evidently the university did not view the inspection with disfavour. It was safe to parade now. Many who had sneered at the country boys who had served faithfully, unobtrusively, for the past four years were now anxious to become officers.

In Dublin I noticed a certain amount of drinking. Headquarters staff officers could be found at the bar in Vaughan's Hotel or drinking in the rooms of the Gresham. We could see men now in relation to living again, after secrecy and withdrawal. Mulcahy, however, never touched drink. I told him about the commission that was forwarded to me by Cathal Brugha. He laughed as if amused. 'That's the MD's own idea,' he said, and did not throw any further light on the subject.

Throughout the country recruiting had continued; the companies had increased in strength, some had doubled their numbers. In many places special companies of 'trucers', as they were called, were organized. We remembered the conscription scare in 1918, when recruits had poured in. When the threat had not been enforced the newcomers had fallen away, and the over-worked officers found they had sweated for men who only wished to save their own skins. We were doubtful about the advisability of continuing to recruit. The division now totalled over thirteen thousand men, but perhaps they would all be needed when the war began again.

I toured the Mid-Limerick area inspecting the country for

suitable ambush, signalling and sniping positions, taking notes and sketches of the police and military posts. When I reached Limerick I placed the car in a garage to have the lights fixed and walked up O'Connell Street. I saw Brian Shanahan approaching. He halted.

'What are you doing here?' I asked. 'Have you permission from your brigade adjutant?'

'No, I have not.'

'Don't you know,' I asked, 'that instructions have been issued that no member of a battalion staff can leave his area without the permission of the brigade adjutants?'

'Yes, we received the order.'

'Well, you'll have to return, Brian. You know that every officer is needed in his own area. There is so much to be done.'

'I have to remain here,' he said. He looked a little confused, but determined. He lowered his voice. 'There's an Irish Republican Brotherhood meeting here today and I have been ordered to attend.'

'All right,' I said and walked on.

The Irish Republican Brotherhood was a secret oath-bound society established in 1858, over sixty years ago, as the Fenian Brotherhood: the Fenians, they were spoken of. Always it had maintained a small nucleus and had been the core of the physical force movement. Some like Cathal Brugha and de Valera did not now approve of it, and the opposition had led to friction. They thought that it had ended its purpose with the Easter fighting; perhaps they feared its political influence, for it sought to control all existing Irish organizations.

As I walked along, thinking of the IRB, I met another of my officers, the Adjutant of the East Limerick Brigade. 'Have you permission from the Divisional Adjutant to visit Limerick?'

'No,' he replied, 'but I must remain until this evening.'

'IRB?' I inquired. He nodded and walked on. I turned back and went down to the centre of the city. On O'Connell Street I would meet anybody I knew. It is the main street of the city, the only street one would care to walk up and down, a habit of the Limerick people in the evening time. I met an officer from Mid-Clare. 'I suppose you're here for the meeting,' he said. 'Where is it to be held?' I asked. He told me the place and time; then I talked of his area and the men there whom I had known.

A little later than the appointed time I walked in to the meeting. There were a number of men present, about sixty, and the proceedings were about to begin. Sean O'Muirthile was seated behind a table. In front of him were sheets of paper, typewritten. He was talking to some Clare officers who stood near the table. My entry was unnoticed. The man who opened the door knew me; he did not ask any questions. The men were seated on chairs in rows facing the table and I sat down amongst a group of East Limerick officers and men.

Sean O'Muirthile struck the table with the end of his fountain pen. He was about to speak when he caught sight of me.

'*Dia's Muire dhuit.* What brought you here? You have not been summoned, nor are you entitled to attend. I must ask you to leave the room.'

I stood up. 'I am sorry,' I said, 'but this is my divisional area. My officers are present. Even some who are not officers. I am responsible for my area and for them to the Government of the Republic.'

A Clare officer jumped up. 'We do not object to his presence. We all know him, to our cost. I vote that he be allowed to remain.' Other officers stood up and said: 'And I also.'

'Very well,' said O'Muirthile, 'he can remain.'

He tapped the table with the fountain pen. The men stood to attention. 'I call the meeting to order in the name of the Irish Republic,' he said, standing to attention himself. The officers sat down. An order was read about the re-organization of the IRB in each area. The circles, as the groups were called, were instructed to take in recruits. O'Muirthile spoke again. 'This order must be put into effect at once. Select the men carefully but increase the strength of the organization. Are there any questions?'

'Yes,' I said, standing up. 'I think it inadvisable to recruit amongst the trucers. They have not been tried. Many officers and men who have been thoroughly tested during the war do not belong to this organization. I see some present here whom

I never considered in any way energetic. All officers in our division are fully occupied now. They have more work than time.' I sat down.

'Any other suggestions or questions?' asked O'Muirthile. Nobody spoke. 'All right,' he said. 'Circles will be strengthened.' Other matters were discussed also relating to organization. O'Muirthile rose. The men sprang to attention. 'The meeting will close in the name of the Irish Republic,' he said.

Afterwards as we walked out to the street I said to a group of Tipperary men: 'Why didn't some of you speak? You think the same as I do about the trucers.'

'We do,' said one, 'but we did not like to say anything.'

Our engineers had been working hard at a gun. I had seen it from time to time at the munition factory. Its pattern changed with time. Rory O'Connor, Director of Engineering, visited our area and was very pleased with the results of the engineering training camps. He saw the initial stages of the gun and laughed. 'It's one up on the Headquarters engineers.' He had no motor-car and wished to inspect other areas. He had not been given a car by General HQ, and although the First Southern had many cars he could not obtain the loan of one from them.

'Headquarters should give you a car,' I said. 'In Dublin there is no lack of cars, some for joy-riding only.'

He shrugged. 'It's hard to get a grant for my department. The Staff don't consider it important.'

I gave him my car. He could do more important work than I could. He remained two days, read through our training schemes and general orders, and was given an idea of the administration of the division. He studied the operations maps and we discussed plans. 'I wish I had known of this before,' he said as he left, but we did not understand his words.

'What do you think he means?' asked Con, after he had gone. 'I don't know,' I said.

The Divisional Engineer, Bob de Courcy, sent us word by despatch rider that the gun was ready. He wished to carry out an official test in the presence of the Staff. We visited the

munition factory in Co. Limerick, which was now equipped
with oil motors. We watched the men casting grenade bodies.
We tested some hand-grenades in the rear of outhouses and
worked out by paper screens the distribution of the splinters.
Sometimes grenades burst all to one side instead of giving a
central distribution. The gun was in a large flat field, covered
with a piece of tarpaulin. Beside it were trays of shells of
different lengths, with and without explosives. There were
slits cut in the shells. The slits contained expanding vanes
which were fan-shaped, connected together by pieces of
elastic. When the shells left the muzzle the expansion of the
vanes helped to direct the flight. The gun was rapidly stripped
and we examined the parts. The barrel was long, about six
feet of cold drawn steel; joined to it was the container of large
calibre. Between the container and the barrel, which could be
unscrewed with a specially-shaped wrench, was a thin
diaphragm of mica. There were two steel oxygen cylinders
filled with compressed air. Underneath the container was a
trigger. When it was pressed a thin steel striker pierced the
diaphragm, the compressed air rushed into the vacuum of the
barrel and gave velocity to the shell. The gun was reassembled. It certainly looked like a piece of artillery. There
were sights on the barrel and the gun could be traversed in
any direction. A flexible steel tube connected cylinder with
container, a pressure gauge on top of the container showing
when the air had reached the required point.

'I've tested the mechanism,' said de Courcy; 'it's quite
safe.' He laughed, showing his isolated top teeth. 'The genus
barracks will rapidly become extinct in this area.' This was
what we wanted. A piece of light artillery, if not some trench
mortars. 'I will use a live shell and hit the target at two
hundred yards.'

A wooden door, backed by stones, had been placed at the
required distance.

'You had better move back a little,' I said.

'I would prefer to remain with the gun,' de Courcy said.
'I'll go down with it if necessary.'

I remembered an experiment we had carried out with a
cannon on the Kerry frontier, so I told the others to get back
fifty yards and we lay down. De Courcy stood upright to one

side of the gun; his assistant, Peadar Dunne, sat on a small stick which ran out at an angle. De Courcy, I thought, is like a sea captain. He has a gun instead of a ship. De Courcy bent down. There was an explosion, a shout, and de Courcy was seen hopping about on one leg. Peadar, the assistant, was stretched on the ground, his face dabbed with blood. Smoke blew around the gun. We ran towards it. The barrel had burst, Peadar's jaw had been cut open, and de Courcy had been struck by a flying splinter.

'Something went wrong,' he said. 'The pressure must have been too great, or we used too much explosive. We'll try again and fire it from a distance.'

The gun was improved, tested again and found to be satisfactory.

When Con and I returned to our headquarters we found two despatches, one from the Minister for Defence asking us to bring the gun to Co. Clare for demonstration. He and de Valera were then inspecting the First Western Division, but he had already met the officers of the Tipperary battalion in my own division. 'The rifles will have to be returned,' Cathal Brugha had said; 'I'm sorry'. As the officers left he called them back, looked at the crestfallen faces and said: 'If there have to be raids, they should be quiet ones.' The officers laughed. Capturing rifles was one thing, I felt; giving them back was another. We had never been accustomed to return rifles.

The other despatch was from the Adjutant-General in Dublin. He gave us seventy-two hours' notice to prepare for hostilities, move our peace headquarters to our active service one, burn any important papers that we could not take with us.

We worked all day and late into the night removing papers and getting our new headquarters ready. The munition plant was dismantled, supplies and explosive were distributed to dumps. Orders were sent out to the brigades to stand-to; columns were ordered to mobilize, and operation plans revised. At last a decision had been arrived at. We sang and whistled as we worked. The uncertainty was at an end. War again, and a ruthless one. At the beginning of the truce the people in our area were staunch; they had offered their money and help for when hostilities would reopen in a few weeks time, as we then thought. Then the daily papers, always hostile to Irish independence, had prepared the way for defection of thought. They hinted that a renewal of the fighting would be impossible, that England would grant a sufficient measure of freedom. There were long leaders and articles on Dominion Home Rule and on Canadian status. Slowly the strength of the national resistance was being undermined.

Before dawn we were ready; the gun and its crew were collected and we set off for Clare. We crossed the Shannon and an hour later reached the Clare hills where we were met by a scout. We were oily from the gun, our clothes were smeared, and we were unshaven. We had come without uniforms for we had not many and were saving them for active service. After a time motor-cars with officers in uniform drove up. The First Western had arrived. We looked a sorry contrast to the gay escort. I apologised to the Minister for Defence, but he smiled and said he understood. Bob de Courcy explained the mechanism of the gun and the action of the parts to de Valera, Cathal Brugha and the assembled officers. A new name had been added, the 'Peadar stick', on which Peadar had sat when the accident occurred at our munition factory. They asked many questions. The gun was assembled and stripped quickly; then set up ready for action. A pile of stones was a target. The gun was fired from a safe distance; first empty, then live shells were used. Cathal Brugha's face beamed. He forgot his wounded leg and was as excited as a schoolboy. He ran after the shells to measure the distance covered. 'We will soon give you an order for a supply of guns,' he said to de Courcy.

On the way home we met Mulcahy in Ennis. He invited me to dine that night with the Bishop of Killaloe, but I asked permission to return at once to our headquarters. He appeared surprised when I told him of the despatch from the Adjutant-General and did not seem to have heard of it. That's strange, I thought. Surely the Chief of Staff should know that his army was getting ready for war.

As we were preparing to leave Ennis a report came in from a friendly Auxiliary that members of his company from

Killaloe were in Ennis and that they intended to shoot de Valera as his car passed into the town. We, the oily gun crew, set off on foot to examine the approaches to the town. We were joined by other groups and patrolled the road until the President's car passed through in safety.

A little later, on 7 December, the full text of the Articles of Agreement was published in the Irish papers. I was in East Limerick and the paper reached me the following morning. The five Irish delegates had signed the articles and had returned to Ireland to recommend them to the Irish people. They had signed under Lloyd George's threat of 'immediate and terrible war' on the Irish people.

I cursed loud and long. So this was what we had been fighting for, what we had worn ourselves out for during the truce.

The Quartermaster of the Brigade was in the room. He was silent.

'But Mick,' he began.

'Damn Mick,' I said.

'There's some catch somewhere,' he said. 'Mick Collins would never have signed it. He knows what he is doing.'

I walked out to my car, a long grey-green body, with a very large wheel-lock so it could turn easily on a narrow road. The windscreen was gone, so had the hood. I drove hard across trenches and pot-holes, bumping, swaying, jerking, but I was not thinking of the car or of the road.

Dinny Kelly met me at the door of the hut.

'Bad news, Officer, a regular catastrophe,' he said as he shook hands. 'Collins is a nice boyho, but he must have been dead to the world to sign the likes of that. I wouldn't be in his boots this minute for all the money in the Bank of Ireland.'

'Were you in Tipp?' I asked. 'How do the people take it?'

'Some of them are pleased, the ones that never did a hand's turn to help. The others are tearing mad.'

A numbness followed my first outburst of rage. I became suddenly very tired. I sat down near the table. I felt like a man who tried to cover his head to escape blows showered on him from every side.

I sat with my elbows on the table, my hands pressed against my temples. I could not think; I looked at the wall where the map of the division hung. I took it down and pinned it on the table and stared at it dully. The area began to shape itself up for me, the contours became hills and mountains, little spots of green became woods and forests, the blue lines of rivers formed valleys. Here was the country we had fought for. I followed the boundaries. Evacuated barracks, burnt or stormed, were marked in green triangles. They showed where the enemy had been driven in on his main lines of communications. Blue circles for police block-houses, blue squares for military barracks. Our small companies dotted in with red pencil. Places where we had fought had crossed swords in purple India ink. The history of the area was before me. I followed our little struggles, our victories, our defeats. We had given ourselves to this land, with death or imprisonment as a reward. Other generations had done this. The dead, what did they think? Small dots on the map showed where men had died. I bent close to the map. Men from the Tipperary battalion, Paddy Moloney and Sean Duffy, commandant, had died fighting, surrounded by Tans, beyond that small dotted double line, the road. In the Cashel battalion, the commandant had died, shot through the heart as he fought from a house. There was the house, a black dot. Up near the hills Tommy Donovan, the battalion comman-dant, had been killed fighting on the streets of Killenaule. I moved across to the adjoining brigade, East Limerick. There the brigadier had been shot dead outside that house, standing in from that thick red line, the main road. Here Martin Conway, the fearless, had fallen in action against police and soldiers, and lower down on the map the wounded Tobin had dragged himself to die, there, outside his mother's house. Here we had been chased, there we had stood and fought.

What was the use of brooding over it? I became angry again as I thought of the men who had betrayed us.

CHAPTER THREE

DECEMBER 1921—MARCH 1922

THE officers and men I met seemed dazed. Some had been crying, their eyes were swollen. We awaited the arrest of the delegates. They had no authority to sign without first referring the matter to their Cabinet. Some of us expected that they would have been arrested when they landed, but nothing happened. The press approved of their conduct; county councils expressed agreement or disagreement. The Catholic clergy as a whole applauded their signing. I sent despatch riders to the neighbouring divisions and found that the First and Third Southern were opposed to the so-called treaty, but that the First Western to a great extent approved of it. Dail Eireann, it seemed, was going to debate the articles. Why could not the President decide the matter.

I went to Dublin to find out what was going to happen, to discover how the army stood. I dropped into McGilligan's, as was my custom when in town. The family, with the exception of Eileen, was in favour of the treaty. Ginger O'Connell, the Assistant Chief of Staff, was there. He was not perturbed; he seemed pleased with life in general. He smiled, twisting his head slightly as he did when he made a pun. Beside him sat Michael Brennan, Commander of the First Western, in uniform; curly hair, handsome face, with Clare accent. He seemed to be on good terms with the Staff now. Formerly Mulcahy and Collins had been hostile to him.

'We're talking about the army,' said Ginger. 'We'll be allowed to have twenty thousand men.'

So that was it; he had solved his difficulties. The organization of an army was the important question!

'How will you build it up?' I asked.

'From the IRA,' he said. 'We expect to get many a good battalion from the Second Southern for the Free State Army. Stout fellows in your area.'

I was silent.

'How many men can you contribute?'

'You'll have to fight in our area if you are false to your oath,' I said. Ginger's smile faded away. 'That's where you'll meet with immediate and terrible war.'

Then I left the room.

The Dail had been meeting daily. Member after member had disclosed his views, most of them at length. Terms of abuse had begun to creep in. The old story, divide and conquer.

The morning after my arrival in Dublin I wrote a letter to the President, Eamon de Valera. I told him that he, for us, had always typified the ideal of Irish nationality, that we trusted and relied on him. I pledged our division to his support if he wanted to take action, and told him that the First Southern Division could be relied upon. That afternoon I met Mulcahy and the Adjutant-General, Gearoid O'Sullivan, in the halls of the National University where the treaty debate was being held. I saluted. They shook hands with me.

'When will the debate be finished?' I asked.

'I don't know,' said Mulcahy.

I asked him if he was in favour of the Articles of Agreement. 'How are you going to vote?'

'I am in favour,' he said, 'but you must disassociate my position as Chief of Staff from that as representing a constituency. I would do or say things as a public representative that I would not do or say as Chief of Staff.'

'I cannot reconcile the two positions,' I said. 'I hereby tender my resignation as officer commanding the Second Southern.'

'You are acting prematurely. I can not accept your resignation. During the months to come we will require all our experienced officers to deal with the new situation, to help to police the country and maintain order.'

I saluted and walked off. At the head of the stairs I saw Cathal Brugha. He ran towards me, gripped both my hands and smiled. 'Well, a chara, how are you?' he asked. I told him I had offered to resign. He linked his arm in mine.

'You must not do that,' he said; 'you are playing into their hands. That is exactly what they would like you to do. Go

back to your division and try by every means in your power to
keep it intact.'

'How is the debate going to go?' I asked. His face became
grave. 'I don't know, but I think we'll win through.'

That night I found Peter Moloney reading a copy of Document No. 2, an alternative to the treaty, which de Valera had
devised. Next morning I met Liam Mellows and told him that
if that document were put forward as an acceptable alternative to the treaty, I would withdraw the support I had
offered.

All that evening I walked from street to street. I was sick at
heart. The splendid dream we had built up was toppling like
a house of cards. I found myself near the National Gallery. I
went in. Often I had come there for quiet, for peace. The
Italian and Dutch rooms seemed filled with ugly daubs today.
I walked out again. It was no good trying to sit and think.
There was no solution now. The majority of the Army Staff
had their minds made up: how long since? O'Connell had
worked the situation out. How often had we vowed, as we sat
around the turf fires, or as we tramped with squelching feet,
the rain dripping into our boots, that we in our generation
would finish the fight? We would save the boys to come from
what we had seen our people go through, when we felt others
would take our places. Was the sacrifice in vain? We were
strong in faith, in spirit, and men. We had built up a government that the people respected and trusted. In our strength
did we do what we had never thought of doing in our weakness, betray the sovereign independence of Ireland? What
would the Fenians have done in their day if the heritage of
their trust had been violated? What would the poor dead
generations, who had toiled, landless, starved, homeless,
beaten to their knees, cowed, disheartened, with the vision in
their hearts. They did not barter. We were to become part of
the British Empire and lose our souls.

That night, in a house in Heytesbury Street, I met Liam
Lynch, Rory O'Connor, Liam Mellows and Seamus
Robinson, the brigadier of Tipperary Three in my division.
The family had talked to us at first and laughed; then when
they had seen our faces they became serious also. We sat
around a polished table in the drawing room. Rory's eyes

were sombre. I noticed the grey streaks in his black hair. Liam Mellows looked energetic, business-like, efficient, anxious to settle down to work. He had been attending the meetings of the Dail.

Liam Lynch was square and determined looking. He tightened his pince-nez glasses as he muttered: 'My God, it's terrible, terrible.'

Seamus was dogged. His hair was touselled. He held his clenched fist underneath his underlip. Somehow he had sensed that one day something would go wrong. There was an old antagonism between Mulcahy and himself. Seamus had too much of the French kind of inquiring, critical logic.

I sat there white-faced, feeling as if I would like to cry. Thought was so difficult when there was no way out. Thinking in the dark only made one's brain turn around the wrong way. If only we could act. That would clarify thought. What to do?

Liam Lynch broke the long silence. 'I wish we knew what the other divisional officers thought and felt. That would make things easier.'

'Have you seen Collins?' asked Rory. 'He was looking for you.'

'Yes, I have. I met him and Eoin O'Duffy. They said the treaty would give breathing space, allow the army to arm and equip; then we could declare war whenever a suitable opportunity came.'

Rory said: 'They mean to enforce the treaty, but we must organize.'

'That's the difficulty,' I said. 'They have their minds made up and have, I expect, organized IRB and the army. We don't know who remains true, and we are disorganized.'

Rory was in favour of breaking away from General Headquarters, and that as soon as the debate in the Dail was over. Seamus and I agreed. Liam Mellows said: 'Let the situation develop. The Republican Army will never stomach the treaty.'

We decided to keep in touch with each other and with Rory's office and find out what men still believed in an uncompromising Ireland. Rory's quiet humour broke the gravity; soon we were chatting and laughing.

That same night when I returned to the house I slept in, I met Con. 'Collins sent four messengers after you here today and this evening. They said he wants to see you at once. It's urgent.'

'I'm not going to meet him,' I said.

We returned to our hut next morning early.

Dail Eireann adjourned until after Christmas. We knew that time was on the side of those who were in favour of the treaty, and had hoped that a vote would have been taken at once before the adjournment, for in the meantime pressure of different kinds would be brought to bear on public representatives, public bodies, and army officers, to support the treaty. During the debates the alternative to the treaty, Document No. 2, which had been discussed at a secret meeting of the Cabinet, and was not meant for publication, had been dissected by the members of the Dail. In fact, the debate seemed at times to resolve itself into a discussion of the rival possibilities of the Articles of Agreement and of Document No. 2. Early in January 1922, the Dail reassembled and when the final vote was taken, sixty-four deputies voted for, and fifty-seven against, but only three accepted the articles on their merits; the other sixty-one supported them as the only alternative to war.

Collins was spoken of as the man who had won the war. The people's war, which had been lost when we were able to win it. Members of the Dail said they voted for the treaty because they were told that the IRA could not fight again. There was not enough ammunition. They had been told by Collins and Mulcahy that the army was in favour of the treaty. Two days after the vote was taken, de Valera resigned as President, and Arthur Griffith, one of the signatories to the treaty, was elected President of Dail Eireann in his place. Griffith stated that the Republic of Ireland would remain in being until the Free State was established, and that Dail Eireann would remain in existence until an election was held. Dick Mulcahy, the new Minister for Defence, promised to keep the army 'in the same position with regard to the government of the Republic and under the same management and in the same spirit as before'. Four days later Griffith called a meeting of the members elected to sit in the Southern

Parliament. A year previously the British had constituted two parliaments, one of Northern Ireland, the other of Southern Ireland. When the Southern Parliament had been convened four out of one hundred and twenty-eight elected members attended. Dail Eireann refused to recognize it. Now sixty-four members were present, including the four Unionists from Trinity College who had last year been the only members who attended this Southern Parliament. The Articles of Agreement were submitted to the body. They approved of them. By their presence they had agreed to a divided Ireland. A Provisional Government was formed before the meeting ended, with Michael Collins as Chairman, and authority taken from the hands of the Dail.

The British began to evacuate the country slowly, handing their barracks over to the Irish Republican Army. Our Headquarters undertook to maintain a certain number of men in barracks, to uniform and equip them, and to give them a small allowance. Some of the Dublin barracks were first handed over, and were occupied by men from the 'Dublin Guards', officered by members of Collins's former intelligence squad. In the country the men in barracks were maintained by running bills, as instructed by Mulcahy, on the local traders.

A meeting of senior officers was held in Dublin. I was in the mountains, the Comeraghs, and the despatch did not reach me in time. When I returned from the mountains I saw Con at the hut. 'You missed the meeting,' he said, 'but you did not miss much. De Valera attended and appealed for unity. He said that no matter what political parties said or did, the army must remain intact.'

'That's all tripe,' I said. It was impossible. There were two parties now, Republican and Free State. Those who believed in an absolutely independent Ireland and those who wished to become a dominion of the British Empire.

Some of the officers of the Headquarters, the Chief of Staff, Assistant and Deputy Chiefs, Director of Intelligence, Adjutant-General, Director of Organization, Director of Training, Quartermaster-General and Director of Publicity, approved of the treaty and would naturally strengthen their political positions by reason of their army ranks. Three of them were members of Dail Eireann.

The Directors of Engineering, Chemicals, Munitions and Purchases, were still Republican. The commanding officers of the First and Second and Third Southern Divisions, of the Second, Third and Fourth Western, of the Fourth Northern, and of the Dublin Brigade were Republican. The commanding officers of the First Eastern, First Western, First and Second Northern, and some of the brigades still undivisionalized, were pro-treaty.

I knew from the conversation I had had with Ginger O'Connell that a Free State army would be built up. I had no longer any faith in Collins or Mulcahy. They would use the army for their own purpose and slowly our men would either be absorbed or would have to return to their farms, businesses or universities.

I went to Dublin to see Rory O'Connor. Count Plunkett told me that he was at home in Monkstown. I took a tram out along the sea front. The house overlooked Dunlaoghaire and Dublin Bay. Across the bay was Howth Head, Howth of the Golden Spears, and the semi-circle of coast connecting it with the city.

Rory came to the door. 'The very man I want,' he said. 'I sent word to you two days ago that there would be a meeting this evening. We must come to some decision at once.'

In a front room overlooking the bay, he played gramophone records, Brahms, Debussy, *La Fille aux Cheveux de Lin*, Ravel's *Jeux d'Eau*, Schumann's *Carnival*. I searched amongst the records for Spanish music, Longas, Falla, Albeniz, but I could find only *La Gitana*. We forgot about the time. Suddenly he started. 'We must go down town now.'

As he placed the records in the albums he turned to me and said: 'Did you ever hear 'The Soldier's Song' sung by a drunken man?'

'Yes,' I replied.

'Well, you'll hear it now.'

He placed four records on the central steel point; on top was 'The Soldier's Song'. The records covered the steel point. He moved the top record until it was inaccurately centred, and released the disc. The words of the song were drawn out, the notes became flat, rising from one false note to another.

' 'The Soldier's Song' is like that to me now,' I said. 'I cannot bear to hear it sung.'

We trammed to the foot of Grafton Street and walked to the Pillar. His office was at the back of Marlborough Street. Women sat with wicker baskets of apples, herrings, bananas, at street corners. 'Three bananas a penny,' they shouted, 'a penny for three bananas.' Women with shawls over their heads, broken boots; children in their arms, snuggled against their dirty blouses. Kiddies ran about on bare feet. It was cold. Their small, torn coats were turned up about their necks. Some had holes in the seats of their trousers, others had a collection of grey, black, brown patches. The houses were tall, four and five storeys. Steps led up to the open doors. Some doors had one hinge missing. Ionic pillars, chipped, broken; cracked semi-circular fan-lights over the doors. The houses of the Dublin aristocrats of the eighteenth century. Here now was poverty, dirt, laughter, song, curses, children, children everywhere. We climbed the wooden stairs to his office and entered a large room. I had been here before, two or three times. A door led into a smaller room where his typist worked. The door was closed now.

The officers he had summoned arrived one by one, the Western officers together. Liam Lynch, McCormick, Tom Maguire, Billy Pilkington, Michael Kilroy, Oscar Traynor: the officers commanding the First and Third Southern, the Second, Third and Fourth Western, and the Dublin Brigade: the areas, with my own division, that had borne most of the fight. Sean Russell and Jim O'Donovan, Directors of Munitions and of Chemicals from Headquarters, were also present. Liam Mellows could not attend. I had not met Kilroy or the other Western officers before but I had heard about them.

Kilroy wore blue smoke-glasses; he had grey hair in amongst the black, a square face. He spoke slowly, haltingly, as if translating from a foreign language, his strong Mayo accent rising and falling. He was older than the others and had commanded the West Mayo column during part of the Tan war.

Billy Pilkington, fair-haired, thin faced, ruddy cheeks, straight, a pair of flashing blue eyes and an insistent directness of speech. He was very much loved by his men; very religious, a fighting saint.

Tom Maguire was quiet looking. He spoke in mono-
syllables, nodded often instead of replying. He had been a
large farmer though he did not look a farmer. He might have
been a teacher in a college.

The room was not well lighted. We sat on chairs forming
three sides of a square, which Rory's desk completed. A
prismatic compass, a map measurer and a celluloid pro-
tractor stood against the ledge of the desk. To one side of
them were coloured mapping inks and small slender mapping
pens. Maps hung on the wall. A large scale map of Dublin; a
map of Ireland with the divisional areas inserted in red
pencil. A pair of prismatic glasses hung on the back of the
door beside a heavy leather jacket lined with wool. Rory's
blue-black skin looked darker than usual; patches of light
rested on the hollows of his cheeks, the dark colour deepened
the shadows.

'We are all here now,' said Rory. 'You all know why you
were summoned. I outlined the reasons in my note. I think we
should regularize the meeting and appoint a chairman.'

He was elected chairman.

'There are officers in other areas who might have been
summoned,' he said, 'but I thought it best to gather a small
group together first. The Headquarters Staff are playing with
words. We are all still the Republican Army, but soon it will
be reduced and disbanded. How is the situation in your area,
Liam?' he asked.

'Some barracks have been handed over there but I have my
own men in them. Recruiting for the Free State Army is going
on, however. It is hard to trace it exactly, but we know some
of the organizers.'

No barracks had been taken over in the other areas.

'We should form a headquarters of our own,' said Jim
O'Donovan, 'and at once.' He spoke with his lips closing on
the words.

'Well, what do you think, Ernie?' asked Rory.

'The sooner we form an independent headquarters, the
better,' I replied. 'The men do not know what to do. Time is
on the side of the others to wear us down. Once we take a
definite step the men will know exactly where they stand.'

'They have the money,' said Billy Pilkington, 'the press, the clergy and the arms. All our areas are being sapped in one way or another. I vote we here and now form an independent headquarters.'

Rory had been writing on a sheet of paper.

'Let's see how this reads,' he said. 'The undermentioned officers had viewed with alarm the attitude of the Headquarters Staff on the question of the treaty. They demanded a convention of the whole army to meet at once. If the convention was not summoned, an independent Headquarters Staff would be formed.'

Sean Russell suggested some amendments. He twisted and untwisted his hands as he spoke, the fingers pressing the knuckles of the other hand. He threw himself forward when he stood up. The lapels of his coat went further back and his body turned to one side. His even teeth showed when he talked. He was the Director of Munitions, but his kindly, ready smile betrayed no trace of his death-dealing work. The statement was revised and read again. The officers were satisfied with it.

Some days after Mulcahy had received the communication he summoned the senior officers to Dublin. We met in the Banba Hall. All the Headquarters Staff, divisional commandants and independent brigades were represented. I carried two guns under my coat as I thought there might be an attempt to arrest some of our number. We sat around the room in a semi-circle, but though there was no break, there was a division. To the right were the men who were Republican, to the left the Treatyites.

Mulcahy said he intended to keep his promise, to maintain the army as the Republican Army.

'A name will not make it so,' said Rory, when the Chief of Staff stopped speaking.

'We intend to cut away from this Headquarters,' said Billy Pilkington. 'All you,' pointing to the Staff and to the officers on the left, 'want to build up a Free State army so that you can march in step into the British Empire. Do it openly. We stand by the Republic.'

'I do not recognize the authority of this Headquarters,' I said, 'nor of Dail Eireann. The members of the Cabinet and of the Staff are imperialists, marking time until we are worn down. They, the Free State, will be maintained with the arms which the British have sold to you.'

The officers protested. Jim O'Donovan turned to Collins. 'You are a traitor,' he said, 'and you should have been court-martialled long since for treason.'

Collins jumped to his feet. There were loud shouts of 'Withdraw', 'Apologize'. Some of our number seemingly did not approve of the word 'traitor'.

Mulcahy brought the meeting to order with a few quiet words. Whatever he felt his face did not show either feeling or emotion. Collins sat with hands propped up, supporting his chin, a fighting expression on his face.

'I will not withdraw the word,' said Donovan. 'It is true.'

Mulcahy had a suggestion to offer. 'We will give you officers permission to appoint two men to attend meetings of the Headquarters Staff to see that nothing hostile to Republican interests is said or done.'

'We'll go into another room and discuss the matter,' said Rory. We left the meeting and talked over Mulcahy's suggestion. Rory asked us what we thought.

'I agree,' said Liam Lynch.

'I don't,' I said. 'We cannot remain in Dublin all the time. Things can happen that will not be brought up at a Staff meeting and that we will not know of.'

The majority were in favour of forming an independent headquarters. Liam Lynch said he would have to leave us in that case. That eventually decided the question as his division was the strongest numerically, was better armed than any other area except in the Dublin Brigade, and had the largest territory. Oscar Traynor and I were appointed 'watchers', as we were called. We returned to the meeting and informed the Staff of our decision. Mulcahy promised to call an army convention in two months' time, at which delegates from every company area in Ireland would attend. The constitution of the army stated that a convention should be held yearly, but there had been none called since 1918. A large number of men in Dublin would have been noticed by the British during the Tan war.

I returned to the south, summoned a divisional council, and placed the matter before the officers. One brigade, East

Limerick, was willing to accept the conditions, the other four were hostile. I had the option of continuing to represent one brigade, many of whose officers approved of the treaty, or of refusing to co-operate with General Headquarters, and commanding four brigades whose officers believed in complete independence. I decided to command the latter. By breaking away from General Headquarters we would not receive any arms or ammunition. We would find it difficult to maintain men in barracks. We would be isolated. It was a definite step, however. Our brigades would know exactly for what they stood, to whom they were giving allegiance. We would find it difficult to get food; we would have to cut down staffs. Many of the men would have to return to their homes.

I was called to attend staff meetings in Dublin, but did not comply. I was ordered to report at Beggar's Bush barracks, the then Headquarters, but refused. The Assistant Director of Organization asked for a permit to drive through my area, as he thought he might be arrested. It was granted. I met him in Limerick and he had a talk with me. Two days later the despatch which he had brought with him and had not delivered, ordering me to attend a court martial in Dublin, was forwarded.

An immediate election was threatened. Churchill was anxious to have an election at once, but the Ard Fheis of Sinn Fein, comprising three thousand delegates, met and it was agreed to postpone elections for three months. In the meantime the final form of the Free State Constitution was to be produced for the people's consideration to vote on. Collins had often hinted in private interviews that the Constitution would be definitely Republican. The meeting was then adjourned.

During this time some of the barracks in the Second Southern had been evacuated by British troops. Our men went up to the gates on the morning of the evacuation with rifles and fixed bayonets to take over the post. Sometimes they were admitted; at others they had to wait until the garrison marched out. We would not allow the Mulcahyite officers to take over the barracks. They were afraid to enter the area. The local battalion staff moved in with a small guard of men; they could not afford to feed many of them. The barracks which formerly held one thousand or six hundred men now housed ten or fifteen. Some of the barracks had been left without a guard after our men had taken them over; the neighbouring battalion could not afford to keep any men there. The empty, unprotected posts had been the scenes of extensive looting. The people from the towns and neighbouring places had taken everything they could lay hands on, gas and electric-light fittings, woodwork, timber, closets, baths. The orgy of loot had developed into destruction in some instances. People seemed drunk as they smashed, tore and carried off material for which they had no use, on their backs, on asses and carts, in trucks. It seemed as if they vented their pent-up feelings of hatred, which they had had to suppress for so long, on the fittings of the former quarters of the British garrison.

I was at the hut when a Limerick officer arrived to see me.

'Dublin officers have taken over the Castle and the Strand barracks from the British,' he said, 'and men from the First Western Division have arrived as a garrison.'

Limerick city was in our division; evidently the Mulcahyites had grown in strength since they dared to enter a hostile area.

'Why the hell didn't the Limerick Brigadier take over the barracks himself?' I asked.

'We did not know they were going to be evacuated. It was news to him when he found that the Clare men had occupied them early in the morning.'

'I will probably arrive in Limerick tonight,' I said, and he drove away.

Limerick was a key position. It had always been strongly held by the British who had attempted from it to dominate counties Clare, Limerick, and portion of Tipperary. A Cork officer arrived that evening to see me. He wished to know if we had any definite plan of action to prevent our men being gradually absorbed by Mulcahy. I told him that our division was acting by itself, trying hard to exist.

'They have paid some divisional officers in our area,' he said. 'They have uniformed and equipped some of them in the barracks. They have organization behind them and know their strength.'

I told him of the Limerick situation.

'What do you intend to do?' he asked.

'I am going there as soon as I write some despatches. Would you like to come?'

'Yes, I would,' he replied.

We motored in to Limerick, where we met the Brigadier of Mid-Limerick. 'I have been talking to a Clare man in the Castle barracks,' he said. 'He seems friendly and when I said you would be in town tonight, he said he would like to see you.'

Late that night a tall, uniformed officer with a soft green uniform cap came to the house. 'I remember meeting you in 1919,' he said, 'in Mid-Clare.' I did not remember his face. I talked casually whilst I tried to remember the last occasion we had met, but could not. 'We thought we were going to Dublin, to Beggar's Bush barracks first,' he said; 'then we found ourselves in the Castle barracks here. Some of us did not like coming in to your area, the others did not mind. They say that you are all rebels and that General Headquarters is going to have its authority recognized in Limerick.'

'We don't want trouble,' I said, 'but the troops in the Castle and the Strand barracks will have to leave.' I asked for the names of the Dublin officers. He gave them to me. I inquired about strengths. He told me the position of the sentries, of the machine-gun posts, the strength of the guardroom, the situation of the officers' quarters. He seemed anxious to give information. He drew rough sketches for me.

'Are you willing to help?' I asked.

'I am,' he replied, 'I'm a Republican.'

'How do you return to barracks?'

'I have late leave. I knock at the front gate, one of the sentries opens it. I flash a light from my lamp when I get inside, tell my name, and then walk across to my room.'

'Are you willing to get late leave tomorrow night? I will have some men here. We will follow you in the gate, gag the sentries, hold up the guardroom and rush the officers' quarters. We don't want any shooting.'

'All right,' he said, 'I'll do that,' and he left the room.

I knew the Dublin officers, Slattery, Stapleton, and Kehoe. They had been members of Collins's intelligence squad.

'They will fight,' said the Brigadier. 'We will have to manage the sentries and the guardroom very quickly, and then lead the men to the officers' rooms. Once we have them prisoners there will be little trouble with the other officers or the men.'

'Whether there's shooting or not, the Free State Army is not going to seize a portion of my area,' I said. 'It will have to be confronted sometime. Trouble might as well begin in this division.'

I sent off a despatch to Seamus Robinson, telling him to let me have fifty to seventy armed men by road the next night. Our scouts would meet them on the Limerick road. The men were not to be told where they were going. In the morning an officer and I walked through the crooked, twisting lanes of the old part of the city, Irishtown. The Castle barracks, known as King John's castle, had been built in the thirteenth century. It had been a portion of the old walls; part of it faced the Shannon and commanded Thomond Bridge and the far bank of the river. The walls were massive, over forty feet high, sloping back out of the river, with a tower at the corner near the bridge. The other walls were modern, as were the barracks buildings. The tower and the river walls were loopholed, with long narrow slits for crossbows, embrasures for cannon. These had now been filled in with stones, leaving small openings for rifles. Lichen and grass grew between the crevasses, and mud and green slime were at the bottom. The river was low, but the tide at the mouth, over forty miles away, reached to beyond Thomond Bridge. We had studied the rough sketches before we approached the barracks. We identified the officers' quarters and other buildings. We again visited the narrow by-lanes. 'This would be a good place to keep our men while we're waiting in the night for the Clare officer,' I thought. 'There are not many houses here.' It was a small lane, deep in mud; puddles of water lay where the roadway had sunk. We crossed the river by the swivel bridge near the boat club and looked at the Strand barracks which was in view of the castle; then we returned to the house we had been staying in near the Tipperary road. We checked off the imaginary men for the raid. Ourselves two to hold up the sentries, two men to tie them up; six men for the guardroom;

eight for the officers' quarters, and ourselves; twelve men for
the men's quarters; a reserve of ten men to remain near the
guardroom, and twenty more men to cover the outside
approaches: total sixty. 'Won't the British and the Clare men
be surprised when they find that the castle has been
captured,' said my companion.

At ten o'clock that night the Tipperary force arrived. It
had numerous cars, lorries, Crossley tenders, a Lewis gun
and seventy men. The transport was placed in a small
bohereen off the main road. A guard was mounted. It was
raining; the wind lashed the rain into our faces as we detailed
off the men and explained what they had to do. We moved
quietly through the muddy lanes, in groups; heavy coats; the
darkness and the rain hiding our weapons. There were few
people out of doors. We reached the lane near the barracks.
After the men had been arranged in order of entry we lay up
against a wall and tried to shelter. The Clare officer was due
to arrive at 11.30 pm. We waited; no officer. Twelve o'clock;
he had not appeared. Perhaps he had been delayed, we
thought. We waited until one o'clock. Then, thoroughly wet
and in bad humour, we moved back to the Tipperary road.

'He must have funked it,' one of us said.

'We're here now,' I said. 'We can't surprise the barracks.
We'd better occupy some buildings and wait till morning.
Where's the nearest large building?' I asked the Limerick
Brigadier.

'The County jail,' he said.

'No, that won't do; we'll be there soon enough. Any
others?'

'The County Home.'

'We would disturb the patients,' I said.

'Well, the only other place I can think of,' he replied, 'is the
asylum.'

'That will do grand,' I said. We all laughed. We drove up
to the insane asylum and knocked at the door. There was no
reply. We knocked again. We heard the rattle of keys
approaching. The door was unlocked; the porter stood at the
half-open door, the heavy keys in his hand. 'What do you
want?' he asked crossly. He was in shirt and trousers, and
wore loose slippers, his hair was tossed.

'We want to enter,' I said.

He carried a lighted candle in his left hand, which he held above his head. The light waved to and fro in the wind. Forms of men, caps turned back-to-front, rifles on their backs, could be seen in patches of flickering light.

'This is the asylum,' he said; 'you can't come in here.'

'That's all right,' I said. 'You hunt up the Master; tell him the place has been taken over until morning. Nobody is to leave without permission.'

We placed men on guard out of sight near the entrance gates; and others stood near the telephones inside. We made tea in the kitchen, then lay on the floors and slept.

Next morning we decided to place our men in the hotels. We took over the Royal George and the Glentworth and billeted our men there. We could not feed them ourselves. I interviewed the hotel proprietors and told them to make the bills chargeable to the division. Before noon I telephoned the Castle barracks and said I wanted to see the Dublin officers. I was told to come over at once as they would like to talk with us. Another officer and I walked across the barracks yard and were met by Slattery, Stapleton and Kehoe. They brought us upstairs to a room over-looking the yard.

'Well,' said Slattery, 'we were expecting you earlier but you did not come,' and he smiled. I wondered if he was referring to our raid. Perhaps the officer had given information.

'I want you to leave the city,' I said. 'You have no authority to enter the divisional area.'

'We have received instructions from the Chief of Staff to take over the barracks here and to hold them,' said Slattery.

'I am sorry,' I said, 'but you'll have to leave. You can wire the Chief of Staff. If you remain here, I'll have to attempt to capture both barracks. I don't want bloodshed, but my area is not going to be invaded. Would you like it if I occupied barracks in Dublin?'

They were uncomfortable; they did not like the situation.

'We have to remain here,' said Kehoe. 'We don't like to because we know you, but we have to carry out our orders.'

Two officers from North Tipperary walked into the room. I knew both; one was Collison, a fine-looking man. 'Hello, Mike,' he said, addressing me. I was known by that name when I organized his area in 1919. He shook hands and smiled.

'I'm delivering an ultimatum,' I said. 'I want these officers to leave Limerick.'

'I don't like to be here; I wish I was out of it.'

'I will give you twelve hours' notice prior to hostilities,' I said to Slattery; then we walked back to our headquarters at the Glentworth.

I sent to Clonmel for more men and explained the situation by letter to the three divisional commanders in Connacht. I asked them for picked officers and men. I received a wire to say that men would entrain for Limerick as quickly as possible. The hotels were unsuitable, but they provided us with food and beds. At last we could have well-cooked, regular meals and sleep again in sheets; the occupation of Limerick was worth while if only for the good meals. At the last moment we could seize the positions that would be of use to us for attack or defence. A staff was appointed and the engineers surveyed the city, visited suitable positions which they reported on, and selected places to be mined. I went to Dublin to see Rory O'Connor. He looked grave when I told him of the Limerick situation.

'We have continued to work with Mulcahy under the 'watchers' agreement,' he said. 'We are waiting for the situation to develop.'

'It has developed in our area,' I said. 'Can you send me some engineers?'

'No, I'm afraid I cannot,' he said. 'You have taken the responsibility on yourself; you will have to see it through. Perhaps an agreement may be reached. Mulcahy and O'Duffy were to have gone to Limerick today.'

'If we don't act soon they will have taken all the important positions in Ireland—Dublin, Athlone, Limerick, and our men will grow tired of the inaction.'

'I cannot help you,' he repeated, 'but I hope there will be no fighting.'

Mulcahy and O'Duffy had arrived in Limerick, I learned when I reached the city. The officers at our headquarters refused to visit them in the Castle barracks. And they declined to visit our officers on neutral ground. I surmised from stray remarks that the conversation on the 'phone was not as polite as it might have been, as they returned to Dublin highly incensed. The western men arrived and were marched off to take over other hotels. Soon practically every hotel in the city was occupied. Sean Moylan of Cork came to see me. He offered to send engineers and explosives. We could blow in the gate of the castle or a portion of the wall and rush the buildings, using explosives in petrol tins with batteries attached. Extra Mulcahyites arrived. We marched and counter-marched to give the appearance of having more men than were actually there. Supplies of land mines had been prepared; the city had been surveyed and supplies of sand, sandbags and barbed wire had been commandeered.

The Mayor of Limerick invited the Castle officers to meet some of our own at lunch. We ate well but there was no result. I required complete evacuation. They meant to remain in the city. The British armoured cars patrolled up and down, as did the armoured cars from the Castle barracks. Liam Lynch was asked to negotiate and he came to Limerick, sent by Mulcahy; he met officers from either side, together and individually. Finally an agreement was reached. All the Mulcahyites were to evacuate the city and hand over the barracks to me. All my men were to leave Limerick save the garrison I would put in the Castle and Strand barracks. We had won without firing a shot. We had maintained our rights. The Connacht men departed to the western divisions; boys who had come from different parts of the country, outside of our command, without the authorization of their officers, left regretfully for their areas. The barracks were occupied by a small guard of Limerick men. I watched the Mulcahyites leave the city. A company of the East Limerick Brigade, formerly members of our division, were the last of the invaders to leave. They hung around. They did not want to go. The knew the Tipperary men were still in the city and they thought of delaying so that they would be the last to march through the streets. That would make the defeat less bitter. I threatened to arrest the officer in charge, and watched them march out. Then the Tipperary men passed through in their lorries and tenders on their way to Clonmel.

I was left to the inglorious aftermath, the collection of the many bills from the hotels of Limerick. We had attempted to include the payment of the bills in the agreement, but we did not succeed. After all, Mulcahy had been responsible for our occupation of Limerick; the bills should have been his to pay.

CHAPTER FOUR

MARCH—APRIL 1922

THE situation dragged itself out. The British were still leaving the country, the Royal Irish Constabulary were being disbanded, and numbers of Auxiliaries had volunteered for service in the Holy Land. The promised army convention was due to be held on 26 March, but on 16 March, four days after the Limerick settlement, Arthur Griffith took the bold step of proclaiming the convention. He threatened to suspend any officers who attended. Our division was the only area that would be unaffected. We were independent of Army Headquarters and of Dail Eireann. It was a challenge to the democratic spirit of the army. 'They must have gained in strength,' said Con, 'to take such a step. The army will hardly stand for it.'

'The army has stood for a lot,' I said. 'Mulcahy and Collins are afraid of a convention. Perhaps they sense they are not sufficiently well dug-in. A new Executive will probably be elected and a new Chief of Staff.'

'I wonder what Rory and the others will do now,' he said. 'It must be plain to them now that the Collins-Mulcahy policy is going to be put through at any cost.'

Next day I received an urgent despatch asking me to attend a meeting in Rory O'Connor's office. That was good news. The longer we hesitated to make a definite decision, the stronger the Staters would become. I wondered how many of the officers who had attended the first meeting still remained faithful.

We met in Rory's office. All the officers who had formerly signed their names demanding a convention were there, save McCormick, the commandant of the Third Southern. He had gone over to Mulcahy. Liam Mellows was present, and a newcomer, a small, dark-complexioned, brown-eyed officer, Joe McKelvey, commander of the Belfast Division. Rory was again elected chairman of the meeting.

'We're in the same position in which we found ourselves two months ago,' Rory said, 'but the situation has developed. We can all see what faith can be placed in Mulcahy's word. He's afraid of the convention. He dares not hold it. He thinks he has the whip-hand now because he has money, is able to pay his officers, and provide them with arms.'

'We'll hold the convention ourselves,' said Liam Lynch. 'We can notify all commands in Ireland whether they are friendly or not.'

'What do the other officers think?' asked Rory.

All were in favour of holding a convention.

'We'd better elect a Chief of Staff before we return home,' said Michael Kilroy. 'It can be a temporary appointment until the army convention is held.'

Liam Lynch was elected Chief of Staff. Liam Mellows, Quartermaster-General. Rory O'Connor, Director of Engineering. Jim O'Donovan, Director of Chemicals. Sean Russell, Director of Munitions. And myself, Director of Organization.

'We'll have to remain in Dublin now,' said Liam Lynch. 'Can you,' turning to Oscar Traynor, the Dublin Brigadier, 'provide a headquarters for us?'

Traynor thought for a while. 'I can,' he said. 'The Gaelic League hall in Parnell Square. Will that suit?'

'Yes,' said Liam, 'that will do for the present.'

We moved in that night. The hall stood amongst the row of houses forming the west side of Parnell Square. Built at the end of the eighteenth century, it had some spacious rooms but it had no office equipment. In the room on the ground floor I had signed as a member of 'F' company of the first battalion over five years ago. The Dublin Brigade supplied an armed guard. Some of the lower windows were strengthened with sandbags, but the building was unsuitable for defence. From my office on the second floor I notified all areas in Ireland about the convention. The constitution of the Irish Volunteers and the organization scheme were hastily printed and sent to divisions and independent brigades. Each brigade was to hold its own convention: each company elected two delegates; each battalion staff elected two; all were to discuss the situation, pass resolutions, examine the constitution and the

organization scheme. And the assembly elected a number to
represent the brigade at the Dublin convention.

On 26 March the general convention met in the Round
Room of the Mansion House. Over two hundred delegates
attended. Representatives also came from the north, the midlands, Wexford and Carlow, those areas in which the senior
officers were Free State. The meeting unanimously reaffirmed
allegiance to the Republic, and agreed to place all its forces
under the supreme control of an Executive to be appointed by
the convention. Finally the Executive of sixteen members was
elected by ballot. They would select from their number an
Army Council of five who would remain in or near the
capital. I was elected a member of the Executive.

The adjourned convention reassembled on 9 April. At a
table on the raised platform sat the Chief of Staff. He had
been elected chairman. I sat by his side; he had appointed me
as secretary. Resolutions which had been forwarded by the
brigades were put to the meeting and voted on, amended,
accepted or rejected. The Executive had been instructed to
draft a new constitution for the army and submit it to the
convention; it was dissected paragraph by paragraph. When
it was ready, I sent copies to all units and the constitution
was amended by the assembly who voted on each paragraph.
The Executive was to continue to meet to discuss and decide
on policy. It was to represent the views of different areas so
that the Chief of Staff could be kept in touch with the situation in distant parts of the country. The Army Council was a
tabloid executive which could meet frequently and advise
the CS.

When the Executive met that night in our headquarters,
Liam Lynch was confirmed as Chief of Staff. He retained the
members of the Headquarters Staff he had already appointed.
The Chief of Staff as member of the Executive possessed the
same influence as any of the other members, although perhaps his words were listened to with added respect. A resolution to proclaim the elections, which were to be held in
Southern Ireland, was discussed at a meeting. The treaty
would be the issue of elections to be held in the twenty-six
counties only. The election was not based on adult suffrage;
no man under twenty-five, no woman under thirty, could

vote, and the ages could be increased by four years in either
case. During the Tan war young men and women had not
added their names and addresses to the register. It would
have given the enemy too much information. Unless England
withdrew her threat of war no election should be held. There
was a majority in favour of proclaiming the elections, but no
decision was arrived at, as a unanimous vote would be needed
to take such an important step.

No arrangement was made to reimpose the Belfast boycott.
A pogrom had continued in the north; begun in Belfast, it
had spread to other parts of Ulster. Directed against the
Catholic minority, it was intensified against all who had Sinn
Fein sympathies. It had started in June 1920 and had continued sporadically. In six days of August 1920 twenty-two
people had been killed, well over a hundred seriously injured,
and more than three hundred slightly wounded in Belfast.
About one hundred and seventy houses and shops had been
burned. The destruction of life and property in north-east
Ulster had been much greater than that in the rest of Ireland
during the years of 1916 to 1921, yet martial law had not been
declared, and curfew restrictions, which had been imposed in
most cities, towns and even villages in the other provinces
during the Tan war, were not in operation. The homeless
people, over twenty thousand, found refuge in the south in the
homes of friendly persons. The Belfast boycott had been
imposed to check the victimization. Unionist firms in Belfast
were on the list; the people in other counties had been
instructed not to stock or sell articles forwarded by their
firms. During the Tan war the IRA had enforced the boycott.
Trains were held up, wagons searched, and boycott goods
burned. During the truce the IRA could not destroy supplies,
but the shops had learned not to stock the goods. Collins had
met Craig, the Premier of Northern Ireland, in London some
months ago. As a result, the boycott which had seriously
affected north-eastern trade had been withdrawn. No guarantee had been received that the minority would be respected.
The Orange Hall, a large building on the other side of the
square opposite the Gaelic League rooms, our headquarters,
was seized by us. It was then the headquarters of the
Orangemen in the south, the organization which had insti-

gated the pogrom. It was held by our armed guard, and here some of the refugees from the north were housed. They had to depend on charity; officially they had not been cared for. Some had a dazed, hopeless look in their eyes. They carried little bundles, all they had been able to save in some instances. The women looked broken; their nerves had been shattered during the period of waiting, always expecting that their houses would be attacked by rifle fire and burned by the mob. Dormitories were fitted up for them; boycotted food supplies were given to them. In the west, mansions and estates were taken over; they provided shelter for others of the homeless.

Our headquarters was unsuitable. It had become too small and we had the barest of office equipment as we wished to economize. Some of us ate in our friends' houses in rotation as we could not afford a mess. Twice it was reported that we were going to be attacked by Staters. Despatch riders and messengers scoured the city for us. We buckled on our guns and hastened to headquarters, waiting for the raid which did not come. We could not have held the building for long, anyhow. It was found impossible to maintain our men in the barracks throughout the country. Mulcahy, since the convention, had repudiated the bills which he had ordered those who had once accepted his orders to run on the local traders. The shopkeepers blamed our men for non-payment. A meeting of the Army Council was held in the Gaelic League hall. It was decided to raid the banks in Dublin and in the country to maintain our men. Mulcahy and his staffs were receiving salaries, being paid and armed by monies subscribed through the Republican loans in Ireland and America. Many needy people had stinted themselves to purchase bonds, the money to be used to defend and maintain the Irish Republic. Now it was being used to undermine it, to win over men, to buy arms, armoured cars and munitions from the British. Ostensibly the arms were at some future time to be used against the British; in reality they were to crush those who believed in the complete sovereign independence of Ireland. Griffith and Mulcahy could compensate the banks. Raids took place simultaneously throughout Ireland. Receipts in the names of the officers in charge of raids were to be given for all monies received.

My staff had increased; a typist and an assistant director, Sean MacBride, son of Major John MacBride executed after Easter Week. The typist had saved what was left of my temper. No longer would I pound, with finger uplifted as I sought the keyboard, tying myself into knots in the process. I was in the Orange Hall one night, selecting tins of Marsh's biscuits of Belfast which would supplement the afternoon tea we had in our rooms, when Liam Mellows came in by the back yard.

'We're going to take over the Four Courts tonight,' he said. 'We're going to have a decent headquarters at last.'

So that's why the Army Council met this morning, I thought. 'It's a huge series of buildings, Liam. They will surely attempt to clean us out tomorrow,' I said.

'We'll see,' he said, and smiled. 'Some of your Tipperary lads are due to arrive any minute. They will act as a garrison. Men from the Dublin Brigade will take the Courts over at midnight.'

We brought the biscuits over to the Gaelic League rooms and waited. There were armed men in the halls and in some of the rooms on the first floor. There was an air of suppressed excitement and of gay laughter—something to do at last. I packed up all my papers and tied them into brown paper packets. 'Are you ready?' said Liam, as I put on a Sam Browne belt and examined the breech and magazine of my long-barrelled Parabellum. 'It's near twelve o'clock now,' he said. 'We'll move down.' We walked along by the footpath near the river, through the dimly-lighted streets. We could see a group of men in one of the lanes off the river. 'They must be the Dublin men,' said Liam. As we approached the Courts the heavy massive buildings took blurred shapes in the darkness. The dome could be seen faintly against the sky. We leaned against the parapet opposite to the main gate. We approached the main gate. Some stooped down and gave the others a back. They climbed over the railings and disappeared in the dark.

'They're going to round up the police, I suppose,' I said. Liam nodded his head.

Dublin metropolitan police guarded the buildings which

were government property, containing the courts of higher
appeal and comprising the headquarters of the legal departments. The main building had been designed by James
Gandon and was now, together with the Kildare Street Club
and the Rotunda, amongst the outstanding edifices in
Dublin. The city had been ill-fated. Two fine buildings had
already been destroyed; the General Post Office had been set
on fire by shells during Easter Week, the Custom House had
been burnt towards the end of the Tan war. The heavy iron
gates of the Courts were opened from the inside. Liam and I
walked through. Inside in the shadows loomed tall forms, the
police, guarded by five youngsters. They were told to march
outside and go home. They answered our 'goodnights' and
crunched away. A sound of marching men. 'What's that?'
asked Liam. 'I don't know,' I replied; 'the Tipperary men or
the Staters.' We waited in the shadows. The marching feet
swung in the gate. Forms carrying rifles appeared; they wore
no uniform, the Tipperary men had arrived. Guards were
posted inside the three entrance gates. We moved up and
down in the dark, meeting members of our staff, trying to find
our way with flash lamps and candles. We went astray in the
dark. We got separated and shouted until we heard footsteps
or voices. It was a huge area of buildings.

One large block was pointed out by Liam Lynch. 'That
will be the Headquarters block. You had best select rooms
there.'

I entered room after room on the second storey. This will
do, I thought, as I located a nice little suite of rooms. I pinned
a sheet of paper on the door: 'Office of the D/O'. I opened
other doors. I found more suitable quarters. I pinned another
sheet on the door. I went further; yet better offices. It was like
being in a Hans Andersen fairy tale. First the boy had filled
his pockets with coppers. He went into another room. Here
was silver. He emptied his pockets and filled them with silver.
His pockets bulged. He found another door; he entered.
Coffers full of gold were in the room. He quickly emptied the
silver and filled his pockets with overflowing gold coins. At
last I was satisfied.

I went downstairs to help to put the position in a state of
defence. Motor-cars and lorries brought in sandbags and

barbed wire. The building swallowed them up. 'It's like putting a strawberry in a bull's mouth,' said a Tipperary boy, as he carried in a sandbag. The majority of windows were barricaded with heavy legal tomes, law books and weighty ledgers, and tin boxes filled with earth. There was an endless succession of windows. The buildings were as big as a city block. Before dawn we were tired, and we sat down to rest. In the darkness Liam Mellows sang come-all-yez, 'The Croppy Boy', and 'Come all ye brave Un-it-ed Men', giving the proper stress and intonation in his inimitable way. He seemed gayer, more cheerful now. Perhaps action, such as it was, after the long period of inaction had made him more light-hearted. Anyhow it was an adventure and the smiling faces one met, the snatches of song at intervals, the ring of voices across the darkness, showed that the men who were tired of the drifting policy now realized that some kind of a decision had been made. We had a good strong headquarters with a well-known name. That counted for something. We had come out into the open; no more hole-and-corner work.

From the flat roof some of us watched the dawn over the city, lifting slowly along the river, creeping up with the gulls from the Custom House. Shafts of light striking the shivering Liffey; a light breeze making little waves in relief. The light climbed up the houses, touched the sturdy Norman mass of Christ Church, moved to the slender spires of St. Patrick's Cathedral and dropped on to the irregular squares and cones of Guinness's brewery. We looked down at the defences and laughed. The barristers and the gowned notables from the Inns of Court never dreamed that one day their heavy legal tomes might defy the law and stop a bullet. We walked through and outside the buildings, attempting to get an idea of the whole. The Four Courts was built in the form of a square, with gaps where there were heavy gates leading to courtyards. Facing the Liffey was the main gate, with a high wall on either side, and buildings of cut-stone continued in each direction until they turned the corner of a street crossing the river by a bridge. Inside the gate was a large rectangular courtyard surrounded by buildings with a pillared colonnade. The buildings continued up the side streets at right angles to the river, an interval on either side for a gate. Two isolated buildings completed the square. The smaller one contained the records and was known as the Records office; the other was large. It was now the Headquarters block. The other large building, on the opposite side to our block, facing the river and separated from us by a courtyard, contained the dome.

We all had offices now; roll-topped desks, typewriters, bookcases, comfortable upholstered and leather chairs, good lighting. Supplies of files, notepapers, sealing wax and office material were supplied by the stationery office below stairs. The Tipperary garrison remained a few days, then returned to their area. They were replaced by less sturdy-looking Dublin men. Paddy O'Brien was appointed to command the garrison. He was above medium height, straight, soldierly, beautifully proportioned. 'The most beautiful body I have ever seen,' said a Dublin officer who had been at the university with me. 'I noticed it often when swimming. He reminds me of the Greek enthusiasm for manly beauty.' Blue-eyed, serious, good featured, tireless in energy. O'Brien selected Sean Lemass as adjutant.

The Records office was converted into a munitions factory. It was the most isolated building for that work. Lathes and motors were installed. Mine cases were made and filled with the explosives manufactured in the building; grenades were cast and filled. Liam Mellows, the Quartermaster-General, endeavoured to import arms. Officers were sent to foreign countries. Sean MacBride, the Assistant DO, a native French speaker, departed on mysterious journeys. Small quantities of arms arrived and were distributed; the garrison was armed with a short light German Mauser carbine. In the cellars I practised revolver shooting with the adjutant of the Courts, using ammunition which I had bought from the Assistant Quartermaster. Our target was a royal coat of arms cast in metal, the lion and the unicorn supporting the crown. They were scattered through the small courtrooms of the buildings. Liam Lynch heard the shooting one day and investigated. Next day an order was issued that there could be no revolver shooting without the written permission of the Courts commander. The Belfast boycott officers were on the ground floor. The director of the boycott, Henderson, was now important.

It was well to be as friendly as possible. Did he not have stores of tobacco and delicacies? My bedroom was in a large chamber. It must have been a conference chamber of some kind. There was a raised dais at one end, above which was the royal coat of arms. The room was panelled with oak; high carved-oaken chairs and upholstered settees were near the walls. There were no beds in the building. I made a couch by placing three of the chairs together, then I wrapped myself in a rug which one of my friends lent me.

We ate our meals in the block opposite, where there was an officers' mess. It was a place to avoid. The typists dined out. The material for the food was good, although we did not believe it until we had inspected the pantries and the kitchen. The cooks might have learned their trades in a sailors' dive on the quays. They were self-made cooks, however, who improved with time. I heard the orderly officer of the day register a complaint to the cooks, while I was seated near the door leading to the kitchen. 'I don't worry about the officers,' one of the cooks said; 'they'd complain anyhow. They think they're soldiers if they grouch enough.'

The minority party, the Republicans, in Dail Eireann were trying to obtain some form of political unity. Negotiations had continued for some time. Liam Lynch attempted to bring about unity between the two armies. A committee of officers from either side, ten in all, met frequently. Liam thought that a joint Headquarters Staff, Republican and Free State, might be reached by negotiation. He had already discussed the defence of the Courts with the Dublin Brigadier, Oscar Traynor. In case of threatened attack on our position by either British or Free State we would probably receive notice from our Director of Intelligence. Positions surrounding the Courts were to be occupied by snipers; some houses were to be lightly held; the Dublin barracks were to be isolated both by snipers and by occupying houses. Movement of enemy was to be hindered by destroying or blocking the canal bridges and barricading the streets. This would confine the armoured cars to certain areas. Attack was to be then directed on the positions occupied by the hostile troops surrounding the Courts.

I went to Connacht on a tour of inspection, visiting country I had not seen since I was a boy, country which had always been a vivid, living memory. I motored from Sligo along the coast out to Erris on the rough Atlantic, where our boyhood hero Ferdia had come from; the mountains of Achill and the cliffs could be seen in the distance as I took the road to Mulranny. Clew Bay again, a circular sweep of water running inland, turning at Westport to go out to sea once more, passing beneath the bare-looking climb of the Rock. The islands shining in the rough water. I spent from early morning until midday looking at the bay near Mulranny. My work could wait. I might never see the bay again. I visited the military barracks in Castlebar, now occupied by our men. I inspected the companies on parade in the barracks square where once from the high wall of Lord Lucan's demesne my brother and I had often watched the British soldiers drill. The towns in the west seemed to have a strange grey lichen appearance; there was no warmth in the buildings. I saw Tom Maguire in Ballinrobe near the lake country, after I had visited rock-swept Connemara.

In the Second Southern area Seamus Robinson had been placed in charge of the division.

On my return journey I visited Templemore barracks in Co. Tipperary. The barracks was occupied by men from Tipperary Two Brigade. They courted the Beggar's Bush Headquarters one minute, the Four Courts the next; the officers did not seem to be quite sure what part they meant to play. I had met Leahy, the Brigadier, a few weeks previously. He said that he hoped to obtain rifles from Mulcahy; he would then hold his barracks for the Republicans. Rifles were always a bait. We fought hard to obtain them, or had paid dearly for them. Many of the men now supporting Mulcahy thought that the rifles given to them would one day be used against England. The Mulcahyites made up his mind for him. 'Two weeks ago,' he told me, 'an armoured car was sent from the Bush and remained inside the gate. A guard was always kept in the car. At night the crew, Dublin men, slept in it. I expect the car was a threat. Our men surprised the guard one night and captured the car. We have it behind one of the blocks. The mechanics are overhauling the engine.'

'We want it in the Four Courts,' I said.

He hesitated for a while. 'All right,' he said, 'I'll go with you.' We inspected the car. It was covered with heavy plates of bullet-proof steel. The engine was long, a Rolls Royce. On top was a revolving steel turret which contained a Vickers gun, capable of long sustained fire without overheating; the ammunition was in strips, side by side, in narrow belts. Near the driving wheel was a long steel rod with a handle projecting into the car; the rod opened or shut the steel flaps protecting the front of the radiator: the engine would overheat if the flaps were not opened occasionally. There were small loopholes which could be closed with small steel shutters; they were for the revolvers of the crew.

We started off for Dublin, the driver, the Brigadier and I. This was a piece of luck. To think that I would return in an armoured car, the only one our men possessed. The car was stuffy at first, but the day was cold. We were soon warm and cosy. On corners the speed had to be considerably reduced as the car was too heavy. We had to wait outside the entrance gate of the Courts until the sergeant of the guard came down to identify me. I had forgotten to get a leave pass before I departed for the west. When I had signed my name and rank in the guard book I was admitted.

Men gathered about the armoured car. They were all pleased. This was an event. The Brigadier went directly to the Quartermaster's office. He was, I suspected, going to drive a hard bargain and obtain rifles in exchange. The following day I saw one of the garrison painting a name below the turret with white enamel—'The Mutineer'.

The press, as directed by the Staters, had given us a variety of names, 'Mutineers', 'Executive forces', 'Rory O'Connor's men', 'looters', 'bank robbers'. Always they were shy to call us Republicans; that name might raise memories even though Staters had proved as well as they could that a Republic had never existed.

CHAPTER FIVE

APRIL—JUNE 1922

WHILST I was in the country other positions in Dublin had been occupied by our men. The Ballast Office, the Masonic Hall, and the Kildare Street Club. Oscar Traynor had been ordered by our Chief of Staff to occupy these buildings; he was reluctant to do so, although two of them had been included in the emergency defence scheme which he had previously outlined for Liam Lynch. The Kildare Street Club was the most exclusive in Ireland and was the headquarters of the ascendancy, always closely linked with Dublin Castle. The Club fronted the grounds of Trinity College and extended into Kildare Street. It was well proportioned, with windows that had solved the problem of space. Now, boys from the Dublin Brigade, some of them undersized, roughly clothed, armed with rifles, replaced the uniformed porters at the entrance hall. They sat in the upholstered chairs where the members once lolled at ease. They played handball and occasionally puffed leisurely at long cigars. The source of the cigars was a mystery. I was friendly with the quartermaster of the Courts; he often brought a pocketful of cigars to my office and said with a grin: 'I can recommend these. I get them in my club in Kildare Street; all the other lords smoke them there, so you may be sure they're good.' Belfast refugees slept in the well-furnished bedrooms and sat somewhat fearfully in the reading rooms.

Executive meetings were held frequently. I was a member of the Executive and the secretary. There was no attempt to define a clear-cut policy. Words ran into phrases, sentences followed sentences. At times I sat holding my head in my hands, dulled, wishing I could stand up, let out a few wild yells to relieve my feelings, before I left the room. I watched the half-hidden yawns of the other members. A drifting policy discussed endlessly in a shipwrecked way. One speaker picking up a sentence, inverting it, developing it as a theme, playing with it. Then silence, in which we all sat in a kind of vacuity. Soon I learned to hate Executive meetings. I got a bad headache even before the meeting began. I thought of them when engaged on other work and shuddered. They were a bad dream; the situation was going to make up our minds.

In Tipperary and Westmeath, at Annacarty and Athlone, friction had occurred and an exchange of shots. Liam Lynch instructed our men in a few instances to evacuate posts to avoid fighting, with the result that they became dissatisfied, thinking that the Executive in the Four Courts wished to compromise and were unwilling to support them, but we would not retire indefinitely. I felt that Mulcahy and Collins were playing for time until they felt strengthened and secure. The longer the army negotiations could be drawn out the better. Some of our men were preparing to leave for their homes. They thought that negotiations would end in compromise and that the question of the sovereign independence of the nation would be lost sight of. In parts of the country organization slackened and languished.

Another little crisis occurred. Some of our officers, including Sean Hegarty of Cork and Dan Breen, had entered into negotiations with Mulcahy. A statement was published in the press which was signed by both groups, appealing for a unification of the army on the basis of the acceptance of the treaty. Our officers had no authority from the Executive to negotiate. They evidently meant to work the treaty and allow the army to gain strength until it could declare for independence. They could not substantiate any agreement arrived at, and their action tended to show how disorganized we were and how individual attempts at a settlement could whittle down our resistance. No action was taken by Liam Lynch at this breach of discipline.

I asked permission of our Assistant Chief of Staff, Joe McKelvey, to organize an operations staff. He was responsible for that branch but nothing was being done. He told me to see the Chief of Staff. I went to Liam Lynch's office and told him how essential it was to have a group of officers working on operations so that in case of war our troops would be able to co-operate efficiently and strike quickly, acting on a carefully thought out, prearranged plan. 'Negotiations will soon end,' he said, 'and everything will be settled satisfactorily. There will be a joint Headquarters Staff and we will see that the Republican position is not jeopardized.'

'I do not trust Mulcahy,' I said. 'I have no faith in him. I have not had it since the day I tendered my commission before the vote on the treaty took place.'

'Well, I think negotiations will end shortly,' he said.

'So we cannot organize an operations staff?'

'There will be no necessity for one.'

'Can I inspect the defences of the Courts officially with the ACS?' I asked.

'All right,' he said, 'do that.'

Next day the Assistant Chief of Staff with Paddy O'Brien, his adjutant and I inspected the Courts. We selected snipers' positions on adjoining roofs from which our positions could be commanded. Range cards of the distances were to be prepared. The defences were divided into sections. The men already knew their individual positions; alarms had been given occasionally to test the speed and accuracy with which they could get ready. The Headquarters Staff, in case of surprise attack, were to act as a section, in charge of a section commander under the control of Paddy O'Brien. The Headquarters officers were to rank as volunteers. We arranged for a sudden night alarm to test the garrison. Of the four gates, only one was used, that on one of the side streets; the other gates were protected with a little barbed wire, and behind them in the open spaces were obstacles. We needed more barbed wire and moveable obstacle rests which could be rushed to places in the interior of the buildings. The windows were not sufficiently well barricaded. Communication between the blocks was in the open. We needed a supply of sandbags to make a passage way between the dome and the Headquarters block, between the munitions and Headquarters blocks. We needed a way of escape if we were suddenly surrounded. The sewer system underneath might be investigated; a tunnel could be sunk and be driven out in two or three different directions under the side streets. There were many recommendations to be made. We made a thorough inspection of the position and drew up a report which we forwarded to the Chief of Staff, but it was not acted on.

The army negotiations continued. To promote a better understanding, Liam Lynch ordered the Dublin Brigadier to evacuate some of the positions in the city. It was understood that the Four Courts would eventually be evacuated.

I had a talk with Paddy O'Brien in his office near the main gate. His adjutant, Sean Lemass, was present.

'The Four Courts will be evacuated next,' he said.

'It looks like it,' I replied.

'There will be a joint Headquarters Staff formed,' O'Brien said. 'When our members on it find out too late that the Staters mean to organize their Free State, they will break away and attempt to reorganize an opposition. But it will consist of Headquarters officers only then.'

'We don't all approve of the negotiations,' I said; 'they are to kill time.'

'That's just it,' said O'Brien. 'I know what I'm going to do. I'll blow up or burn the Four Courts rather than hand them over.'

'I'm with you in that case,' I said.

Next day barrels of petrol and paraffin were stored in the cellars and in dark corners, unknown to the rest of the Headquarters Staff.

In the meantime, de Valera and Collins had at last come to an agreement known as the 'Pact'. It was submitted to and passed unanimously by Dail Eireann. A statement was issued that:

We are agreed:

1. That a National Coalition Panel for this Third Dail, representing both parties in the Dail, and in the Sinn Fein organization, be sent forward, on the ground that the national position requires the entrusting of the Government of the country into the joint hands of those who have been the strength of the national situation during the last few years, without prejudice to their respective positions.

. . . . .

6. That after the election the Executive shall consist of the President, elected as formerly; the Minister for Defence, representing the Army; and nine other ministers—five from the majority party and four from the minority, each party to choose its own nominees. The allocation will be in the hands of the President.

. . . . .

Signed —
Eamon de Valera
Miceal O Coileain

The terms of the Pact were submitted to the adjourned Ard Fheis representing the Sinn Fein organization. The terms were unanimously approved. Michael Collins, addressing the Ard Fheis said: 'If, as has been said, the agreement imperils the treaty, we have to face the situation in this manner: that we have made an agreement which will bring stable conditions to this country and if those stable conditions are not more valuable than any other agreement, well, then, we must face what these stable conditions will enable us to face.'

On 26 May, three days after Collins's speech, Griffith was summoned to London. Four days later Churchill announced that the Provisional Government would not receive further supplies and that evacuation of British troops was suspended. Evidently Churchill feared the Pact. Next day Collins went to London. He returned the same day. Five days later Collins and de Valera issued a joint statement reaffirming the Pact. At a public meeting in Dublin Mulcahy and Collins advocated the Pact; it was still more important than the treaty. Two days after, Collins was called to London where he remained for a series of conferences. On the eve of the election he addressed a meeting in Cork. 'You are facing an election here on Friday,' he said, 'and I am not hampered now by being on a platform where there are Coalitionists, and I can make a straight appeal to you, to the citizens of Cork, to vote for the candidate you think best. . . .' He had broken his own Pact. On the morning of the election, the Free State Constitution which was to have been issued before the election, with the King freely scattered throughout its paragraphs, was published in the Irish papers—too late to be read by the electors in the country.

Rory O'Connor came up to my office that afternoon. 'Would you like to visit your university?' he asked.

'No,' I said, 'not yet, but as things go I'll be returning there shortly.'

'We are paying a little call to the university offices. They have just finished counting the votes. It would be interesting to know if our Free State friends there have voted for Panel candidates.'

With two officers we drove to Merrion Square. We walked upstairs to where some professors were chatting, seated inside the counter which railed off a portion of the room.

'Is the count finished yet?' asked Rory, addressing a clerk who stood behind the counter.

'Yes,' he replied, 'it's just finished.'

The ballot box stood on the counter.

'In that case,' said Rory, 'we'll borrow the box. We are anxious to know if these gentlemen,' pointing to a group of Collins's supporters, 'have kept their word.'

'You can't do that,' said the clerk.

The men inside the counter jumped to their feet and shouted 'Looters!' 'Robbers!' We carried the heavy box outside to the waiting car and drove away. 'We'll be in a very awkward position if they have kept their word,' said Rory, as we entered the gates of the Four Courts.

The university ballot papers contained the names and addresses of the voters, so that individuals could be identified. That evening a group of us examined the papers. The Republicans had voted for Panel candidates; a few of the Staters had, but the majority, including some of their outstanding men, had broken the Pact. The result of the election was published later. Ninety-four Panel candidates had been returned; fifty-eight of them were pro-treaty. The Dail was due to meet on 30 June.

At the meetings of the Executive the situation was discussed endlessly. Some favoured an attack on the British in the north, giving them two days' notice first. Others thought we should attack them in Dublin. A fight would probably unite the Staters and Republicans; some of the Staters would want to fight with us. The only solution appeared to be the British. They would, we expected, attack us before the two days had elapsed. We of the Four Courts were the centre of the armed Republican resistance. We had to defend the independence of our country, and whether we made mistakes or not, we were going to make a last attempt to prevent the stampede of the nation.

Our Director of Intelligence had been for some time past in communication with the training nucleus of the new police force, the Civic Guards, who were based in a hutted camp in Kildare town. Following the precedent of the Royal Irish Constabulary, the force was being trained in the use of rifles, revolvers and hand-grenades. One night I was summoned to McKelvey's office.

'There's a chance of getting arms,' McKelvey said. 'Some of the Civic Guard officers are willing to come over to us. Some who are not willing may be talked into giving their rifles. Two lorries of guards are to proceed towards Dublin around midnight, bringing arms and ammunition. Be careful now. We don't want any shooting. Our convoy will start later tonight.'

'Do you know the names of any officers or men involved?' I asked. He mentioned some names. 'A few are friendly,' he said. I knew two of the officers he mentioned; once I had helped to organize their area.

A Crossley tender, the armoured car, and a line of motor-cars were outside in the courtyards being overhauled for the journey. Then we started off, in cars separated at intervals so as not to attract attention. On the main road near the entrance to the plain of the Curragh we halted until all the cars had joined us. I walked down the road towards the Curragh with two others until we saw the lights of a lorry approaching. We held up our hands and shouted 'Halt!' The lorry pulled up.

A voice said: 'Who are you?'

I replied: 'From the Four Courts. We want to talk to you. We see no way out of the present situation but to attack the British. That would reunite both forces.'

'I would not mind having another whack at the British,' said a man. 'Nor I,' said another.

'We want to have as many arms as we can before we give them notice,' said the officer with me. 'We ask you to give us your weapons, and if any of you wish to come back to the Courts with us, you can do so.'

'When do you intend to attack?' asked a voice from the rear of the tender.

'We'll wait until the new Dail meets, then we'll know exactly how many armed men we can have. If we don't fight before the British leave the country, we will be left to face each other.'

One man came over to me. 'There's my rifle. We have fought the British together.' Another gave me a revolver. 'We know you. Here's my gun.' They handed over their weapons by degrees. 'Don't forget that we are Republicans. We'll be ready to fight for Ireland when we're needed.'

Most of our convoy led by Tom Barry and Rory had proceeded towards the Kildare police camp, while we pulled in at the side of the road and waited. One of our men climbed a telegraph pole and cut the wire when we heard cars coming across the Curragh. 'They may be Staters from the Curragh camp,' I said. We could see the lights of seven or eight cars, 'No,' said a voice in the darkness, 'I think they're our own.'

Men jumped down and ran towards us. They were laughing and talking. 'We were given the arsenal.' said one. 'Rory and Tom Barry talked the guard over.'

Rory came up to where we stood beside the tender. He was smiling. 'They have given us all the rifles and ammunition they had. They even gave us tenders to remove the stuff. Some of them are coming back to the Courts.'

'You can have our tenders, too,' said a guard. 'You might as well make a clean sweep.'

'There may be a hell of a row tomorrow,' said another, 'but we don't mind now. It will be worth it.'

We arranged the convoy and distributed our men. Those police who had joined us shook hands with Rory and me. The other guards marched along the road in the dark. They would have to face the music tomorrow. Those men who had disappeared into the darkness had risked their positions, their pay, perhaps their liberty, to provide us with arms to fight the British who had divided our nation.

The convoy started back for the city. We wondered if we might be halted before we reached the Courts. I sat in a tender on a pile of rifles. The men whistled and sang. We were all in good spirits and reached the Four Courts before dawn with our treasure trove.

Liam Lynch had decided to summon another convention. He as Chief of Staff could have decided on war and have issued instructions to all our commands to prepare for it. Officers in charge of areas could have been interviewed. Instead a convention was called and members of it were entrusted with an operations decision which the Executive could have decided at a meeting. Liam Lynch was not in favour of the project so perhaps that explained the convention. A convention would mean that the enemy would be immediately informed of all questions discussed and would

receive a report of the proceedings; after the last one there
was an account of the transactions in the press the following
day.

The new convention met on 18 June in the Mansion House.
We knew that the Staters and the British would receive a
report. A resolution proposing to declare war on the British,
first giving them and the Staters seventy-two hours' notice
prior to hostilities, was submitted to the delegates. Some were
annoyed because they considered a resolution of that nature
fatuous; it was not a matter for a convention but for the
Executive. Others were confused and thought it meant
seventy-two hours' notice from that moment, though it was
worded clearly.

The resolution was narrowly defeated. Liam Lynch and
some of the officers from his division had opposed it. Rory
O'Connor and many of the men who had supported it stood
up and left the room, stating that they were going to the Four
Courts and had their minds made up on what they were
going to do. I remained until the meeting was over. That
evening I had some difficulty in getting into the Courts; the
guard at the gate had been strengthened. No member of the
Executive or of the Staff except those who had voted for the
resolution would be admitted. Our members were again
reduced. Soon the Four Courts would be left with a garrison
only.

Joe McKelvey was elected Chief of Staff by the members of
the Executive who were in favour of war.

During the following days we had visitors to the Courts;
civilians came to offer their services at the entrance gate.
They said they had heard that we were going to fight the
Provisional Government. They were obviously British officers,
or a certain brand of secret service men; they were searched
in the guardroom and interrogated, then told to return to
their barracks or to Dublin Castle. A few were shown up to
my room, where we talked while the DI instructed men to
follow them when they left. They were traced back to their
source, the British barracks or the Castle. We wondered
what they had come for. Possibly to get a shrewd idea of the
defences, such as they were, from the inside, or to locate the
offices of the Headquarters Staff for reference in case of a

sudden night assault. We did not wish to take them prisoners; it would have served no useful purpose. Already we had one prisoner near the guardroom. He was a professional gun-runner. He entertained us with stories of Mexico and of the South American republics. He passed comments on the hotels in Dublin; there was only one where a person could eat in comfort. I expect the food from the officers' mess was not much to his liking. He was rather tall, well dressed, with light fair hair and a slight moustache varying between fair and white, well pointed at the ends, he must have used some kind of grease. He was accused of trying to double-cross some of our agents in Belgium and Germany who were attempting to purchase arms. He protested vigorously. This was an outrage, it was the first time he had ever been arrested. He was told it might be the last time, and his smile, showing a few gold teeth, dwindled away. His nasal voice was not raised so often now.

We were told by our Director of Intelligence that some of the members of the Headquarters Staff and of the Executive were likely to be shot by men who had served on Collins's intelligence squad during the Tan war. I do not know what truth was in the report, but we took additional precautions, carried our guns always and slept near them. One night after midnight I was walking towards the Four Courts along the quays from O'Connell Bridge. As I came near the Courts a man jumped out of a doorway, an automatic in his hand, a cap pulled down over his eyes. He shouted 'Hands up!' I jumped forward and seized his gun. He pressed the trigger, but there was no report. I recognized his voice as we struggled; he was the quartermaster of the garrison. He had forgotten, luckily for me, to remove the safety-catch of his weapon. The neighbourhood of the Courts was being held up; passers-by were diverted to the upper bridges and to the side streets. The officers of the garrison were exploring the sewers, endeavouring to make a line of communication that would lead out of the position. The adjutant, Sean Lemass, managed to fall into a sewer and he smelled to heaven.

Sir Henry Wilson, former Chief of the Imperial General Staff, was shot dead in London on 22 June by two London Irishmen. We believed that Wilson had been shot through

instructions from the Irish Republican Brotherhood, that is
through Collins, O'Hegarty and Mulcahy who were
members of the Supreme Council. Two of Collins's trusted
men had been in London before the shooting took place.
Arthur Griffith, who was not connected with the IRB, sent a
message of sympathy to King George and to Wilson's family.
The English accused the Four Courts Staff of instigating the
shooting. The Four Courts officers had nothing to do with it,
for the truce, so far as the British were concerned, had been
observed. The motive for the crime was not apparent.
Perhaps Collins may have wished to appease some of the
Northern officers who were members of the IRB and who
required some assurance other than promise of arms. The
establishment of a Free State would cut them off from the
remainder of the country. Some of them believed that he had
deserted them, others he had promised arms to. Wilson had
been responsible for the reorganization of the Ulster Special
Constabulary, a kind of territorial force, armed and
equipped. Whether Collins, for he was the dominating factor
in the acceptance of the Articles of Agreement, wished to
break with England, eventually, it is hard to say. His per-
sonality and influence had helped to coin the saying: 'What is
good enough for Mick Collins, is good enough for me.' Many
men had followed him, thinking that he would beat the
British, the masters of duplicity, by his own duplicity and
probably he wanted to give weight to his promises by aggressive action. He was the controlling influence in the Irish
Republican Brotherhood. It seems strange that this organization, which for over sixty years had been the backbone of the
separatist, physical-force movement in Ireland, should have
been the strongest element to support the treaty. It did not
work openly but its effects could be felt. Collins was now
what was called a 'stepping-stoner', one of those who agreed
to accept the treaty as a stepping-stone to the Republic.
Many sincere Republicans followed him blindly. He used all
his many influences, as member of the Supreme Council and
as Chairman of the Provisional Government; his former
ranks in the Republican Army—Director of Intelligence,
Adjutant-General and Director of Organization—had helped
him to maintain touch with groups and individuals.

Personalities rather than principles seemed to have swayed many. Men talked of what such an officer had done, recounted his many exploits and what he had suffered for Irish freedom. We regarded a tradition as it was reflected in the living present. There were so many temptations: power, position, money, the appreciation of a grateful public. We ourselves always felt humbled, for any of us might succumb. We gave the men who had fought and worked credit for the past, but when their present action negatived the past they were only a danger to the cause they had once served. To uphold the sovereign independence of Ireland, to maintain it, seemed easy enough in theory, but there were so many by-paths. The line of least resistance led away so often from the path. One had material values to consider, which led away slowly from the spiritual values.

The main result of the shooting of Wilson was to focus attention on the occupants of the Four Courts. Next day Rory O'Connor and I, instructed by Joe McKelvey, Chief of Staff, visited the offices of the Provisional Government, formerly the College of Science, looking for Mulcahy, the Minister for Defence. We were instructed to see him in person. We walked past the military police on duty and entered the building. A clerk directed us to the office. We knocked and went in. Mulcahy's secretary was seated at a table. He jumped up in surprise. He became startled-looking when he recognized us both.

'What do you want here?' he asked.

'We would like to see Mulcahy,' said Rory; 'we have a little business to discuss with him.'

'He is not here at present,' said the secretary, backing towards another door. 'In that case,' said Rory, as we reached the door before the secretary, 'we'll just look in to see how he keeps his office.' We opened the door.

Mulcahy, in uniform, was seated at a table, writing. He turned around at the noise of the door. He stood up when he saw us. He looked surprised, then sat down again.

We stood in front of his table.

'What do you want?' he asked. He spoke concisely, as if he wanted to deal with us quickly. He did not ask us to sit down.

'Our Chief of Staff instructed us to see you in person and

here we are,' said Rory. He produced a typewritten sheet
folded in an open envelope and handed it across the table.
'We would like you to read this, please.'

Mulcahy read the writing. It stated that in case we decided
to attack the British, we would give their Commander-in-
Chief, and the Minister for Defence, seventy-two hours'
warning.

'We would like you to consider it,' said Rory.

'All right,' said Mulcahy, 'I'll send a reply.'

'In writing this time,' said Rory, 'there have been too many
verbal exchanges.'

'Yes, in writing,' he said.

We said 'Good-day' as we reached the door but he did not
reply.

We stopped at the secretary's desk in the other room.
'You'll never be President of the Free State now, your career
is ruined,' said Rory. 'Dick is raging at you for allowing us to
walk in unannounced.'

Macready, Commander-in-Chief of the British forces in
Ireland, was summoned in haste to London. As he relates
himself:

At six P.M. on the 22nd June I reached the Royal
Hospital to be greeted with the news of the
murder of Sir Henry Wilson in London. An hour
after I heard of the sad news, a telegram arrived
calling me over to London. I confess that I was
somewhat taken aback when asked if the Dublin
Four Courts, in which Rory O'Connor had been
established with his Republicans for the past
two months, could be captured at once by British
troops.

This conversation took place on 23 June, the day after
Wilson was killed.

Next day soon after arriving in Dublin and whilst
I was going over the details of the scheme with
General Boyd, whose troops would carry out the
operation if it materialised, a telegram came
ordering it to be put into effect the next day.

On the following day word came through from
London that the Government had reconsidered
their original decision and that no action was
to be taken against the Four Courts.

The situation had become tense, something was bound to
happen, how or when nobody knew. We were drawn closer
together in the Courts. There was an air of gaiety, a greater
sense of comradeship. We learned to know each other better.
For months we had busied ourselves with administration; our
relations were those of staff officers building up resistance.
We discovered little personal things; we talked of our homes
and of our friends. We discussed books and sang old ballads.
Late in the night we could be found talking in each other's
rooms. The feeling of comradeship in common danger bound
us closer together, it helped us to comprehend our deeper
feelings and ideals, gave us more understanding; we became
less impersonal. Rory talked of his experiences in working on
the Canadian Pacific Railway; Liam Mellows told us of his
escape from Ireland after the Easter Rising and of his visit to
Germany. He showed us the huge Zeppelin night-binoculars
which the firm of Zeiss had given him. He spoke of hard,
wretched days in the United States, of his imprisonment
there.

Commandant-General Leo Henderson, the director of the
Belfast boycott, was arrested by Staters when enforcing the
boycott on a Dublin firm. He was removed under escort and
imprisoned in Mountjoy jail. Joe McKelvey sent for me that
evening after he had discussed the arrest with Liam, Rory
and some other officers. Rory was busy working on his
tunnel, which had been neglected of late.

'What do you think we should do?' McKelvey asked.
'I think we should arrest an officer of equal rank,' I said,
'and hold him prisoner in the Courts until Henderson is
released.'
'Whom do you suggest?'
'Collins, Mulcahy or O'Connell,' I said.
He thought for a moment. 'O'Connell would suit. Do you
know where you could find him?'

'Yes, he's generally in McGilligan's. I'll wait until he leaves the house.'

I took a car and three men. We crossed the city and halted a little above McGilligan's on the opposite side. We saw people enter and depart. After an hour or more I saw Ginger O'Connell leave the house. He walked towards the canal bridge. We followed slowly. The car halted at the bridge. I walked after O'Connell. I touched him on the shoulder.

'Ginger, you're under arrest,' I said. He turned around quickly. He looked startled. He saw a gun in the hands of a man behind me.

'Into the car,' I said.

He began: 'What do you mean? I bloody well— '

'Into the car, quick, Ginger,' I repeated.

He sat down in the back seat, a man on either side. 'Keep quiet,' I said; 'we don't want to hurt you or tie your wrists.' He began to struggle when passing through Westmoreland Street. 'Sit on him,' I said. He was placed on the floor and a man sat on him. As we came through the gate he said: 'I hope they blow the hell out of you.'

I left our prisoner in the guardroom and reported to the Chief of Staff.

'I have Lieutenant-General O'Connell in the guardroom, sir,' I said.

He laughed. 'No, you haven't?'

'Yes, he's below.'

He telephoned to the quartermaster and told him to prepare a room for Ginger. 'You'd better telephone to O'Duffy,' he said; 'you might as well complete the operation.'

I rang up Portobello barracks. 'I want to speak to the Chief of Staff,' I said.

After a delay I heard O'Duffy's 'Hello'.

'Hello, this is O'Malley, Director of Organization speaking.'

'Hello, Mr. O'Malley. What do you want?'

'I have to tell you that Mr. O'Connell, your assistant chief, is now in custody.'

I heard a surprised 'What?'

I repeated the information.

'He will be released in exchange for Commandant-General Henderson whom you have now in prison.'

'Is that all?' he asked.
'Yes, Mr. O'Duffy. Goodnight.'
'Goodnight, Mr. O'Malley.'

*   *   *   *   *

That day Churchill had stated in the House of Commons:

The presence in Dublin, in violent occupation
of the Four Courts, of a band of men styling
themselves the Headquarters of the Republican
Executive is a gross breach and defiance of the
Treaty. It is not unfair to make the new Irish
Parliament a request in express terms that this
sort of thing must come to an end. If it does
not come to an end, and a speedy end, then it
is my duty, on behalf of His Majesty's Government,
to say that the Treaty has been formally
violated.

Lloyd George said:

Here you have three or four hundred young men
seizing the Courts of Justice of their capital,
near the centre of their Government, where
they have an organized force, and they
permit them to run a sham Government in the
name of the Republic. I do not want to use
the language of menace, but it is essential
that that should be brought to an end, and
speedily.

CHAPTER SIX

JUNE 1922

THE following day members of our intelligence section reported that a Stater officer had paraded the square in Wellington barracks with a wreath to bury the Republic.

Not until ten o'clock at night did rumour of attack become definite. We were told by a Franciscan friar from Church Street that the Four Courts would be attacked after midnight, that Free State troops were on their way to Dublin from the Curragh of Kildare; the Dublin garrisons had been recalled to barracks; any member of our Executive found on the streets was to be arrested. We realized how inadequate were our defences. Members of the HQ Staff talked the situation over with the garrison staff. Captain O'Brien looked at me as he came to the table; then he lifted his eyebrows to say we're in a nice mess now as a result of this Headquarters Staff. Joe McKelvey talked about strengths of defences.

'They're hopeless,' I said; 'nothing has been done. Get in touch at once with Traynor, the Dublin Brigadier, to arrange for snipers to hold outposts in a large circle around the Courts, and get his men ready to hem in the barracks occupied by the Staters.' O'Brien agreed with me. 'We must not fire a shot or give any provocation,' said McKelvey.

'You mean,' said Mellows, 'that members of the Executive will not resist arrest if attacked outside the Courts in the next few hours?'

'Yes,' said McKelvey.

'I don't agree,' I said. 'There is no food in this place, I have just found out. I am going out with a lorry and an escort as soon as this conference is over and I intend to use weapons if any one prevents me from bringing back food for the men here.'

The majority vote was that there should not be any resistance or provocation. Army records of importance were collected and sent to what was considered a safe hiding-place. Trenches were dug inside the heavy gates to prevent armoured cars moving in from outside. Our engineers brought out mines and began to dig up the paved blocks of the street near the Liffey. Stater armoured cars drove up; men got out of them and cut the wires connecting the mines to the batteries inside. Our men stood there helplessly, as they had been instructed not to fire under any circumstances. Some thought that the Staters were looking for a flimsy excuse to create an incident which would right themselves in the public's eyes in an attack on our position. I, and a few, believed that the Staters were slowly driving for power; any temporary negotiation would give them time to strengthen themselves and to weaken us. We should have occupied positions around the Four Courts, the city bridges, the approaches to their barracks, and have blown up their armoured cars as hostile reconnaissance units before an action. Free State armoured cars patrolled the city and interfered with the laying of mines; our outposts had to withdraw as they had not received instructions to fight when molested. Our touring scout-cars were chased as they moved up town around British and Staters' barracks to find out information; sentry patrols in the streets were held up.

I went out in a Crossley tender to get food, and I ordered the men to bring rifles and a Thompson gun. 'I have been instructed not to open fire,' I told the crew, 'but I'm going to bring back food whoever dies for it.' The sergeant in charge with my party laughed. 'All right,' he said; 'we'll back into any armoured car that gets in our way and go for the turrets.' The delay whilst shops opened for us made us tense. An armoured car passed us but did not interfere. On my way back from a bridge where men were using picks to make a mine-bed I saw men from an armoured Lancia jump down quickly. They held up four of our men some distance in front of me; they searched them. I drew my revolver from its holster and held it through the pocket slit in my coat but I was not interfered with. I had decided that I would not be taken a prisoner.

Inside the Four Courts men moved barbed wire, cleaned and checked ammunition, fitted rifle-slings, cleaned rifles,

automatics and machine-guns, and laid out spare parts.
Captain Paddy O'Brien saw that the officers rechecked the
ammunition, examined the weapons, and knew the positions
they were to occupy. Dr. Jim Ryan arrived with nurses and a
group of Cumann na mBan girls to help him. A temporary
hospital was fitted up on the ground floor of the Headquarters
block; large supplies of medicinal equipment, bandages, lint,
gauze, bottles of iodine, picric, and splints were carried in
and arranged on tables.

Lancia lorries drove up outside all the heavy gates, backed
their cars broadside or tinkered with the engines, and the
crews walked away. 'What do you want?' our men in the
guardroom shouted. No reply. 'What the hell are you doing?'
What was their idea anyhow? The gate guards wanted to get
permission to fire as the Lancias could contain explosive
charges which would blow the gates and entrances to bits. No
permission was given.

Across the river in the darkness men were moving into
position. We could see the dark shadows advancing.
Armoured cars purred their gentle throttles, heavier Lancias
drove up and down. Their troops entered the Four Courts
Hotel and the adjoining buildings which fronted part of the
Courts. They opened the Bridewell gates, opposite the Headquarters block across the street, and marched in. We could
hear them as they prepared the position inside; lights
appeared in the windows, sandbags were placed to form loopholes; now they could command portions of the open yard
inside the Courts. Our position was being slowly surrounded. Houses commanding the courtyards and the
windows facing the yards were now occupied. The Staters
were taking advantage of the fact that we did not want to
open fire on them. The Courts was already a trap. A report
came in that artillery was on its way from the British lines.

I suddenly found that I was cold, due more to tenseness
than the air. 'We're like rats in a trap, Paddy,' I said to
O'Brien as we inspected positions on the roof of the Headquarters block dominated by men in the Bridewell.

'I know,' he said, 'I wish I had power to make the whole
Headquarters Staff leave, then I could fight it out as a
soldier.'

In the rotunda, under the dome, Headquarters officers met
again to talk, seated on the ground in a half-circle. Some were
in favour of leaving for the country to take charge of areas and
to assist as staff officers.

'We don't know what the country will do,' said Liam
Mellows.

'The West will fight,' I said, 'and the Tipperary men.'

'Our men are disorganized,' he continued. 'We don't know
what the First Southern Division will do. They will fight, of
course, later, but they may not be able to help us. We have
created the Four Courts situation. We should face the
responsibility.'

Rory nodded. His face was quiet as if he was thinking
deeply of other things. 'I think we should stay here,' he said.
'It's unmilitary, but we represent the Republic at present. It
is now going to be attacked; we should be here to defend it.'

'We can defend it,' said O'Brien. 'I think Headquarters
Staff and the members of the Executive should leave at once
for the country. It's not too late yet. They have work to do
outside where their influence can be felt. They can organize
the country and then advance on Dublin. We can easily hold
out here for some days.' The majority wanted to remain in
the Courts. In a way, that was unfair to the commander of
the garrison as his position was already not properly tenable
by reason of Staff decisions.

'I wonder will they use artillery,' said Joe McKelvey, as if
talking to himself.

'They have no artillery,' said Peadar O'Donnell. 'The
British might lend them some. Perhaps both will attack
together. They might use Stokes guns. What's artillery like?'
he asked, turning to us. There was silence. I was also thinking
of its effect and of what Stokes fire could do. Would it be bad
on the nerves and would I show my fears? I tried to visualize
accounts I had read of artillery bombardments.

'You get used to it,' said Seoirse Plunkett. 'It's not bad.' He
and his brother Jack, sitting together, had been in the GPO
during Easter Week 1916, as had some others of the garrison.

Rory and Joe McKelvey began to draft a 'Proclamation to
the Citizens of Dublin'. Rory asked me to help him but when
I had read a few sentences I laughed. 'I doubt if anyone will

read one of our proclamations,' I said; 'I'm against the use of
too many words just now.'

The Dublin Brigadier, Oscar Traynor, arrived and talked
to the Chief of Staff. He brought the proclamation out with
him to have it printed.

At 3.40 am, a soldier handed in a message to the guard at
the main gate.

The officer in charge,
Four Courts.

I, acting under the order of the Government, hereby
order you to evacuate the buildings of the Four Courts
and to parade your men under arrest, without arms, on
that portion of the Quays immediately in front of the
Four Courts by 4 a.m.
Failing compliance with this order, the building will
be taken by me by force, and you and all concerned
with you will be held responsible for any life lost
or any damage done.

By order
Thomas Ennis
O/C 2nd Eastern Division

Paddy O'Brien ordered the guards company to fall in by
sections. He read the message to them and they laughed. It
was the first time the Staters had ever asked us to leave the
Courts.

'You are to command the Headquarters section in the
rotunda,' he said to me. 'Fall them in.'

'But I'm not the senior officer,' I said, 'and anyhow I
shouldn't be in charge, for a crowd of Staff officers are no joke
to handle. I'd sooner have a group from the guards company.'

'I'm putting you in charge,' said O'Brien, 'and you know
why.'

I came to attention and saluted. 'Yes, sir, I'll do my best.'
He gripped my hand hard. 'It's come at last,' he said quietly,
then he walked into the darkness.

Liam Mellows was walking up and down under the dome,
a rifle on his back.

'Liam,' I said, 'Paddy O'Brien has placed me in charge of

the HQ section. I don't think I should be in charge of men like you.' He put his arm around my shoulder. 'We'd all prefer to serve under you, don't you know that, for you have had the most experience of any of us.' He patted his rifle barrel. 'God, it's good to feel myself a soldier again after all those futile negotiations,' and his face beamed.

I examined rifles and small arms, checked on the ammunition and first-aid supplies. There were batteries, cables and land mines to one side, but no appliances to fight fire from incendiary shells and grenades.

Underneath the dome the garrison had gathered. A Franciscan, Father Albert, in his brown habit, the hood over his head, his feet sandalled, spoke to us. 'I'm going to give you general absolution, boys.' His worn, thoughtful face was troubled. He looks like the Saint Francis of my imagination, I was thinking as I looked at him, his face modelled by his kindly, unselfish spirit and his unfearing tenacity. Father Dominic, my fellow prisoner once of the dark cell in Dublin Castle, stood close to him.

We all knelt down. Some of the men gripped their rifles instead of joining hands; others held their revolvers. We were dedicating our weapons as well as our lives. Then he made the sign of the cross over us. 'Say an Act of Contrition now.' The disjointed murmur of voices. 'O my God, I am heartily sorry for having offended Thee'; then the priest pronounced the absolution. *Ego te absolvo.* A pause when he had finished. 'We'll say now an Our Father and three Hail Marys for Ireland,' and the responses came loudly in Irish and in English. Our faces were tense there, kneeling in the light of the candles. The electricity had been cut off by the attackers. 'We'll place ourselves under the protection of the Mother of God and under the mantle of Brigid,' Father Albert said; then: 'God bless you, boys.' The tears were running down his cheeks. Men stood up slowly. Some were still on their knees.

'Company, fall in by sections!' shouted O'Brien. The sections drew up in line, two deep, with an interval between. 'Company attend!' There was a click of heels in the night. 'Company, by sections, number!' The simple parade ritual had another meaning now; it became alive, as if for the first time the words had been uttered, and as each man shouted his number he asserted his resolution to fight.

'Order arms! To your posts!' he shouted. Five sections ran
quickly to their action positions; the sixth, the HQ section,
remained beneath the dome. I looked at my watch nervously,
forgot the time I had just seen, then looked again and forgot
what I had tried to observe. The minutes were slow in
coming. Artillery and trench mortars, incendiary shells,
armoured cars and tanks, of these I was thinking in a confused jumble, and of my relationship to the section. Would
artillery fire shake my knees and confidence, and would I
disgrace my section?

'Time's up,' said Rory, and as he spoke a machine-gun
from outside echoed across the night, to be answered by a
shout from each of our sections. A heavy boom came next,
and we knew artillery was being used; the crash of an
eighteen-pound shell announced that those who stood in arms
for an independent Ireland were to be attacked by some of
their former comrades.

'That's Mulcahy's answer to our last note,' I said.

Now that fighting had begun, problems that could have
been easily solved a few days ago came up. Communications
between the blocks was in the open. The dome area was cut
off from Headquarters block, the latter from the Records
office. The space was covered with rifle and machine-gun fire.
One man was hit as he crossed behind me. Paddy O'Brien
and I found men to work on a sandbag barricade but there
were not enough bags to make a covered bullet-proof passage
between the blocks.

I climbed up the iron ladder of the dome, pausing as I
heard a wind sound of bullets crossing its space; they made a
shrill whistle as they passed. Up above, dawn was coming up
the river, risen to the roofs and spreading slowly towards
Kingsbridge. This was the second dawn I had watched from
the Courts. I could see the old city rising from the river,
gradually in Parliament Street, steeply in narrow Winetavern
and streets towards Christ Church and the Castle. Light
climbed up the house-tops and along the ridge of church
spires towards the west; slight flashes, soon indistinguishable
with full light, showed snipers' nests. I could follow the quays
up to the corner of O'Connell Bridge and down by the older
houses to beyond the Mendicity Institute. The river bordered

the most colourful part of the city, haphazardly pleasant the disparity in roof heights and the colour contrasts of shop fronts. Beyond the corner of Winetavern Street was a gun. I saw its recoil as it fired. This gun was firing with open sights at an easy target, the corner of the Courts facing Morgan's Place. Slowly the top storey was crumbled, the stone stairs shot away, and men were lowered to the floor below by using knotted blankets. Behind, on Mary's Abbey side, was a second gun at the end of Chancery Street. It looked as if the enemy could advance and occupy any position they thought necessary; the third and fourth battalions of the Dublin Brigade which might have interfered with enemy positions and guns across the river did not seem to make much of an impression on them.

Men of my section worked picks and shovels to tunnel under the open space whilst some of the section in Head-quarters block tunnelled to meet them. It was slow work. 'I wish we could tunnel between Headquarters and munitions,' said Paddy O'Brien, 'but we'd have to go right under the cellars.' The other tunnel which Rory and the engineers had begun three weeks ago was unfinished; it would take a long time to complete. It was originally to have run to Patterson's factory in Church Street. Rory O'Connor had been in charge but the work was not determined. It ran nearly as far as the street and was water-logged; it had been kept dry with a hand-pump but would need a full section-strength to con-tinue the work; the enemy would know of its scope and direc-tion as two of our garrison had joined up with the Beggar's Bush troops. We had not sufficient men. There were between a hundred and eighty and a hundred and ninety men in the garrison, but to hold the Courts under present conditions we would have needed at least two hundred and fifty. Practically all were on duty at a time. The reserves of each section for counter-attack were very small, and we had no central reserve to fall back on. As I walked about between sections, the buildings seemed to consist chiefly of windows, about five or six windows to each man. They could not all be barricaded; only a few had been made bullet-proof, but rifle-grenades could always be lobbed in, and movement under fire was a little difficult. The roofs were dominated by buildings close to

them, and by snipers from St. Michan's tower and from the
top of Jameson's distillery, but one tunnel was completed by
the end of the following day. We could not make another as
we could not spare the men. The munitions block containing
the Records office was isolated. Paddy O'Brien and his
adjutant went the rounds frequently during the day, inspecting sections, crossing to munitions which was commanded by
the Bridewell prison less than thirty yards away. The passage
was narrow; Thompson guns and machine-guns spattered as
they ran across. I went with him at times. The telephones in
the sections buzzed at intervals. We answered the operator at
the main switch and reported the situation in the sections to
our commander. Then the telephone did not work; the service
had been cut off.

Ginger O'Connell was removed to another room in the
centre of the building, the safest room we could find. The
shells were pounding the walls, large gaps appeared, and
O'Connell's former room was hit by successive shells a few
hours after he had left it.

'How are things, Ginger?' I said to him.

'Oh, all right. The shelling doesn't seem to make a deep
impression.'

'Well, I suppose you know the plan of attack well enough.
A few of the old Chinese tortures would help in a case like
this. But you know this is an easy place to take.'

He smiled, nodding his head.

'What about books, Ginger? I have a pile in my room and
can bring them over. This isn't as exciting for you as it is for
us. I will bring you a mixed lot, war and peace; indeed I'll
bring you Tolstoy's *War and Peace*.'

'I'd like to read it,' said Ginger, 'but I think it will be
browsing because I won't have time to finish.'

I crossed to my room and brought him back an armful of
books, Von Lettow-Vorbeck's campaign in German East
Africa, the defence of Duffer's Drift, and interesting short
military stories. He did not seem very anxious to read.

Matty McDonnell was hit in the ankle as he crossed the
open space between the dome and Headquarters block. Two
Red Cross men were bringing him back on a stretcher to the
hospital when a machine-gun opened up on them. They

dropped the stretcher and ran for cover, closely followed by McDonnell. Charlie McAuley dressed his wound and prepared to extract the bullet. As the surgeon was operating, bullets from the Bridewell direction came in through a door. Then Father Dominic thought of our great mainstay. The Law Library was close by. He took two men with him, and soon columns of books blocked the door against illegal bullets. Within four hours of the attack five men had been wounded, four of them by snipers from the Bridewell and St. Michan's Church.

The Records office, munitions block, was held by a section of young lads under Tom Morrissey, all of them orderlies who in peace kept communication between staff officers and who served food in the mess. Morrissey was handed a Thompson gun, which he had not been trained to use, as he went into position. At first the section lay down behind the roof parapet, protected by sandbags. Free Staters held Hammond Lane factory to the north and the Four Courts Hotel behind them. Snipers from St. Michan's shook the bones of the brothers Sheares in the vault below, and maybe the large black spiders amongst the mummified corpses, but they soon drove our men to the first floor. Here there were no sandbags. Before evening they could not fire on Hammond Lane, nor could they open a door. They had used books, ledgers, and records on tables to protect themselves from the enemy in the Four Courts Hotel. They had no food; it was brought across under machine-gun fire. There was a gun in the Haymarket which bashed in the west side of their building; soon railings and concrete foundation were blown away, leaving a gap from the street to the rubble front behind. The inside was a jumble of lathes, moulds and mine cases; hand-grenade bodies lay in heaps; electric detonators, electric wires and explosives were piled between the racks which held the records. The men facing the Bridewell held the roof until it could be no longer held, and a few had to lie out for a further twelve hours until darkness covered them. In the lower rooms there were explosives, including a large amount of TNT. This was the real danger for a direct hit could explode it and blow up the block around it.

It was cold at night, under the dome. We sat leaning

against a wall, with a blanket around our legs; others lay flat
on the flags, or sleeping against a pillar. We talked and
argued in a friendly way, except about the shortage of food,
lack of ammunition, and the completely hopeless position for
defence of the buildings through this section's fault. When
some of us had made these matters clearer than was wished
by some of the section, the discord ceased. Men are very kind
to each other when in danger; it seems a strange time to make
a man gentle, but here everyone was kindly and solicitous,
each trying to put himself last when it came to physical comfort. Rory and Liam were wearing leather motor-jackets
which kept them warm at nights. At the end of the first night
I thought of my sleeveless leather jacket which I then wore.

Rory handed me the printed proclamation which he had
helped to write: 'To the Citizens of Dublin'. It now adorned
the dead wall spaces and the pillar boxes of the city. 'The
situation is well in hand,' he said, and laughed.

Then he quoted:

> And how can man die better
> Than facing fearful odds
> For the ashes of his fathers,
> And the temples of his gods?

He usually said those lines when anything went wrong, in a
bantering way, but often before he had finished the smile had
gone. He sat there, his face becoming set as he finished. There
was silence under the dome.

Paddy O'Brien, with his adjutant, often with myself, went
around to our posts at intervals to gather information and to
check on shell damage to the buildings. Our fire had to be
very particular and the natural tendency for men in action to
fire luxuriously in excitement to be stifled. 'The Mutineer'
went slowly up and down the yards between three blocks but
out of reach of direct hit by the guns on the Liffey side, concentrating fire on snipers' posts with its Vickers gun.
Cumann na mBan girls carrying despatches came up to the
side-gate under fire as the chains had to be opened to give
them entry. They brought us news of the outside; one
brought ammunition given to them by Free State soldiers.

Mary Comerford slept on sacks of flour. O'Connell Street
had been occupied by Oscar Traynor and his men. They
were endeavouring to advance towards the Courts, but they
had occupied in strength the east side of the street and it
would be difficult to cross it. On the south side of the river our
men of the third battalion had their headquarters in the Swan
public house but they did not seem to make any impression
on the bombarding guns. It seemed a haphazard pattern of
war. A garrison without proper food, surrounded on all sides,
bad communication between their inside posts, faulty defences, girls bringing ammunition from attackers, relieving
forces on our side concentrated on the wrong side of the
widest street in the capital.

Our men were wounded as they lay behind sandbags on
the roof. Paddy O'Brien, Sean Lemass and I climbed the
dome by the thin iron ladder. A wooden partition provided
the only protection in places. Bullets entered with a buzz and
changed to a duller, muffled note as they crossed inside. From
a flagstaff on the dome hung a tricolour. The Republican flag
hung limply now as there was little breeze, but as we watched
it ruffled into an eddy, showing the scars. Bullets had torn a
piece out of it, there were eye-holes across it, the wooden pole
had been nicked in places and long splinters hinged off it.

'They must be hard up for a target,' said O'Brien scorn-
fully.

Along the quays towards O'Connell Bridge we could see
Free State troops through our glasses and on a church tower
and roofs near at hand there were snipers. Paddy O'Brien
laid his rifle and sighted slowly. 'About seven hundred yards,'
he said. 'What do you think?'

'I think Paddy must be about right,' said Lemass.

'I'd allow somewhat more,' I said.

We saw a green-coated soldier fall in front of a Lancia.
Another came forward. The rifle echoed again and another
man lay by the Lancia. 'I got them all right,' said O'Brien,
his eyes shining with excitement.

Across the river were the guns, eighteen pounders, protected by a barricade of armoured Lancia cars. Two cars
made a V slit, a loophole through which the muzzle of the
gun protruded. We watched it recoil when it fired. We used a

machine-gun and rifles from the top. We spattered bullets off
the paved roadway, firing in front of the cars, endeavouring to
make the bullets ricochet and zing upwards towards the gunners. In the distance we could hear machine-guns and rifles
attacking the positions in O'Connell Street. We looked down
on our position. Morgan's Place had been battered. Munitions block was in a more ragged condition, and the corner
near the gun shop had been battered at the lower storey. The
roof of Headquarters block had been holed but the far end of
it was intact.

'Munitions is getting it most,' said Sean Lemass, 'and the
garrison are kids. We should have put older men with them.'

We were now tunnelling across to munitions underneath
the cellars. Explosives would have made the work easier but
those blocks were a mass of explosives, some of which would
detonate. Slowly the work went forward as men were tired
and they had to remain at their posts continuously. A meeting was held under the dome. If the tunnel could be pushed
forward quickly, reinforcements from the nearest post, Headquarters, could come in case of attack. 'The young lads were
hard to hold,' Morrissey, section commander of munitions,
said to me the last time I had seen him. If the Four Courts
Hotel could be rushed, we could burn it out completely; we
had sufficient grenades for a storming party. The Chief of
Staff and others thought that by burning out the hotel and
adjoining buildings, munitions and Headquarters blocks
would be left very open to artillery fire and it would
encourage the attackers to use incendiary shells and
grenades. It was decided not to attack. Mines were laid
throughout the yards in case there would be an attempt to
storm with armoured cars and tanks. Already one of our outside mines had been exploded by accident. It had left a nice
crater in the street as a warning, but the section commander
in charge made an equal crater in the mind of the unfortunate
who had touched off the switch.

Paddy O'Brien met me after the staff meeting. 'Munitions
is a weak post, Paddy,' I said, 'insecurely held. I'm afraid the
tunnel will not get through in time.'

'I know,' he said. 'The only thing left for me is to burn it
out, and I think I'll do that. Make the garrison come in first
and then put the place up.'

'Don't bother about artillery,' I said. 'Gunners, if they're any good, can hit any few square yards of this place. A building doesn't make a bit of difference, save they might like to fire over open sights. It's hard on you, Paddy. The only hope for this place is to put Headquarters section in munitions and let it be blown up.'

'That would help,' he said with a smile, 'but there's the future to think of.'

He had decided to burn out munitions as he felt it could no longer be held. The block contained the Irish archives and it had suffered more than any other of our buildings from shell fire. The last report from its section commander was that unless the Four Courts Hotel was taken, he would not be able to hold his position; at present his only safeguard for his men was the ground floor at the rear facing the dome. Landings and windows could not be properly protected even on that side.

'Paddy,' I said, 'our strong points are mines and explosives. The broken mortar and the rubble of the outer walls are a fine defence, and mines, we have plenty of mines. Even if we withdraw the garrison, save for an observation post or two, mines could be scattered through the building and used on attacking parties. They will hardly get past a series of mines unless they come in waves.'

'They might bomb us from the air,' he said. A plane had passed slowly over the Courts during the previous day. 'The Mutineer' had slewed up its gun but had not fired; too difficult a target anyhow. The British were observing the results of artillery fire and they would report to their new allies.

Simon Donnelly of the Headquarters section, who had once escaped from Kilmainham jail with Teeling and myself, was in difficulties. He had a very tight-fitting pair of shoes and he talked about his sore feet to a rather unsympathetic audience.

'I have a new pair of shoes in my room, Simon,' I said. 'I think they will fit you.'

I crossed through the tunnel which now connected the dome with Headquarters block; there was a very definite aroma as the tunnellers had struck a sewer on their way. I reached my bedroom. The door had been drilled and

splintered by bullets; I counted about forty holes, two of them
made by a shell. My leather portmanteau had been cut and
torn, my clothes and books damaged. I picked up some of my
books from a shelf. Baudelaire, two *al fresco* prints, Tintoretto
and Piero della Francesca, a portfolio of drawings. There
were two bullet holes through a copy of Vasari's *Lives of the
Italian Painters*. Authors had been drilled and torn out of all
proportion to the number of books. 'Bad luck to them, anyhow,' I said in the direction of a piece of artillery gone
through a Synge illustrated by Jack Yeats. 'They mustn't like
books or anything to do with books.' It's a funny thing for you
to be thinking of your possessions at a time like this, I
thought, as I left a smashed pair of field glasses back on a
chair. Maybe it takes misfortune or war to prove that possessions are not important. Cuchulain had suffered most of
all. Mrs. Hutton's bulky translation of the epic contained a
shell splinter which had gashed *Mesca Ulad*: demon chariots
were now careering around the Four Courts in the form of
armoured cars and Lancias. I turned over another undamaged volume of Vasari, old garrulous Vasari, and sitting
on my bed read his remarks on Andrea del Sarto. The royal
coat of arms had suffered; the lion's head was missing and the
horn of the unicorn. A volume of Montaigne had escaped
shell and bullet. He would have been a good man to have here
with us; he could have joined our philosophic discussions
under the dome. I put him in my pocket where he lay beside a
thin copy of Shakespeare's Sonnets which I had been reading
last night. Beneath a red plush chair I found my bright yellow
boots, untouched; a terrible colour to wear. Simon will have
his pair of shoes, I thought, as I strung them by their laces.

I moved through the building watching curiously the effect
of shell fire; most of the section had been withdrawn. The
large central hall where we had given a concert on the night
of the Bodenstown pilgrimage to the grave of Wolfe Tone was
a wreck. Shells had come through the glass roof. Fragments of
wall, chairs, railings and tables were scattered everywhere.
The concert had been an expression of feeling on behalf of
singers and listeners. Old traditional songs had been received
in a taut silence for negotiations with Beggar's Bush had
broken down. There had been rhetoric in the speeches, but

one quiet talk about the danger of immediate strife had made all realize that it was our last concert together. A shattering crash made my body stiffen. A shell had come through the roof and had torn away a ragged hole of wall. I dropped to the ground; as I lay there another shelled plaster off the wall in a cloud of smoke.

'Here they are, Simon,' I said when I got back to the dome. Simon tried them on his feet; they seemed to me to fit him. He stood up as he tested them while we laughed at their colour.

'I can die in your boots,' he said with a grin.

In the evening one of the guard from the room over the gate reported that there was a messenger outside. Sean Lemass and I unlocked the chains. The messenger was a Cumann na mBan girl. She had a bicycle with her and she wanted to bring it inside the gates. Bullets whizzed. 'Leave it there,' I said. We all dashed for cover. She carried a despatch from Oscar Traynor to the Chief of Staff: his men were working their way down towards Mary's Abbey; he had received word from a very good source that the British had threatened to attack us next morning unless the Staters attempted to storm the Courts. Joe McKelvey wrote a note telling Traynor to push on down as far as he could and to try to get his men across the river and snipe the gunners more effectively. The girl went into a room to secrete the note. We shook hands with her at the gate and wished her a safe journey, and watched her cycle down the street. I told Rory about her wanting to take in the bicycle.

'They're great girls,' he said. 'They treat fear so impersonally. I suppose they really think we should have captured the guns by this.'

That Thursday evening Lieutenant Ned Keller was sent by O'Brien to withdraw the orderlies from munitions and then to destroy the building. When he reached the door across the bullet-swept passage from the Bridewell he was fired on from inside the building. A voice shouted: 'You're a prisoner.' The first of our posts had been captured.

We had heard very heavy fire that evening, concentrating on munitions, but as spasmodic intensity was a routine now, no one had paid much attention. After the Staters had blown

in the heavy iron railing and its concrete support for a
distance of twenty feet, they then blew in the whole side of the
building, concentrated fire, and rushed across. The orderlies
looked up to see green uniforms on a balcony shouting down
to them to surrender. In a rush for cover young Cusack and
Wall were shot; the remainder surrendered.

CHAPTER SEVEN

JUNE 1922

I WAS seated on the floor under the dome, watching Jack and Seoirse Plunkett testing mines with galvanometers. Suddenly there was a burst of machine-gun and rifle-fire.

Paddy O'Brien rushed in from Headquarters block. 'Our Lewis opened up on Staters coming along the quays. They were rushing this building; some were dropped but others got in.' There was a sudden scurry of men near me. Some in panic ran towards the guardroom, others were preparing to move in different directions, others shouted orders. Chairs and tables were carried forward as obstacles.

'Throw up rough barricades of wire,' I said, 'leaving an open space under the dome. Lay mines forward of the obstructions and mine the passages.'

Paddy O'Brien hurried towards that part of the building where the attackers should be, shouting the name of the section commander; I followed the sound of his voice in the darkness. There was a dark, fearful silence in front of me. I heard his voice again in the distance; I met him in the passage, returning.

'I don't know what to make of it,' he said. 'I can't find any of the section. You'd better go back with me to the others.'

Under the dome Rory, Liam and the Headquarters section were unwinding bobbins of barbed wire amidst the loose stones and mortar blown in by the shells; some were placing mine cases, others had piled furniture to interlace with con-certinas of wire. Another group was building a barricade of stones and rubble.

O'Brien strode over to a man who was winding wire around the legs of a chair. 'You were in the advance section. Where's the officer in charge?'

'He's out near the front gate,' said the man.

'Why the hell did you come back from your post?'

'Because we should have been relieved six hours ago. We've
been near the gate for the past two hours trying to sleep.'

Paddy O'Brien went towards the gate.

I took four men forward with me up the passage towards
the Staters, to hold up any advance until the barricades and
mines would be ready beneath the dome. We heard footsteps
in the dark. 'They're making a hell of a row,' whispered a
man.

The noise ceased; then it began again. The sound of their
boots boomed up and down the passage. We were lying flat
on the ground. My heart beat fast; I felt myself trying to hold
my breath. 'Let them get past us,' I whispered to the men
who lay beside and behind me at right angles to the main
passage. 'Open on them when I shout, but not before that.'
The noise came closer. We heard their voices.

'They're our men,' said a voice beside me. 'For God's sake
don't shoot.' We allowed them to pass by and then halted
them. They were three men of the advance section who had
not heard the remainder retire.

'The Mutineer' fired through the windows of the buildings
in front of the dome, raking from every angle, trying to locate
the attackers. Paddy O'Brien was talking to Rory and to Joe
McKelvey when I came up. 'I have a counter-attack
prepared,' he said, 'and the mines are ready. Can I blow
them now?' It would mean a result Paddy and I had agreed
on: the blowing of a gap in a building which could then of
itself form a barricade, with a peppering of mines in front of a
holding party. Rory said: 'If you blow the mines you'll make
a big hole in the building.' Paddy O'Brien came to attention
quickly. He saluted, then walked away.

I met Dinny O'Brien, Paddy's brother, moving off from the
dome up a passage. Candles were stuck into pieces of
masonry, making a Rembrandt etching; men were cleaning
rifles behind a barricade, others were making neat shelters of
stone. Dinny's mild blue eyes were lighted with excitement.

'What are you up to?' I asked; I might have known there
was trouble about by his smile.

'Oh, we three are going up to bomb the Staters.'

Chummy Hogan, his number two, chuckled. Young Page
was carrying a Lewis gun on his back.

'I'll go with you,' I said.

'This is great gas,' said Chummy, as we picked our way slowly up a jet-black corridor. I did not feel too cheerful. Where did these men inherit their gay insouciance, as if war was an everyday, trivial matter, and why was I up here, I thought again, as Chummy stood up to fire. To share danger with these other men or to safeguard Headquarters section? My doubts were resolved by the throbbing of the Lewis. 'Shorter bursts,' I whispered, 'and don't talk in between shots.' Dinny laughed aloud.

We emptied automatics and revolvers through doors to right and left of us, then we hurled ourselves through until by experience we found that contact with the floors and bruised shoulders did not help. We crawled along passages whilst Page fired over our heads, or Chummy held the Lewis to his shoulder until he received a torch signal. At last we reached a heavy door which was soon pocked with bullets. We tried to force the door but it held firmly. The Lewis gun fired in bursts of five. A pause. There was no reply to our fire. 'They must have barricaded it well,' said Dinny. 'We might be able to get in the windows from the yard.'

We held another council of war under the dome. We squatted around on the flags, our coats buttoned up around the necks. We had slept at short intervals and were tired.

Traynor's men had some positions near Mary's Abbey. They held houses in Capel Street. Automatics and small arms were being sent down to other houses, but a link-up with us seemed remote. Our wounded would not be allowed out save as prisoners, and we were not sure of what treatment they would receive or what might happen to them. We had about fifty rounds per rifle now; there were five Thompson guns with numerous drums but not so much ammunition, two Lewis guns and the Vickers. Information about enemy positions on the north side of the Liffey was meagre, and inaccurate, some of us thought.

'This is a rat-trap,' Paddy O'Brien said. 'The walls are pretty well battered already. The big guns will blow the rest of it on top of us. We'll make a sortie tonight in full strength and fight our way to Mary's Abbey.' He drew out our advance on a large sheet of paper. 'I'll take the advance guard, with 'The Mutineer'. The main body can carry some of the wounded in the Crossley tender and the rest on stretchers. You,' he said, turning to me, 'will command the rearguard.'

'All right, Paddy,' I said, 'that suits me.'

The Lancia outside the main gate would have to be hauled away by manpower as an explosion would create too much initial suspicion. We had not much food. We had had little sleep. The men were tired and the absence of a really decent feed must have been felt by all, although no one allowed his stomach to speak for him, but the decision cheered us up. We felt as if this rat-trap could at last be left behind. There was no sense in remaining here any longer.

Later I saw McKelvey, Rory and Liam talking to Paddy O'Brien. 'We're discussing the sortie,' said McKelvey as I stepped into the group. 'Rory says that if we wait for the morning we can get out through the sewers. What do you think?'

'There's been a lull in the firing for the past two hours. I think it looks like an attack at dawn. I think Paddy O'Brien should be allowed to carry out his plan; at least we can feel like men if we fight our way out.'

He said: 'The Staters have armoured cars and Lancias in the streets; we have only one armoured car. It's a long chance, that, of fighting our way out.'

The decision was to remain. There was silence for a while. Paddy O'Brien became the disciplined deferential soldier again. 'We'd best strengthen our side of the building,' he said, 'and prepare to receive an attack.'

We waited for the dawn. It was cold on the flags and our food was scanty: tea and Belfast boycott biscuits. There was silence all around the Courts, broken now and again by a rifle crack. Dawn came but there was no mass attack. Heavy firing began again and we manned positions and waited. Rory came over to me. He looked worried.

'The morning tide has flooded the sewers,' he said. 'So that's that.' He smiled as he recited.

> And how can man die better
> Than facing fearful odds

Paddy O'Brien was hit on the head by shrapnel splinters. He looked very white seated against the wall of a court-room beyond the dome, with a blanket around his legs. Blood had brightened his heavy bandage. 'How are things outside?' he asked.

'Never mind about the outside,' I said. 'How do you feel?'

'A bit dizzy and weak in the head.'

'You'd best wrap yourself in blankets and keep warm.'

Above on the Judge's Bench someone was conducting a judicial inquiry into our supplies of Mauser and Lee Enfield cartridges; the rival claimants lay in opposing heaps.

'Did you hear about the sewers?' I asked.

'Yes,' he said, 'but don't say anything to the men.'

'An explosion may come at any minute,' I said. 'That will solve all our difficulties. We'll go up together.'

'That will be a good end,' said Paddy, as he shook my hand.

Our nerves were getting taut, perhaps with strain. I felt emotional surges in myself and a desire at times to cry. Front and flanks had been pounded steadily, top storeys were out of reach, corridors were involuntarily barricaded with fallen masonry from ceilings and walls. I told Paddy O'Brien about each post when I returned to the courtroom. He looked weak as he lifted himself up from the blankets.

'I want you to take charge now, Ernie,' he said. 'I can't think clearly any more. But I wish we had tried to fight our way through last night.'

I hesitated. 'No one could replace you, Paddy; surely you know that. Why don't you make the Chief of Staff respon-sible?'

'I'm asking you to take charge now,' he said, 'for I can't hold on much longer.'

'All right, Paddy, I'll do my best.'

It was decided to remove the wounded together with the doctors and the girls. I spoke to Dr. Jim Ryan. He did not want to leave. His kind, sensitive mind felt every pain the wounded men experienced.

'But you must leave. It's an order,' I said. I lowered my voice. 'We are expecting the munitions block to blow up. That's really one of the reasons, but don't tell it to anyone.'

A cease fire was ordered, and the wounded, the nurses and doctors passed through the gate. Armoured cars patrolled the outside approaches but at a respectful distance, as they were evidently afraid of mines.

The munitions block had been on fire for some time now. The roof had caught first. Slowly the flames crept or dropped down to lower storeys, then on with a rush, crackling, as if reminded of their work. 'The Mutineer's' gun had been hit; our engineers had worked on it by candle-light and a Lewis now replaced it. 'The Mutineer' moved up and down the yard, raking the windows of the occupied building but there was no reply. The Vickers was a loss. It was a heavy gun and could keep up sustained fire without overheating, but ammunition was low. Some of the Mauser rifles were out of action also; the barrels began to glow when the rifles had been used quickly and the luminous sights had dropped off. Outside, flames lighted the courtyard, shining on the armour of 'The Mutineer' as it moved slowly on patrol. The glare was reflected by windows on our side. On our right flank flame was our guardian. Behind us was a hinterland of mines. We had withdrawn from most of Headquarters block, but at any moment the tons of explosives in munitions might detonate, or the TNT, a half-ton of it, in the cellars. The fire roared and crackled. Suddenly I thought of my books, maps and papers in my office rooms, my notes and the small handbooks I had practically completed, my library and my clothes. A strange time to be thinking of property, I thought, as if to scold myself.

'What day's today?' I asked.

'The 30th of June,' said Peader O'Donnell. 'The Dail should have met today.'

'Are there any TDs with us?'

'Yes, Liam Mellows, he's a TD. He could address us today.'

'How's Ginger?' I asked. 'I hope he's all right.' We had removed him from room to room trying to find where he would be safest. But one room was as safe as another by this. Stray shells blundered against the pillars of the colonnades or dropped into or through the rooms. Ginger sat beyond the dome, wrapped in a long heavy coat, amongst some of the men.

'Hello, Ginger,' I said; 'how goes it?'

'All right. I wish you had laid in more food.'

'I wish we had more ammunition,' I said. 'We'll have to move forward soon. They're a long time blowing hell out of us.'

He had been more cheerful the first day. Perhaps he thought he would be rescued at once. The Staters had pinned their faith in armoured cars, machine-guns and big guns. They were what mattered in their minds. Money talked, but artillery boomed. Their faith seemed to fluctuate between the two.

We went forward, thinking that we could hold the building lightly; the men were gathered into a kind of semi-cellar near the gate. I was in the guardroom with Dinny O'Brien, trying to listen for movement across the street but all I heard was my blood thumping when I listened too intently. We went out to the main gate and put our heads against the bars. 'I expect we can blow that car away,' I said, pointing to the Lancia.

As we stood near the gate there was a loud shattering explosion. The pillars of the gate shook. A blast of air seemed to rock about us. I was thrown heavily against the iron bars and fell to the ground; groping with my hand I felt Dinny beside me. The munitions block and a portion of Head-quarters block went up in flames and smoke. Large pieces of stone and wood crashed around us, papers feathered down. I had seen the sky behind me as I fell. Yellow-white, topped with dark balloons of smoke.

'That's the first explosion,' said Dinny; 'the other should come shortly.'

A thick black cloud floated up about the buildings and drifted away slowly. Fluttering up and down against the black mass were leaves of white paper; they looked like hovering white birds. A half-burnt broken volume fell at my feet. I picked it up. An account of the Secret Service money paid by Dublin Castle to informers in the year 1798. I thought: in a hundred years' time will the new Records office contain an account of the Secret Service money paid out in 1922? I had expected that the other buildings would have gone up also.

The flames in Headquarters block raced on towards the undamaged part of that building. I was badly shaken.

Rifle bullets hit off the bars of the gate and whirred. We dashed for the window and scrambled through into a room. The windows were unprotected. We could see the gate and the houses across the street. There was a series of small explosions in the yard and against the walls. Grenades came through the windows and burst in our room. We crouched on the floor near the wall; I felt the dust rise into my nose and mouth. We were not hit. 'Rifle-grenades,' I said. 'Get back to the corridor.' We moved into the corridor. 'Those houses opposite must be occupied,' I said. 'We'll go back to the others and see are there any killed or injured inside.'

The yard was littered with chunks of masonry and smouldering records; pieces of white paper were yet gyrating in the upper air like seagulls. The explosion seemed to give an extra push to roaring orange flames which formed patterns across the sky. Fire was fascinating to watch; it had a spell like running water. Flame sang and conducted its own orchestra simultaneously. It can't be long now, I thought, until the real noise comes. The dome had been lifted by the shock. 'We thought it was going to leave us for good,' said a man with a Thompson gun as I passed under it. The dome was an old friend by this. Its proportions gave a kind of dignity to the small humans gathered below it. The majority of the garrison was crowded together in the semi-cellar, but some were out in the adjoining rooms which had gaping holes from the shells. Rory was talking to one side with Joe McKelvey. He called me over.

'We've been discussing surrender. Ammunition and food are low and the flames will soon reach this block.'

'There's no hope of relief from the outside,' McKelvey said, 'and you know the sewers are flooded.'

'We're not depending on the outside,' I said, 'but on ourselves. What do you think, Rory?'

'I think we should surrender.'

'And you, Liam?' I said, turning to Liam Mellows who was looking through a shell hole.

'The Republic is being attacked here,' said Liam. 'We must stand or fall by it. If we surrender now, we have deserted it.'

'Let's hold on for a while, Rory. I'm thinking of rushing the houses near the main gate.'

Rory handed me a message from Oscar Traynor which had recently arrived.

I have gone into the whole position re your
situation, and have studied the same very carefully,
and I have come to the following conclusion: to help
me carry on the fight outside you must surrender
forthwith. I would be unable to fight my way through
to you even at terrific sacrifice. I am expecting
reinforcements at any moment.
If the Republic is to be saved your surrender is
a necessity.
As senior officer outside I take it that I am
entitled to order you to make a move
which places me in a better military
position. This order must be carried out
without discussion. I take full responsibility.

I re-read the document. 'This command is directly under General Headquarters,' I said, 'and this is GHQ at present. This order is a face-saver, and I don't like it. The Dublin Brigade has failed to get through to us. Now they are fighting on their own hook. So are we.'

We heard shouts outside. 'Stretchers outside the guard-room,' I was told. Inside men fixed bayonets, standing-to, while Dinny O'Brien and I unlocked the heavy chains. Father Albert had come back with doctors in white coats, and nurses wearing white bands on their arms on which were small red crosses.

'We want to remove the wounded,' said a man in a white coat. We unlocked the chains. They followed us in through the window.

'Are there many killed, my son?' Father Albert asked anxiously.

'Shaken, Father,' I said, 'but no one badly injured.'

'We'll bring out the wounded,' said a doctor. 'Is that all? We have stretchers for forty. Who's in charge here?' he asked.

'I'm in charge,' I said. 'My name's O'Malley.'

'I don't agree with you,' he said, 'but you're a great crowd.

Don't you think you have done your duty? Can't you surrender now?'

'I'm afraid not,' I said. 'We're going to hang on.'

Father Albert had been talking to the Headquarters Staff,
strongly urging surrender so that the lives of the garrison
would be saved. 'Padraig Pearse had to surrender to save the
people,' he said to me. 'The movement went on when he was
dead. And besides, the people are changing. I have heard
many of them curse the soldiers in green.'

'Padraig Pearse fought a good fight,' I said. 'We haven't
done so. We're not men just now, we're a symbol, and I think
we should hold this place to the last. No, Father, we won't
surrender.'

McKelvey, Rory and some others of the Headquarters
section were for surrender. Liam Mellows and I were against
it. I went up to the Chief of Staff. 'I think you should leave,
sir, with the wounded,' I said. 'I know they'll get through. It
would be better if senior members of the staff were not taken
here.'

'That's a rotten thing to say to me,' he said, tears in his
eyes. 'You are asking me to desert the men.'

'I'm not,' I said. 'I'm in charge of the garrison now and I
don't look on myself as a staff officer. I don't want the HQ
staff taken in case of an assault.'

Father Albert shook hands with us in turn. I helped him
out of the window to the gate and locked the chains in position. The firing began again, slowly, reluctantly it seemed,
then it intensified.

Dinny O'Brien and I were at the main gate again. We
looked through the bars into the houses opposite and at an
angle tried to look up and down the narrow street. 'Dinny,' I
said, 'we must find if those houses are occupied. We'll charge
across the street with a number of men, break in the doors
and hold until we can get the rest of our men across. 'The
Mutineer' can rake the windows and doors with fire. Then we
can return and blow up the Lancia so that 'The Mutineer'
can make a dash up town.' Rifle fire went high, then lowered
on to the gate; it pinged off the bars.

'What do you think, Dinny; are those houses held?'

'I don't know,' he said, 'but someone is taking an interest
in us just now.'

'I'll wait for a while,' I said.

'I'll wait with you,' said Dinny.

A bullet cut the strap of my field-glasses which were hanging round my neck. They fell to the ground. Dinny picked them up. 'They're not broken,' he said simply. Small explosions began around the yard; we threw ourselves on the ground. 'Rifle-grenades,' I said, as splinters cut glass across from us. 'That's not so nice. We're a pair of owls; we can't find out this way. Let's go in.'

We climbed into the first large room and watched the houses across the street. The small explosions continued; there was a smash of glass at the end of the room. 'Those bloody houses are held,' said Dinny, 'but no matter.'

There was another explosion, but I did not think it so severe as the first shock. Again masonry was hurled through windows and about the yards. Dust swirled around in the corridor. We leaned against the walls. They swayed to and fro. There was a strange buzzing in my ears. Shattering explosions: grenades fell into our room and burst. The noise seemed to shatter my ear drums. We threw ourselves on the ground whilst splinters went around the walls. I held my hands to my ears and my body shook. My nerves began to twitch. My mouth was filled with grit. The bursting noises seemed to thud and rethud against my ears.

'Dinny,' I whispered, 'I'll stay here. You go back, pick thirty men for a charge; bring ropes, sledge hammers, the Thompsons and the Lewis, and bring the Plunketts with mines and batteries. The rest can cross under our covering fire.'

Dinny moved across to the corridor. I crouched on the floor. After a time, it seemed a long time, he came back. He looked very grim and swarthy.

'More than thirty volunteered,' he said, 'but the others want to surrender. What do you think of that?'

I went back with him. The men had been for some time crowded into the half-cellar; there were unprotected windows in front. 'What's this about surrender?' I asked.

There were shouts. 'No surrender!' 'We want to surrender!'

'All right,' I said. 'Keep quiet about it.'

In a corner a group of us discussed it. The Chief of Staff
and Rory and some others were for immediate surrender.
Liam Mellows would not discuss the matter. 'I've already
told you what I thought, and still think.'

'The men have done their best,' said McKelvey, 'and it's
not their fault.'

'All right,' I said, 'let whoever wants to surrender go out
and surrender. Some of us will stay here.'

Suddenly I began to cry. I tried hard to stop but I could not
keep back the tears. Seoirse Plunkett came over to me. 'You
know what to do with those who want to surrender,' he said;
'you can stop that. And it's no use crying.' Seoirse was always
a rock of gentle determination.

The morale of the men had been broken by their crowding
together in cellars where they could do nothing but listen to
the fire directed against the walls and hear the explosions. I
thought for a little. If we allowed some of the garrison to
march out and we remained to fight our way out, they would
be disgraced. They had all done the best they could; it was
we of their Headquarters Staff who had left them here to be
trapped. I suddenly thought of the dead. Had we maintained
the tradition? What would our dead comrades of the Tan
war, the men of 1916, the Fenians and the others think? The
majority were not afraid to die. A surrender would be harder
than having to fight it out. I might force an issue by threats,
but I wanted to fight with men who were volunteers.

'Very well, sir,' I said to the Chief of Staff, 'we'll go out
together and surrender, but let's use up our ammunition
first.'

Some of the men broke down and cried, leaning on their
rifles. Others scattered through the front rooms and fired
enraged volleys in the direction of the big guns along the
quays and at the houses opposite. A white towel hanging
from a sweeping-brush was thrust through a bullet-shattered
hole in the glass. After a time the firing in front slackened.
Father Albert was driven up with green-uniformed soldiers in
a motor-car.

'The garrison want to surrender,' I said to him as I stood at
the gate, 'and I wish to discuss terms.'

'We will go to Brigadier-General Daly,' said a green coat.

'He's in charge of the attack.' I handed Father Albert an
envelope. 'That is for Daly and I would like a written reply.'
In the enclosed note I asked Daly if at this late moment we
could unite to attack the British before any further blood was
spilt between us.

We sat together under the dome, the men nursing their
rifles, somewhat weary now that the tension had eased. I had
often wondered why men who were not afraid to die should,
when they had weapons in their hands, surrender to what
they thought was certain death. I thought, as did the others,
that the members of the Headquarters Staff would be
executed, but that was not a factor that weighed on our
minds. Now that surrender had been decided the men were
quiet, each, I suppose, trying in his own mind to see into the
future.

Rory O'Connor sat beside me with his back against a
pillar. He looked in the dimmed light more than ever like a
Byzantine portrait, the dark blue-black shadows on his face
recessing the lines.

'What's the book?' he asked, for I had closed a small
volume as he sat down.

'Shakespeare's Sonnets. I'm trying to find a little peace
before the answer comes back.'

'Well, what does he say on the situation?'

'I can tell you that at random for I know a number by
heart:

> The painful warrior famoused for fight,
> After a thousand victories once foil'd,
> Is from the book of honour razed quite,
> And all the rest forgot for which he toil'd.'

'Has he any more hopeful message than that?' he asked.

> 'Ah! do not, when my heart hath 'scaped this sorrow,
> Come in the rearward of a conquer'd woe;
> Give not a windy night a rainy morrow,
> To linguer out a purpos'd overthrow.
> If thou wilt leave me, do not leave me last,
> When other petty griefs have done their spite,
> But in the onset come: so shall I taste
> At first the very worst of fortune's might.'

'So shall I taste at first the very worst of fortune's might,' he repeated. 'Not that that sounds much better.'

Father Albert returned. 'Daly says the garrison is to parade on the quays outside the Four Courts and he has not been authorized to accept conditions.' I sent back word that we wanted terms for the men but were not particular about the officers as we expected they would shoot us. Father Albert, departed, but no reply came back.

'Who'll take charge of the surrender?' asked Rory.

'The Headquarters Staff,' I said, 'for they have directed operations all along.'

There was a silence. I did not want to take the surrender, neither did the Chief of Staff. To surrender was not shameful, but actually to hand over to the troops outside was undignified. There was some debate as to who should make the surrender, but as I was in charge I decided to make it myself.

'All right,' I said to the Chief of Staff, 'I'm OC. I'm responsible, and I'll take the surrender. Company, fall in by sections. We're not going to march out with our arms. The men outside have broken their oath to the Republic. Pile arms and ammunition in the room beyond. Gunners will smash machine-gun parts. Strip automatics and throw the parts in the burning block. Then parade on the quays.'

The machine-gunners stripped their guns, jumped on the parts, twisted and battered them; their hands were torn and bleeding but they did not heed, they smashed in a frenzy. The men walked out of the gate in groups. The rifles and revolvers were heaped in a large room. The Courts' quartermaster with Peadar Breslin and I remained there to pile them up. Paraffin was slopped around the floor, and then with blinding flashes incendiary grenades were thrown; flames flared on the rifle pyre, licking the butts and the woodwork. We watched for a time, tears of rage in our eyes.

'Let's go,' I said; 'the men are all outside by this.'

We could feel the heat of the burning buildings as we crossed the ground. I stripped my long-barrelled gleaming Parabellum and threw the top mechanism into the flames of Headquarters block. I had scarcely fired a shot.

'Wipe your faces,' said Peadar Breslin, 'I can see the lines of the tears.' We wiped our faces with our handkerchiefs. The handkerchiefs were black and grimy when we had finished.

The men were standing outside watching the flaming buildings. 'Fall in,' I ordered, 'by sections.' The sections fell in two deep, dressed, and were numbered off by the section commanders on the quays to the left of Church Street bridge, facing the river. Only when we were on the quays did surrender seem worse than it was inside.

Paddy Daly and Tony Lawlor came up to us, smiling. They wore green uniforms. Daly carried the shoulder tabs of a brigadier-general.

'I am surrendering on behalf of the Republican garrison of the Four Courts,' I said. 'I want to discuss terms with you.'

'There are no terms,' said Daly. 'This is an unconditional surrender.'

'I want terms for the men,' I said. 'I am surrendering my command as prisoners of war. Are you going to see that they receive prisoner-of-war treatment? And I demand terms for my men.'

'I have received my instructions. No terms.'

Soldiers in green uniform with fixed bayonets marched up. They stood on guard around us. How hateful the green uniforms seemed now. An officer gave an order to the prisoners to form fours. They looked at him and laughed. He ordered again and was told to 'Go to hell. Who do you think you're talking to?'

Amongst the officers was a Clare man. I walked over to him. He was in uniform and carried a captain's tabs. 'Hello. I did not expect to see you here.' He looked confused and ashamed. 'We were rushed into it. We did not realize what we were doing and we were into it before we knew. I'm sorry.'

We shook hands and walked towards the Liffey parapet. 'I have some papers in my pocket,' I said, 'and I want them delivered.' I mentioned the name of the house. 'Will you bring them for me?'

'I'll do it,' he said. 'Anything you wish.'

'They're to be kept in safety till I send out a note. On your word of honour now?'

'On my word of honour I'll deliver them safely.'

I slipped him a bundle of papers as we both stood looking into Anna Livia, the river that flooded our sewers. 'Here's an offering to Mother Liffey,' I said as I flung my long-barrelled Parabellum out to the centre of the Liffey. 'I was very proud of that gun and now my pride is in the mud.'

I walked back to where the men were standing. All the officers still wore their Sam Browne belts and holsters, empty holsters. A photographer set up his tripod in front of us.

'I won't let you take a photograph,' I said.

'But it's for the papers,' he said, as he settled the tripod.

'No photographs, and I mean it.'

He looked towards the bayonets of the Staters as if for permission. 'If you don't move quickly, we'll throw you into the Liffey.' He gathered up the tripod and melted away.

MacManus, who had attended our training camp in the Galtees, came up grinning. He had seen service against the Turks in Gallipoli. His face was blackened. There were holes in his green uniform tunic, the edges were singed, it was open at the neck. 'Damn good show,' he said. 'When you let off that mine we were in the block opposite the Bridewell. Two of our companies were nearly blown up.'

'We did not fire a mine,' I said. 'It was the spirit of freedom lighting a torch. I'm glad she played her part.'

Daly came over to me. 'I want you to move your men up the quays to Jameson's distillery.'

'All right,' I said. In fours we marched along by the river, then up side streets, surrounded soon by a crowd; some curious, some cheered us, others muttered words of sympathy. 'Look at the poor boys, God help them. Who'd ever think it would come to this.' In front was an armoured car, beside us Staters with fixed bayonets. We marched across an open paved square and halted in front of the distillery. Daly told me to lead the men inside. We entered the yard; the ground floor windows had iron bars and the wall of the yard was high. I dismissed the company. We walked through the rooms to find out what our temporary prison was like. The house was a high one, containing offices. Outside was the open space, rectangular in shape. An armoured car moved up and down. Soldiers in green uniforms were scattered about the square. Outside a crowd of men and women had gathered; they climbed up the railings above the basement and asked questions about friends and relations. Some of the boys threw out their holsters and belts through the windows to people they recognized, asking them to keep them in safety.

On the stairs I met a Stater in uniform. 'What do they intend to do with us?' I asked. I had escape in my mind.

'I think they will remove ye all soon to Mountjoy prison. They might at least treat ye decently.'

'Perhaps you'd like to help,' I said.

He looked at me straight. 'I'll do anything I can.'

'Then try and get a few uniforms or uniform coats and caps as quick as you can.'

'All right,' he replied. 'I'll look for my pal. We'll be back later.'

I found soap and water to wash the grime off my face and hands. I took off my leather jacket and placed it in a corner; I wanted to be ready whenever an opportunity came to escape. Sean Lemass was scrubbing himself beside me. We tidied our hair and clothes as best as we were able. 'They're going to move us to the Joy soon, Sean, so we'd best make up our minds as to whether we'll go or not. I'm sure we can get out of this place if we try hard enough.' The bars of the lower windows could be prised apart but that would be difficult to do as the outside was jammed with people and we were not sure how friendly they might be; besides there was the armoured car a few yards away.

A company of Staters, headed by Daly, marched into the yard of our building. They stood at ease in two ranks, the butts of their rifles on the ground. Most of our men were there in groups. 'That's a good chance,' I said to a man.

He looked at the Staters. 'Indeed it is.'

I went over to Rory O'Connor. 'Let's rush them now, Rory,' I said. 'They can't use their rifles quickly. We could disarm them and hold the building.' Rory shook his head.

'It's not dishonourable,' I said; 'we have not given our parole.'

'No,' said Rory, 'it's not dishonourable.'

The fight to him had been a symbol of resistance. He had built a dream in his mind and the dream was there; failure did not count and he evidently did not sense defeat. With me the fight was a symbol only if it had dignity or significance. A stout resistance at the beginning would emphasize the difficulties ahead for the Staters and make waverers uncertain of overt allegiance to the Free State. If we disarmed our guard, it would turn the laugh on our opponents, and then we could join our men in O'Connell Street.

Daly came over to me. 'Are you sure that all your men are unarmed?'

'I think they have no weapons, but I'm not sure.'

'Can you find out?' he asked.

I knew that he hesitated to search the men. I shrugged my shoulders. 'You can find out for yourself if you wish,' and walked away. He watched us as Rory and I went towards the door leading to the stairs. When I returned to the yard the Free State troops had gone away. Sean Lemass came over to me in a hurry. Normally he was very calm, but now he was excited, trying hard to keep his breath as he spoke.

'I think there's a chance of escape. The small gate here,' pointing towards the front corner of the yard, 'leads into the next house, the manager's house, and we can walk right through.'

'Let's go now,' I said. 'I'm not going to discuss any further decisions with the Headquarters Staff, but we'll send word to them to come if they want to.'

Joe Griffin, our Director of Intelligence, and Paddy Rigney, joined us. We opened the small gate. There were two Staters standing near by but they did not seem to notice. We opened the back door of the house and walked through the kitchen into the hall. A man and a woman were standing at the front door looking into the street, evidently the manager and his wife. I said: 'Good-day. Please excuse us passing through your house, it's rather urgent,' and walked past into the crowd.

The armoured car was moving back slowly towards the crowd of people but no one looked twice at us as we crossed the large square. As we turned the corner we heard a shot but we did not look back. We ran when we were out of sight. Rigney had already left us.

'I'll leave you here,' said Joe Griffin.

'I suppose we'll meet at Philippi, Joe,' I said as we shook hands.

'Where will we go, Sean?' I asked.

'Over to the south side. We'll try Paddy O'Brien's house.'

'But he's not at home.'

'Yes, he is,' said Sean. 'The ambulance men who took him out of the Courts were friendly; they said they'd take him to his own house.'

We passed down narrow streets to the river side. There was a noise of shooting but it was some distance away. We crossed the Liffey below Church Street bridge and walked on the south side until we were on Merchants Quay opposite the Four Courts. Cordons of troops kept the gathering crowd away from the approaches across the river. The Morgan's Place end was smouldering, it would soon be a ruin. The dome was perched to one side. There was a spot to the right of the colonnade through which an entry might have been made; the corner near Chancery Lane was battered to the ground storey; and over all hung smoke from Headquarters block behind. The walls were very battered; gaping holes, lathes and pieces of smashed wood jutting out amongst the crumbling upper storeys. 'It's terrible to see them fighting amongst themselves,' said a man beside me. We moved on through the crowd. The burning buildings had a fascination for us. We stood leaning against the river parapet for a long time, the buildings reflected in the sky and river. An old woman moved in beside me; she began to cry. 'The poor boys, the poor boys, they were all killed inside, God help them.' 'No, they weren't,' said Sean, 'and there are plenty more to take their place.' She looked at us in doubt, then sobbed as she tried to speak. 'God bless you and guard you for those words,' she said.

We reached Paddy O'Brien's house behind the Castle near the Coombe and knocked at the door. Paddy's sister opened it. I saw the surprise on her face as she recognized Sean. 'Oh,' she said, 'oh, come in. How on earth did you get here? We heard you were all prisoners in Jameson's.'

'Oh, we did not like the distillery, so we left it,' said Sean. She smiled. 'How's Dinny?' she asked.

'He's slightly wounded, but he's all right; he's a prisoner with the others.'

'How's Paddy?' I asked.

'He's very weak. He's in bed upstairs but he's restless. He wants to get up and go out.'

We climbed the narrow stairs. Paddy was in bed, pillows supported his back. He looked very pale, and shaken. His face was the pillow colour, relieved by a dark band of blood on his bandage. We sat on the edge of the bed.

'I'm sorry, Paddy,' I said. 'You would never have surrendered.'

He turned his face into the pillow. After a while he said: 'Yes, it's terrible; that's the worst of two commands, the Headquarters Staff and mine. We could have fought our way out that night.'

'Well, it's over now,' I said.

'You'd better leave the house as soon as possible, Paddy,' said Sean. 'The Staters will probably raid for us, and they'll miss you also.'

'What are you two going to do?' he asked.

'We're thinking of trying to make our way to O'Connell Street to join up with the men there, or leave for the country and hasten the men who are marching on Dublin.'

'The Tipp men are due to arrive soon,' said Paddy. 'They should be in Blessington by this.'

'We'll go to Blessington, then.'

'And I'll be with you as soon as I can walk,' he said, with a set face.

CHAPTER EIGHT

JULY 1922

NEXT day we took a tram to Dalkey. The tram was held up passing through a Free State outpost near Blackrock and we were searched, but a girl had my attaché case. We walked into Bray and found the barracks smoking but little damaged; our men had left for Blessington two hours before in such a hurry that they had not burnt their papers. What South Dublin had been doing since the attack on the Courts I could not imagine. A man walked over from the hotel door. He was the American gun-runner whom we had released a few hours before the attack on the Four Courts began. He inquired for Liam Mellows and Paddy O'Brien. 'I liked them well,' he said. 'I sure am sorry about O'Brien. They were good boys in there.' He flashed his gold-toothed smile. 'I'm waiting for the next boat, glad to go; this country of yours is too sharp for me.' 'If you send us a consignment of trench mortars,' I said, 'no one will quarrel with you about excess profits.'

I commandeered a motor-car and the two of us turned off the road near the Glen of the Downs, up by the Sugar Loaf mountain and crossed towards the Sally Gap. The country was bare and treeless, stretches of heather and soggy bogland, practically unreclaimable. A bird on the wing, a plover, or the startled quick rush of a snipe. It was strange to have such a wilderness within twelve miles of Dublin. Not a house in sight; treeless heather hills, bluish gaunt mountains in the far distance—that was a relief to the eye after a haphazard study of classical line in the Courts. We crossed the narrow military road built after the rebellion of 1798; Michael Dwyer and his men had then fought in the hills near Imail. That fighting in our country had given large armies of British a surprise; with the road the mountainous areas would then be more easily penetrated, they thought. The British were always ready for the last rebellion. The road was narrow and bad. We overtook a convoy of South Dublin men. An old man halted us. 'I heard tell,' he said, speaking slowly, 'that there's fighting in Dublin. What do you think they're fighting about now?'

'It's hard to tell you in a few words,' I said, 'but I think they think they're fighting for a younger generation.'

He stood in the road and looked in our direction. The Blessington road wound high into wooded slopes; below was a saucer-shaped depression holding the Liffey valley and the city; rising ground in north County Dublin, foothills to the south, and the sea shining on the edge.

Blessington was almost one long street below the hills; there were men from South Dublin there already. It lay under the mountains, making access to the plain easy, and would be worth holding. A defence scheme was hastily drawn up. Sean Lemass, I appointed Director of Operations, Harry Boland, Quartermaster. Harry's gay face lighted up when he had work to do. The bank was taken over as headquarters; engineers were sent out on the roads with an engineer from Trinity College to dig up the metalled surface and lay mines to prevent the approach of armoured cars. Movable barricades were placed near the village.

Next day the Tipperary column of seventy men came in a char-a-banc, Crossley tenders and touring cars. They had taken nearly a week to come less than eighty miles; with energy the men could have reached Dublin in the first twenty-four hours. Michael Sheehan was in command; he had been Quartermaster of Tipp Three towards the end of the Tan war. He was noted for his careful—to others, miserly—hoarding of ammunition. To Mike a round of ammunition was a jewel. Men were always impressed with the importance of every round he reluctantly parted with. He was older than the rest of the men. A long weather-blown face, splashed with freckles, a lean neck, a grin gaping from a toothless mouth which blurred his words. He had a slow manner of speaking. He would never be bustled, never found without a stinging remark to answer the jibes of 'you young fellows', as he called us. It was good to see Tipp men again.

In a long string of cars we moved towards Dublin at mid-night. We had about one hundred and thirty men, mines and explosives. Our advance guard would capture and hold some canal bridges; the main body was to take the College of Science where most of the Ministers of the Provisional Government had barricaded themselves. That seemed to me more important than holding a street on the north side of the city. We intended to park three miles from Dublin and then send back the transport to Blessington, but we were halted before we reached that point. A messenger from Oscar Traynor said he was disbanding his men. Staters had pumped petrol into the O'Connell Street positions from armoured cars; the buildings were on fire, they were held by about forty men who were putting up a show of strength. Later he sent out rifles in a Red Cross car; the Red Cross, it seemed, could be pressed into IRA service when needed. Rifles were rifles; all thought it legitimate for us to abuse the Red Cross, but for no one else. We returned to Blessington.

Tom Derrig arrived from Dublin next day. He had a contemptuous wave of the hand when he spoke of anything or anybody he did not like. That dismissed an argument, it was all *raimeish*. He was more of a politician than a soldier, I thought, looking at him with new eyes for I was searching for officer material. His western accent was strong, inflected; he spoke clearly and pressed down his hand for emphasis. 'The kids were great, trying to attack armoured cars with revolvers, and the women . . .' Cumann na mBan girls had learned to drive motor-cars under fire; they practised gear changes up and down streets and back lanes until they felt themselves sufficiently skilled to act as despatch carriers. He laughed at the decoy mines which the boys had placed on certain streets. The Staters were afraid to advance in their armoured cars, but the 'mines' were empty petrol tins with wire running to a house near by. Cathal Brugha and de Valera had joined up as volunteers when the fighting began. Erskine Childers, in charge of publicity, arranged for the gathering of news, and its printing. He walked through streets heavy with rifle and machine-gun fire, from his office to the Gresham Hotel, IRA headquarters, seemingly unconscious of danger, gravely preoccupied with his work, his light mackintosh coat a conspicuous mark. My brother Cecil, a medical student aged twenty, had a command in the Gresham. The Staters sprayed

the buildings with petrol, after shell fire. When flames ate
through the houses it was decided to evacuate O'Connell
Street and a rearguard under Brugha was left to cover the
retreat of the others. The girls had refused to leave. They
recited the proclamation of Easter Week: 'The Irish Republic
is entitled to, and hereby claims, the allegiance of every
Irishman and Irishwoman. The Republic guarantees
religious and civil liberty, equal rights and equal opportunities to all its citizens, . . .' Why, if men remained, should
women leave? The question was debated with heat in rooms
of burning buildings, under the noise of shells and the spatter
of machine-guns. Cathal Brugha had to exert his personal
influence to make them go.

We talked of the Dublin fighting. Some were uncritical. To
me it had been hopeless. We had failed to profit by the
experience of Easter Week. Dublin had failed to learn its
lesson, a commonsense lesson. In 1916 a definite plan had
been prepared and acted on, although due to the counter-
manding order of MacNeill only sixteen hundred men turned
out instead of some three thousand. Joe Plunkett, it was said,
had worked on his Dublin plan for three years. Some positions held during the Rising, Jacob's factory, Boland's mill,
the Four Courts, had not been directly attacked. That
allowed the British to concentrate on Pearse's headquarters,
the GPO. The few central buildings had been too strongly
held; those which had not been attacked might have thrown
out more snipers and have held more small blockhouses. In
the recent Dublin fighting, the eagerness of our Headquarters
Staff to allow the Staters to attack first meant that the Courts
was hardly worth keeping in the end, as it had no strong
points holding approaches and none of our snipers went
beyond the building. The Dublin Brigade had first taken
Barry's Hotel far up on the north side, then they had moved
to O'Connell Street positions which possessed no particular
advantage. They had occupied buildings on the east side of
that wide street, whereas if they meant to relieve the Courts
the west side should have been held. No attempt had been
made to hold the bridges on the Liffey. Driblets had advanced, had captured places from the Staters, but had been
stopped not by the green coats but by orders from Oscar

Traynor. The operations scheme as roughly outlined for Dublin was a defensive and an offensive one, yet when the attack began as we knew it must, though we dismissed the thought of it from our minds as much as possible, we found ourselves waiting until the building was pounded about our ears by artillery fire. We had had enough men to isolate certain barracks and to attack others. Positions held by skeleton forces could have induced Staters to attack them. By pinning them to ground, by carrying out the original plan which would have meant much hard fighting, we could have restricted the enemy movement, held Dublin until relieved, and have stimulated the fighting spirit in our men throughout the country. At any rate we should have been able to hold all approaches to the Four Courts until help arrived.

It was not of much use now to fight in our minds the Dublin fight. I had surrendered my own command; there was no excuse that I could see for that, and I felt a sense of disgrace about it that no extenuating circumstances could explain, nor could I find peace of mind about it. Yet the others did not think I had done anything wrong; nobody said what should be said about such a personal failure. Most were not dissatisfied with the events of the past week. To me it savoured of a demonstration, and when compared with Easter Week it appeared ludicrous, almost a gesture. A good fight would justify ourselves in our own eyes, I thought, and establish us in the minds of the people. Deep down they could be stirred by something they would adjudge as heroic, however else it might appear to those taking part in it. I was annoyed by this calm acceptance of our lack of planning as heroism. They expected the country to be roused and to fight, yet we had no direct touch with our greatest strength, the First and Second Southern Divisions, and what was happening in Connacht, which was mainly Republican, was a mystery. Our actions were idealized rather than tested critically so that there would be a standard for further fighting. The fighting seemed to fit into the general romantic feeling of the sentiment about it.

The Staters held positions in Enniscorthy; the IRA there were not strong enough to attack, but kept the garrisons

inside with snipers. From the men on the Tipp column we
heard that Kilkenny city was being attacked by our men from
the Second Southern. It was a key position; we would go on
there first, then move down to Wexford. Liam Lynch, acting
again as Chief of Staff, was in Limerick but he had not built
up his communications lines. I instructed the officer commanding South Dublin to hold Blessington as a base, harass
and attack posts in the neighbourhood, worry the Curragh
camp. Soon, I thought, the men in the south would have
captured all posts and would then link up with Blessington
and prepare to move against Dublin.

I was inspecting the transport of the Tipp column before
we set off, when Paddy O'Brien came up. He looked weak
and unfit, with a large bandage around his head, but he was
able to walk. His eagerness to help was greater than his
strength. The blue eyes in the pale face seemed to fight a
battle with his body. He was going to help again, his body
must obey.

On a stretch of road in Co. Carlow, bordered on the left
by low hills, we saw three lorries of armed men approaching.
I was with three motor-cars of the advance guard. I signalled
the convoy to halt, then dismounted my men and moved
across country in extended order, endeavouring to outflank
the others who had halted and were lining banks and hedges.
I sent a scout forward with a white flag to see who they were.
The scout signalled to us to advance. They were some of our
men from Carlow who had captured a barracks from the
Staters.

Near Carlow town we met Mrs. Tom Clarke coming from
the south in a car. I asked her if Kilkenny had been taken by
the Tipperary men under Dinny Lacey. 'No,' she said, 'it has
not even been attacked.' It would be best to help the
Wexford men. We turned our cars back and proceeded
towards Ballymore Eustace.

We remained that night at Castledermot, a small village.
A night alarm was sounded, whistles were blown, men tried
to get into their breeches in the dark. As usual, I could find
one leg, with another man trying to insert himself into the
other. A shouting of 'They're coming!' 'They're coming!'
Men in their shirts snatched rifles in one hand, trousers in the

other, and lay down near the windows; others barged round looking for a door to get out through, shouting for their officers. I carried my trousers in my hand until I got outside the door. Women were crying and wailing in the houses along the street. It was a false alarm, nothing more. Two motor-cars had arrived from Limerick with despatches. We could not discover who had first imagined the attack; nobody seemed to know anything about it. Everyone was now supremely reticent about who had first given the alarm and who had passed it on without inquiring.

We summoned Carlow to surrender and were refused. Paddy O'Brien had reconnoitred the town and decided that the police barracks could be rushed, and that the military barracks was not very difficult to deal with, but Enniscorthy asked for help as they had attacked the Free State garrison there.

After dark next evening, we reached Enniscorthy. We heard the noise of firing as we approached, occasional shots only. Paddy Fleming, in charge of the Third Eastern Division, a tall, lithe boy with a half-nervous, wholly charming smile, met me on the outskirts of the town. 'We were just sniping until you arrived,' he said. There were three posts held by Staters: the old castle, a police barracks and the post office. Our men moved up from house to house near the castle; they occupied positions in rear of the barracks which fronted a wide square.

Next day Paddy O'Brien, Fleming and I, with some others, rushed up a narrow lane towards the post office. We reached the building without a shot being fired. The windows were barred. Boys smashed the glass with the butt end of rifles and threw in hand-grenades. The noise of bursting cases, then silence. A sudden rifle crack and a boy beside me fell. A few more sharp cracks from some distance I could not find, then Paddy O'Brien in front staggered and sprawled forward. His collar and neck were stained with quickly flowing blood. I banged slowly with my revolver in the direction of rifle fire; I reloaded and emptied again. When I looked behind me I saw the men carrying Paddy disappear round the end of the lane. The other man lay flat on his back. He moaned; his face was a whitish grey. His eyes were staring. I pulled him in close to

the wall. I took cover beside him against a shallow gate
entrance and heard him begin an Act of Contrition, say 'O
my God ... O my God I am heartily sorry ...', slowly,
haltingly, seemingly unconscious. It must have been a habit
with him to be able to say it just now when he was dying. He
struggled to the last words. There was a little shuddering
gurgle and he was dead. At the gate above me was a Wexford
officer. He was pressed against the gate but he was too fat to
be under cover; his posterior protruded and shook with
nervousness. I laughed. He turned his head in surprise. Then
when I had pointed out the cause of my mirth, he laughed
too. After a time we ran down the lanes, but no further shots
were fired at us.

Paddy Fleming met me in the street outside. 'The post
office can't have been occupied,' he said; 'the Staters must
have left it. Those would be snipers from the castle who fired.
They must be hidden in the houses opposite their post.'

Paddy O'Brien was lying on the floor of our dressing
station; he bled through his plugs and bandages. 'Don't talk
to him,' a Cumann na mBan girl whispered. 'He's been shot
through the lung.'

We collected petrol and explosives to blow in the outer-
yard gate of the castle, then to blow in the front door and fire
the building. A deputation of priests came to see me. They
wanted me to withdraw from the town to prevent further
fighting. 'I can't do that,' I said, 'I'm here as a soldier, and
I'm going to storm the castle soon. If you really want to
prevent bloodshed, it would be better to interview the
garrison and tell them to surrender, otherwise they haven't
much hope. I'll arrange for a cease fire for an hour.' They
said they would talk with the garrison. After the hour was up,
a Free State officer carrying a white flag was led blindfolded
to our headquarters. 'I wish to arrange terms of surrender,'
he said.

Outside the castle, a squat round tower which had been
modernised with small windows, the Staters were drawn up
two deep. They surrendered their rifles, with a Lewis gun. I
allowed any officer who had fought during the Tan war to
keep his revolver. The officers, one by one, gave me their
solemn promise that they would not bear arms against the

Republican forces again; their men gave a promise to their officers. We watched the green coats march out of Enniscorthy.

'It's well worth our while to bring a few priests about with us,' I said to Sean Lemass. 'They'd save fighting if we allow them to talk to garrisons.' He grinned.

Three priests came to see me. They asked me not to burn the castle or the police barracks. I promised them I would not. I had no intention of burning the buildings. We visited the castle. The water-tank on top had been punctured by bullets; water dripped through the rooms, down the winding stone stairs; it flowed out the door. It must have been uncomfortable for the garrison. Our men smashed the roof of the police barracks to prevent its being reoccupied. Armoured plates protecting the windows were removed in lorries.

The nuns were nursing the wounded in the hospital where Sean Lemass and I visited Paddy. His face was white and bloodless, with a light touch of yellow at the contours and turned to one side on the pillow. He opened his eyes slowly when we sat near him; pain lined his face when he tried to smile. I had spoken to a nun before I saw him. 'There is no chance. He is dying fast, and we were so fond of him,' she cried.

'Paddy,' I said, 'we have to go. There are other posts to be cleared in this area.'

He spoke slowly, in gasps of pain. 'I'm sorry to ... leave ... you ... so soon. ... Fight ... well ... Ireland ... *Beannacht De.*'

He fell back exhausted. His eyes were closed and he moaned. Sean and I stood looking down at him. Here was dying the best of our men; would we ever find another like him. Was it worth all this seemingly eternal fighting? Ireland was an inspiration and a curse. Did we only realize universal sorrow when we bitterly felt our own? We talked with the Free State wounded in the beds on the opposite side of the ward. We spoke in a dulled way. They shook our hands in sympathy. We walked over on tiptoe to Paddy's bed. 'Paddy, we're going now,' I whispered. I did not want to leave the bedside, but there was nothing I could do. The blue eyes had lost their shafting light and were dimming; he tried to speak but could not. I bent and kissed him.

'The capture of this place was never worth his loss,' I said, as we walked away.

'No,' said Sean gloomily. 'I wish we had never come near the damn place.'

Ferns surrendered without much trouble. Our convoy passed through the leafy lanes and little dells of Wexford, close to the foot of Mount Leinster heaving itself sheer out of the hill country; in the distance the steep bare slopes of the Black Stairs mountains. We took Borris. Tom Derrig with a Lewis-gun section of Tipp men did not turn up till after the surrender; he had gone into MacMurrough Kavanagh's house for a feed. We waited in Newtownbarry on the Slaney, a peaceful, quiet town; on either side of the river the slopes were wooded. There was an air of placid ease about the town. I was expecting trained engineers; explosives, and a few capable officers from the south. I intended to clean up posts as far as Dublin. That would leave Kilkenny city and the Curragh camp to be dealt with later when we had tested the men in barracks attacks and in semi-open fighting.

News came from Dublin that Cathal Brugha was dead. Cathal Brugha, we thought, the man we most needed now. We had many memories of him: 1916, badly wounded, fighting on after the retreat of his men, the grey look of pain in his face in later years. He had been an athlete; he had worked without pay in the Gaeltacht, organizing, trying to help its people to live. A stern disciplinarian, his integrity undoubted, he had given way slowly to the shooting of police and detectives and intelligence officers; he would not allow us to shoot women spies. When the Tans had burned supplies, houses and creameries, he had consented to a campaign of destruction in England, the burning of factories, docks, ware-houses, the gutting of farm supplies. In 1918 when con-scription threatened, he had brought over a number of men to England: their Cabinet must be wiped out if the English actually attempted to enforce conscription. At the end in Dublin he made his remnant of men surrender; then, revolver in hand, he had run towards the waiting ring of soldiers. They called on him to surrender. He rushed on and fell gravely wounded; later he died. I knew what he must have

thought before he rushed out. We had destroyed an effective
resistance by the surrender of the Four Courts; the death of a
prominent TD and former Minister for Defence was needed
to compensate. He had preferred death rather than outlive
the dishonour of his former comrades. That, to me, was a
policy of desperation, and it was unsoldierly. Dying to carry
out orders in a job of work was one thing, seeking death was a
different idea. I expect that he had seen the futile way in
which we fought, the air of induced martyrdom in the
Courts, and the mysterious occupation of O'Connell Street.

We sat in silence for a while. Then one after another told
some little story of him. He lived again in our little group.
The quiet indomitable face, steady grey eyes, the tightened
reserve of his mouth, the slow smile and sturdy air of independence, the uncompromising.

We moved to Tullow. We had asked Liam Lynch to send
mobilized columns up country to attack posts simultaneously
before the Free State could recruit and consolidate. I was
arranging for attacks on Carlow and Athy with the help of
Carlow men.

I had inspected a barracks held by our men in Baltinglass
and wore a Free State officer's cap with the badge removed.
Returning by motor-bike and nearing Tullow, I heard a
'Halt! Halt!' when close to the town. A boy was walking on
the footpath, holding a rifle in one hand, one arm around a
girl. He swung up his rifle nervously. I rushed at him on the
motor-bike. I knew he was from our Tullow garrison and did
not want to use my revolver which was tied to my wrist by a
lanyard and resting in a clip on the handlebars. My uniform
cap was back-to-front; probably he took me for the enemy,
and he might shoot even if I halted. 'Drop it, you fool,' I
shouted. He pressed the trigger, then worked at the bolt.
Before he could load, I had jumped on him.

'Holy God, it's you,' he said. 'I thought you were a Stater.'
He was from the Tipp column. I had often met him with
Dinny Lacey during the Tan fight.

Later, news from Enniscorthy. Paddy O'Brien was dead. A
doctor with two nurses arrived from Dublin. My young
brother, Charlie, aged seventeen, had been killed on the third
day of the fighting in O'Connell Street. He had refused to

leave his post. I had not seen him during four years,
throughout the Tan war, but I had then seen him a few times
in the Four Courts before we were attacked, all too few the
times I now understood. I had been isolated from my family,
and had never gone home since I left the house in 1918.

A despatch came late at night to say that the Enniscorthy
officers had broken their promised peace. They had rushed a
small post with an armoured car and had killed a number of
our men.

In Tullow I received a despatch from New Ross. Sean
Moylan, Director of Operations on our GHQ Staff, had
arrived there with two hundred men, including engineers and
machine-gun sections. Evidently dissatisfied with the spirit
there, he returned to Cork without any explanation. We
cursed him and his officers; our Headquarters came in for
their share. What the hell did they mean, anyhow? Was this
going to be a movie scenario or an attempt at a fight?

A despatch from Liam Lynch: I was appointed to act as
Assistant Chief of Staff, organize the provinces of Ulster and
Leinster, proceed to Dublin at once and there build up a staff.
Misfortunes seemed to pile on top of me.

I tried to think in terms of the new command but I seemed
to be sagging across a dark log; a worm gnawed at my brain.
All I could see was the futility of the order. I did not now know
the officers or men in Ulster or Leinster, save in Carlow and
Wexford, and I knew little of the physical nature of the new
command. I had been present at an election in north-east
Tyrone, but the IRA was not well organized there now. I had
never been in Belfast. Both these areas were now under the
government of the 'Six Counties'. I had organized Co.
Donegal, Co. Monaghan, Westmeath, South County
Dublin, parts of Longford and Offaly, but that was three or
four years ago. The officers would not be the same, the
mentality of the people would be different.

There was no such thing as a stereotyped command
amongst our divisions. Unlike as in regular armies, one could
not find when moved to another unit the same system, a fixed
standard of training in officers or men. Where to begin? It
would be necessary to stay in Dublin, run it as a headquarters, and attempt to strengthen its resources so as to help

weaker outlying areas. Wicklow, County Dublin, Meath, south Louth, the counties half-circling the capital could hardly be counted on. It would be difficult to move about in Dublin, better to remain in the country in a good area, but there was no good area. To the south the old Second Southern took in Kilkenny, the greater part of Tipperary and half of Limerick. I knew north Cork, a portion of Waterford, nearly all of Clare, north Tipperary and south Offaly. Now with my rough knowledge of Wexford and Carlow I felt I would be of more use back in the Second Southern. I had cycled or tramped across it. I had helped to organize it during the Tan fight. I knew people in country districts, some in the towns, and I understood the type of men there. I could grade the officers in each battalion, knew those who were dependable, those who showed possibility of development, who would lead, who needed to be pushed. Now I was to go to a strange country, a disorganized country as far as I could sense. I was unfamiliar with its people and their ways. It would take some time to gain knowledge of the situation in Dublin. This was not the time to sit down and think in terms of what an area could do; the time needed one who could act quickly, who knew his own mind, the possibilities of his command. Dublin itself, the nucleus from which our strength should radiate, I did not know; the political and military situation had changed so often in the past few months. Some who had been kind to me and in whose houses I had stayed would now be on the other side; I would have to fight against their menfolk. Bitterness was due to increase as the Staters controlled the press and that press had always been hostile to complete independence. We had no way of influencing the outside mind save by our actions and immediate relationship to the neighbourhood we happened to be in. Our lassitude in the Four Courts was against us. I should have known all the areas around Dublin whilst I had been in the Courts, as I could have inspected them thoroughly and have made my own appreciation of their situation. It served me right, I thought, for my lack of interest in staff work during the past few months. I would lose time now in the beginning, and time was on the side of the others. Tan war experience would no longer suffice, as this type of fighting would need semi-open warfare. Columns would have to be larger and their men be trained to take the offensive in attacking positions and in driving the enemy out of towns and cities. Intelligence, the tapping of enemy sources and the quick handing on of every type of information, should be the major service on our staff, with engineering a close second.

The Free State would concentrate on Dublin, militarily and politically. The British would supply them with field guns, armoured cars, rifles and ammunition supplies. They could recruit amongst British ex-soldiers, disbanded Irish regiments. Men who had been careful to conceal their opinions during the Tan fight, or who had been hostile to us, would now help them actively. There would be no shortage of money. The middle class was in power and could use its imperial connections. They could borrow money, make jobs for their men, make use of technicians, and rely on now friendly imperialists. Irish Catholic clergy would support them; a powerful, open and hidden, influence. We were disorganized, comparatively unarmed. Unless our Connacht and Munster men moved on into Leinster, effective opposition would be broken up piecemeal and we would be soon crushed.

I would have to work in the dark. I did not like my new appointment. It was as if I had to begin life over again. Anyhow, it was no use moaning about it; often in trouble we had quoted Wolfe Tone's saying in his diary:

'tis in vain for soldiers to complain

I talked to Mick Sheehan of the South Tipp column; the men did not want to remain in the south-east if I left for Dublin, in what was to them a foreign area. They did not know the country or its officers, and would prefer to return to Headquarters at Clonmel. I paraded the column for inspection for the last time, shaking hands with officers and men, and I outlined their best route home to follow till they reached the river Ware. The char-a-banc and Crossley tenders hummed and chirred; then in swirling dust they headed for Tipperary. I felt suddenly lonely without my men when I heard the last distant rumble of their cars. Whilst they were with me I had a staunch portion of the old division; was dealing with men whom I knew.

Our force was now small. Sean Lemass, Derrig, some despatch riders on motor-bicycles, a few Carlow men. We reached Baltinglass on a Saturday night. The barracks occupied by our men had been attacked by officer cadets from the Curragh, but they had been beaten off.

The inhabitants were not friendly. Next day we went to Mass at the chapel in the town, about twenty of us. Outside the chapel were two sentries in charge of the rifles as we did not wish to carry them inside. The sermon was about ourselves. We were looters, robbers, murderers. The Hand of God was against us. Some of the officers stood up to leave, but I motioned them to remain. If we were going to be insulted when we could not hit back, we might as well be dignified. The sermon continued. The people should have nothing to do with us, neither help, aid nor shelter us. We were outlaws, rebels against authority. It was good to get out in the fresh air again.

CHAPTER NINE

JULY—SEPTEMBER 1922

IN the city a room was found for me to work in, on top of a prim Georgian house not far from Mount Street bridge. It was a studio; there was an easel in a corner, tubes of paint and art books on a sunk-in shelf, paintings and sketches on the walls. A skylight gave me a way out in case of a raid. Madge Clifford, my typist, got ready our office for work, defence and escape. A step-ladder was placed under the skylight; a heavy chest of drawers was moved so that it could be suddenly pushed against the door; two blocks of wood nailed to the floor would back it with support. In the night I crawled over roofs to know my way in the dark. Madge could sit for her portrait if there were only a few in the raiding party.

I attempted to gather a staff together. Tom Derrig became Adjutant and Director of Intelligence; Sean Lemass was Director of Communications; Harry Boland, Quartermaster; Austin Stack in charge of Accounts and Records. I would find officers for Engineering, Supplies, Chemicals, Munitions, Transport, Organization and Publicity by degrees. It was a difficult task as I did not know the officers personally.

The lawyer who owned the house was at the seaside, but his wife was nervous. She told me that she had seen suspicious men at the top of the street, and two women were lingering beside the railings opposite. She was afraid for me. That was a hint to leave. I found another house where I was welcomed. Offices of the staff were at first close together on different sides of a fashionable square which we called 'the front', but later we had to disperse and I had to go beyond the canal to another house in quiet surroundings. Too many visitors were coming to see me and I could not use a place for long for fear attention would be attracted, especially as I had to stay with people who were known to be separatists.

I walked to keep appointments, daily crossed the canal bridges to visit staff offices. I wore a brilliant tie and a hat sporting peacock feathers; surely no one would suspect me with such a flaming tie. Our new Director of Intelligence told me that he had seen an enemy report: I had been noticed crossing the canal two mornings in succession at different times, and walking down Leeson Street with a newspaper in my hand. That was the *Irish Times,* then a good blue-gut Unionist paper. I thought it would emphasize my respectability if I was questioned. Usually I carried a .45 revolver in a holster.

An urgent despatch from the DI early one morning. Men in plain clothes stationed at the canal bridges with orders to shoot some of us on sight. That was to be expected. I used a bicycle now. It was best for moving about. One could turn suddenly, or dash down a side street or back lane. I studied the lanes and by-lanes connecting the main thoroughfares. I changed my hours, never crossing the same street in succession, always returning to my headquarters by a circuitous route. In the streets or on the bridges one might be spotted as one cycled past, but by the time the man or group had recognized who it was and be prepared to fire, one was possibly out of pistol shot or out of sight. Bridges were dangerous. I cycled up slowly, scanning the footpaths in an apparently casual way, then made a quickened descent on the far side, often feeling a twinge around the shoulder blades where I expected a bullet to land. The real danger would come from armoured cars, from lorries of troops, or a sudden hold-up by men in plain clothes, or from touts spotting our houses. Some officers saw touts all the time. At first we had to use the houses of our friends, of people who were known to be Republican; in some of them Collins, Mulcahy and O'Connell had held interviews and staff meetings during the Tan fight. As organization improved, the Cumann na mBan girls took the strain off my friends and selected places that were not well known.

Dublin, the Command Headquarters, was weak; the officers and men were being picked up and it was extremely difficult to get operations carried out. We had to deal with opponents who knew our individual officers by sight and were aware of their efficiency, energy or experience, mentality and degree of training. They had a rough idea of what we would do in a given situation, the method of our attack, which of us were most to be feared. The British had been striking in the dark. They did not know our officers personally. We were an invisible army who melted away when they tried to steam-roll. The people supported us then, and informers were hard to obtain. Now the people, on the whole, were against us; they were willing to give information. The newspapers had led them to believe that we were small disorganized groups. Catholic clergy of all ranks pounded pulpits and re-used their favourite adjectives. We now had to face ourselves and not the English.

Oriel House was the centre for the new detective force, the Criminal Investigation Department, the CID. It had an unsavoury record; prisoners were interrogated and ill-treated there to extract information, and its members raided throughout the city. The men were untrained in detective work, but they were handy with their guns and they were tough; some of them had been attached to our intelligence in the last fight. Their work was espionage. They wore civilian clothes, were well armed, and carried out hold-ups on the streets. Unlike the old detective department, the political branch of the DMP who had stalked about ponderously like giants in a story book, they varied in height, and, remaining individual, they were difficult to identify and avoid. Above all, they knew a good number of our Dublin men opposed to them. A civilian intelligence system was also being organized and it co-operated with the CID and with the military intelligence force. The intention was to have in each street a man or woman who could observe the life on that street and report regularly.

I had a sense of unreality about our work in Dublin. I walked through the people in the street; amongst them might be one of the CID or a military intelligence officer perhaps out looking for me. At any time there might come a rush of men, or an officer or green-coated soldier in a passing lorry might recognize me, and the normal life of the street could be broken by revolver or rifle fire. In the country it was different. We carried arms openly, our watchfulness showed in move-

ment and expression, we were on the alert and prepared. In
the city eyes had to be veiled with casual glances. Even
though we could pick out the touts or spotters we could not
take too obvious an interest in their movements. The men
who bumped against me purposely with a muttered apology
would feel my hip pocket gently but deliberately. My Webley
revolver lay over my heart· a quick short draw would displace
it from its tight-fitting soft holster. Every morning, instead of
my daily dozen, I practised quick draws and grips with either
hand. I had to train myself steadily to certain facial expressions, to try to appear disinterested on the streets, and to
prevent my eyes from staring too hard. I practised muscle
changes until they would seem natural.

We talked of disguises: dyeing hair, changing features,
wearing wigs, fixing eyebrows. I changed my loose, long
stride to a short quick walk, but when I was thinking of something I stretched my legs. If one's appearance was changed,
one would have to grow into the character part to fit it
unconsciously, otherwise the result would draw attention. I
would not dye my hair or eyebrows: theatricals savoured of
the dramatic. I could not last long anyhow, I felt.

One day as I was cycling past University College,
suddenly I noticed men on the path to my right; further on
towards Harcourt Street to my left were three men. When I
passed this second group I felt a twinge in my spine, the old
sign of unease, and this time it had some sense in it. There
came the quick sharp report of an automatic, then two further
shots and a whistle as something passed me. I bent lower over
my handlebars to make my body target as rectangular as
possible, then turned to the right and was soon under an
arch. Truly a bike was the correct approach to an underground movement. It prevented you from being tailed by
touts on bicycles as one could always turn quickly down a
laneway which made the spotters too obvious, or halt to fight
which then put them at a disadvantage. During a sudden
street raid it gave a good view of a street, and if approaches
were cordoned off, I could leave the bike against a curb,
knock at a door, and with some impromptu remark walk
through the house to the back gate.

Beyond the canal bridges I had other houses to sleep in,

where I kept late appointments. We changed the houses frequently to avoid attention, but I was still limited to a few for meeting country officers. I held staff meetings in the morning at eight o'clock; for a time in Kay Brady's in Leeson Street. The Staters would hardly be properly awake at that hour, I thought; nor was it the custom for the IRA to rise early. There was little activity in the mornings. Our staff dribbled in slowly, generally a meeting beginning three-quarters of an hour beyond its timing. Austin Stack came twice dressed as a Protestant minister in a peppery grey suit, his grave face suiting the disguise. The door of the house would be left slightly ajar, or it could be opened by pulling a cord, for a delay at a door might mean that a spy or passing tout would identify someone. I had a collection of yale keys. Large and small keys for front and back doors. I had to work steadily at key drill until I could in the dark remember the feel of the particular key that fitted a lock. I knew how to get into houses over back walls at night, and through side-gates, and where to find unlatched windows.

The Adjutant, Tom Derrig, came to my headquarters. An ex-British Army officer had walked into Tom's office in his sister's house by mistake. The brother was Free State, the sister Republican. He had known Tom during the Tan war. 'At it again, the same old game,' he said, withdrew with apologies and closed the door. We discussed the various angles of the incident. 'It's all right,' I said; 'he won't give information without first telling you.' Tom agreed. He did not move his office. There was no raid.

It was difficult to organize the Command, to find out who was in charge of an area. I knew the names of most of the senior officers in Leinster and Ulster. I had met many of them when I had been Director of Organization in the Four Courts. Their names had given me no inkling as to their worth. It was difficult to get in touch with the divisions and independent brigades of the Command as no lines of communication had been established; despatches could not be forwarded. The first step was to build an efficient communications system. Sean Lemass undertook the work, helped by Cumann na mBan Headquarters, but it was disheartening. Soon the words 'Are you in touch with' became a joke with us. Large stretches of the communication route which we had outlined on our maps were hostile, or the friendly units there were disorganized. Special messengers had to bridge the gap, to establish contacts. Slowly the system was built up. Commands existed on paper often. The months of indefinite action had produced lassitude and uncertainty. We had drifted so long that our men had become tired. Our intelligence service was not good, yet we had fairly good information but were not strong enough to act on it.

During the Tan war the girls had always helped but they had never sufficient status. Now they were our comrades, loyal, willing and incorruptible comrades. Indefatigable, they put the men to shame by their individual zeal and initiative. The men in many cases were supine, lethargic. The wave of disgust at the signing of the treaty had made some cynical, others indifferent. The shame of men of our own blood dividing our country, walking into the British Empire, had dulled rather than enraged them. On the other side they saw good men whom they had trusted and who had fought well in the Tan time. They were more inclined now to dissect motives, to question orders, to think the fight was hopeless. Many saw themselves fighting their one-time friends. I was fighting imperialists. The one-time friends as far as I could see did not mind fighting us.

We were hard hit in Dublin; frequent raids, numerous arrests and uncertain outlook had taken a big number of officers and good men. We should have been strongest in the capital. During the Tan war the Republican Government had concentrated there; the Dublin Brigade was strong and activity had been pushed to the uttermost. Our victories now in the south and west did not carry as much weight as a simple well-planned operation in Dublin. Public opinion was most rapidly affected in the metropolis. A small active service unit of twenty to twenty-five men was started in the city. It worked in groups during the daytime, endeavouring to bomb lorries on the streets: difficult work on account of the hostility of the civilian population. It needed good pistol shots most of all. That would mean less civilian casualties and more military, but the shooting was poor. I suggested operations to the Brigade but its officers, perhaps unwittingly, placed obstacles in their own way, and battalion officers had not much initiative. I expect we, on the whole, felt cowed in the city. I wanted to form a column from amongst my own staff. The intention was to show to our commands the possibilities of a small group, handled with energy, seeking the offensive, but it was not favourably received at a staff meeting. I thought it better that we should act as a column rather than as fountain-pen officers whose instructions and orders were not being carried out. And time was with the enemy.

I inspected areas in the neighbourhood of Dublin. One could better appreciate then the difficulties of the officers and men. Michael Price was the officer commanding the First Eastern, and he undertook the work of endeavouring to organize the scattered units there. Liam Lynch had protested against his appointment. Cork officers for some not very clear reason did not like Price, but I did. His officers were worn out when I met them, constantly hunted, little sleep, a small command now spread over a large area. I went north to Monaghan where the officers were sitting down; I outlined attacks for some not very willing officers.

Harry Boland, our Quartermaster, a close friend of Michael Collins, was deliberately shot during a raid in Skerries and died a few days later. He had been a general favourite, his gay cheery face always brightened up our meetings, but it was impossible to make him take proper precautions; he could not adjust himself to the new conditions. Joe Griffin, our new Director of Intelligence, who had been with him, was arrested. His successor was shot while attempting to escape. Austin Stack was the new Quartermaster. He had to have special rooms built to hide arms, ammunition, and people. Now there were sliding panels and portions of rooms walled off with secret entrances, all the settings for a good mystery story. The Director of Chemicals, Jim O'Donovan, had been arrested but escaped; he came into a meeting where I was appointing another man to replace him. The Assistant Director of Organization, Tod Andrews, who had been wounded, had succeeded in escaping from Wellington barracks. The headquarters of the Command Engineer had been raided, papers captured, a few land mines and explosives, and some of the staff. One officer had been badly wounded in the leg, but had managed to escape. Through the Directors of Chemicals and Munitions, workshops were established and grenades manufactured; I had intended to wait until we had made a good supply of explosives before we began to fight in Dublin and the immediate neighbourhood. The weapons we needed most were automatics and revolvers, hand-grenades, rifles and incendiary grenades, land mines, Thompson guns or sawn-off shotguns, and quantities of explosives. Positions could be stormed with mines; gates or doors of buildings blown in. A charge inside a building would have a shattering effect; it would blow away the ceilings and maintaining walls. Used against a building from the outside we would need twenty to forty times as much explosive to shatter it. Our munitions factory worked as hard as its staff were able. The shops were changed constantly. All the time our men were being arrested. In the evening I was never sure what member of my staff was missing. I often replaced a casualty with a boy who had succeeded in escaping that same day from a prison or an internment camp. The Quartermaster-General in the south did not send explosives or supplies. We wished Liam Lynch would soon arrive in Dublin. Then he could understand the situation and realize the importance of the capital before it was too late. It had been lost to us since the beginning of the fight. The Dublin Guards had been sent to Kerry so the Free State garrison was not very strong in the city, but their intelligence service had local assistance in every company area and was getting a good grip.

One night, returning from a meeting of South County officers, I walked across the city. At the meeting reports and despatches from battalion areas had been given to me, which I padded to a roundness in my socks. I did not carry a gun. I was close to Baggot Street bridge when I saw a car without lights move up slowly to the bridge; there were four civilians in the car. Something wrong with their lights, I thought. A car on the opposite side at the bridge began to swing its beams up and down, then across the street. It moved down on the wrong side, on my side of the street. It was an armoured car. There was no laneway or gate near me. The searchlight focussed on three men in front of me, then on myself. I'm trapped, I thought; the car without lights must have picked me out. The armoured car came to a halt. Men with guns in their hands jumped down, shouting: 'Put them up!'

The three men held up their hands. I did not, as I thought I had been recognized. If they meant to shoot me, they would not shoot me with my hands up. Damn them, anyhow. I moved in under the muzzle of the machine-gun in the turret. That wasn't going to riddle me first. Two men stuck revolvers against my chest. They searched my pockets. They did not pass any remarks about my hands not being held up.

'What's the idea?' I asked, waiting to jump and snatch a gun.

They did not reply. They searched me thoroughly, felt the lining of my tie, the inside of my collar, under my armpits. One of them felt my socks on the outside, patted my trousers, ran both hands on either leg down to my boots. They did not say anything.

'Have you finished now?' I asked.

'Yes,' said one, 'you're all right. You can go ahead.'

I walked away slowly. I did not take a natural breath until I had crossed the canal bridge.

Another night I was cycling from Upper Leeson Street towards the canal when I heard a sudden 'Halt there! HALT!' as I was close to the bridge. The voices came from either side of the footways, and as I swung my bike around I heard rifle shots. I dropped to the ground with my bicycle, and as figures rushed towards the rise of the bridge I fired a few rounds, and then ran back to the pathway on Mespil Road. The figures disappeared but their rifle fire shook the night. To go down the canal was now impossible. To return by Leeson Street seemed as bad, as I would then be under fire from either side. I went quickly back for my bicycle which was in no man's land, fired quickly at both sides of the bridge, reloaded and cycled away. As I looked around the corner I found going on what Irish newspapers would describe as a 'fierce battle' or a 'determined encounter', but it seemed to be between the opposing sides of Leeson Street bridge.

Michael Collins was killed in an ambush in Co. Cork.

Those Free State people who had once glorified the ambush now spoke of it as a cowardly form of murder. Arthur Griffith had died of a cerebral haemorrhage. Republican rumour, always busy, said it was due to severe shock when he found that Collins and the IRB had been implicated in the shooting of Wilson, former Chief of the Imperial General Staff. Many Republicans were in high spirits. The two men more than any others responsible for the treaty were dead. Religious ladies nodded heads in significance. 'Yes, it was a judgement of God.' He was now on our side.

Funerals went to Glasnevin cemetery. Soldiers in green uniforms marched, with arms reversed, after bands playing the 'Dead March', following their dead. Our men were buried quietly; women mostly as mourners. The CID were nosing for men. Cumann na mBan girls in uniform, some with eyes shut and faces screwed to one side, fired a volley over the graves with revolvers or automatics.

I moved my headquarters to the suburbs and remained with a young curate for two weeks, but it was an isolated house, difficult to approach.

Eamon de Valera came up from the south to Dublin early in September. He stayed with Austin Stack in a house in Upper Mount Street known as Mrs. K's, where he had contact with Republican TDs and through Stack with our Command. They had a room prepared. There was a space concealed into which they could retire in case of a raid; already they had used it successfully, and many ingenious devices were worked out.

I met Dev to talk over the general situation. His face was pale; worn lines made his jaw seem longer. He was worried. I was worried myself, but talked of the Command as cheerfully as I could. He could not see, I felt, a military win on our side, and now he had no direct say in the conduct of the fighting. All I could point out was a slow increase in sympathy and morale amongst the people even in this bad area, which would eventually yield political results. He talked of negotiations with Collins. 'Signing the Pact was the worst day's work I ever did for the Republic.'

I was anxious to have a full meeting of the Executive called but it had been postponed. Only when I met officers who really knew each of our areas could I rely on their intimate knowledge for an appreciation of their particular and the general situation. In the south a line had been held along the Suir by our First and Second Southern Divisions, and across the Shannon below Limerick city, with its rear and flanks in the sea. They had placed themselves on the defensive, a fatal point of view, and they were slowly being driven back. Provincialism may have induced the line, such decentralization suiting a piecemeal guerilla warfare, but no series of minor tactical victories by us in Connacht and the south could make up for our weakness in the capital. The Staters pushed on slowly. Our line served no purpose that I could see. The offensive was with the green coats who landed in Cork and Kerry by sea, and occupied towns. The troops had been withdrawn from Dublin so we availed of the opportunity to build up the organization as best we could, for it was essential that we should be strong in the enemy's headquarters. At night the various posts were sniped; machine-guns rattled, but the enemy could afford to waste ammunition.

I went home, to Iona Drive, Glasnevin, to see my people. It was now September 1922. My last visit had been in May of 1918. Mulcahy had suggested then that I had better go home to see them. Evidently he had been approached by my parents or by someone who knew them. The suggestion had been emphasized so thoroughly that I had taken it as an order, but I did not remain longer than twenty minutes. Father, naturally enough, had said what he thought of me, my approach to medicine, and the futility of my Volunteer connections, and I, who acted under what to me was then a command, did not say anything.

Now they had changed. Father and mother were glad to see me. My elder brother Frank, of the King's African Rifles, who had died in East Africa, was in a grave at Dar-es-Salaam, and I was now the eldest. The next to me was with the Nigerian Frontier Force; the next, Cecil, had been arrested two weeks before when attempting to cut a railway line and was now in Maryborough jail; the next, Charles, had been killed in action in O'Connell Street. The two younger ones, about fifteen and sixteen, who had been out during the Dublin fighting, were attached to Fianna Eireann; they slept at home but were expecting raids at any time. Although father and mother did not approve of the decided views of the younger members, yet their unity made a difference.

A boy had been born since I was last home. He was a 'publican, he whispered to me. I was called 'Uncle Jack' by the household for fear he would talk to children in the neighbourhood if he knew who I was. Before I left he called me into the hall. 'You're not Uncle Jack, you're Ernie, but I won't tell.'

I came home once a week, but they were nervous for fear the people would recognize me, or that the house might be raided while I was in it. The neighbours would not recognize me, I felt. Father and mother were now ostracized by most of their neighbours, who refused to speak to them or to acknowledge their presence. Others were insistently rude and gave air the benefit of their opinions. Yet none of these had ever lifted a hand to help us during the last scrap, nor had they helped the Empire save by their inflated sense of righteousness. At least they might have remembered that in 1918 we had saved their manhood from being conscripted by their friends. The outraged bourgeoisie were determined to defend this Free State of theirs, which had been handed them on a platter cooked à l'impériale. My friends opposite, good Unionists, were now, save for the Buckleys next door, the only local people who kept their humanity and were still kind to my family.

Monsignor O'Hagan, Rector of the Irish College in Rome, was anxious to meet me. He had already seen Mulcahy, Provisional Government Minister for Defence, and was attempting to effect negotiations. He was anxious to see if a settlement could be made. I knew of O'Hagan's work in Rome where he had fought hard and ably against British diplomatic pressure on the Vatican. Always he had insisted on the national status of his college, which had formerly been considered an appendage to Beda, the English College in Rome and the focus of our country's most persistent enemies, the English Catholics. I had been warned that he was a trained diplomat but I found him sympathetic and direct with me when I met him at home.

There was little I could do to help him save to report our conversations to Eamon de Valera and to Liam Lynch. We had taken the oath of allegiance to the Republic; we meant to keep it. We would fight until we wore the Free State down, or were wiped out ourselves. Negotiations would have to be conducted through de Valera and Lynch. I had no personal suggestions to offer, but as he intended to visit the Staters' HQ, I asked him to mention the systematic torture of our prisoners and the deliberate murder of men, mostly in this Command; he could tell them to curb their murder gangs. Agents could be controlled if they wished to control them. That would at least prevent intense bitterness.

Coming from a meeting of officers in Kay Brady's house late one night, I was walking near the kiosk at Leeson Street bridge when an open car, travelling fast without lights, rushed across from Wilton Place. I had time to see four officers as I jumped, then the edge of the radiator struck me from behind. I was thrown forward and fell on my back.

I lay there for some time. I must have been stunned, for I heard a man say as he helped me to get up: 'I thought you were dead at first and I was afraid to go near you.' I sat on the footpath for a while until my legs were able to bear me; then I wobbled along, crabwise, sitting down to rest whenever my legs folded up. My hip had been injured. It was lucky, I thought, that the soldiers had not stopped to investigate their victim as my pocket was filled with documents.

Oriel House was now famous as a 'knocking shop' where prisoners were battered and tortured. I was anxious to have their headquarters captured, with its papers, and I thought the attempt would not be difficult. I had been put in touch with a friendly CID man who wished to meet me. Some of our officers thought I would be trapped when I went to meet him, or they looked on the whole move as a plant so that I would be tailed back to my headquarters. Although I was advised not to, I met him in a house we rarely used. I thought him all right as we talked and then, relying on instinct, trusted him. He seemed willing to help in any way he could. He described Oriel House, the number and position of sentries, rooms where the arms and records were kept, telephones, and the general house routine. I took notes. Afterwards some of his answers to random questions could be verified. I drew plans of the building which he amplified. Oriel House was old and strongly built; it held the corner of a street. The CID must have felt secure for their defences were not thorough. Their general feeling of irresponsibility helped to bring this about as the men were rather uncontrolled. They drank hard, were encouraged to be offensive and destructive when on raids, and they had helped military intelligence to murder some of our lads.

Oriel House was in the Third Battalion area. I sent my information to Joe O'Connor, commandant of the Third, having first established some of my informant's details; but he did not seem eager to use it. At last I told him that I would get some men from the First Eastern Division and try to take the place myself. He decided to use his own men. The best time was in the evening when the CID men would have finished a meal and be less careful. The door was held on a chain. Three men were to knock at the door, give the name of a man then out on duty, and hold up the guard. Others would enter behind them, make for different landings and there seize telephones, documents and arms. There were about fifty rifles and small arms there, and that in itself was worth a raid. If unable to retreat in time, our men were to hold the building as long as they could, throw out snipers, and withdraw under cover of dark.

Michael Price, OC of the First Eastern, was in town on the night of the proposed attack, with his acting brigadier, Brennan, and Commandant Paddy Mannion, whose father had been an inspector in the Royal Irish Constabulary. I intended to be near the scene, with Sean Lemass, when the attack began, as I was concerned about the job which I had insisted on. When I told them where I was going, Price and the other officers asked to come with me, for my own protection, if it was nothing else, they said. I did not want to bring them into danger as their own areas needed them badly, but as they pressed their point, I gave way.

We walked down the east side of Merrion Square. I was in front, Price behind me a little to my right, the others about

twenty feet further back. Our men were to hold up the guard
at half-past eight; we would go in five minutes afterwards. We
waited at the corner of the square. A few revolver cracks. We
saw men rushing out of Oriel House; some ran up a lane to
one side.

'Something wrong,' said Mick Price. 'We'd better slope
away.'

I did not like to leave until I had word from the Third
Battalion; someone might be able to explain what had
happened, and their commandant knew I would be waiting at
that corner. An armoured Lancia approached noiselessly
from Merrion Street. It was close to the corner of Clare
Street before I first noticed it. Soldiers were kneeling inside
with rifles pointed at either side of the street. The Lancia
halted twenty yards away from where we stood. The soldiers
got down and spreading out to either footpath began to
search passers-by.

'We'll move away slowly,' I said, 'and keep to the house
side of the square. If we see the Staters ahead of us, I'll knock
at a hall door and we can go through the house to the gate at
the back.'

When I looked back I saw Staters on foot advancing up the
street we had just left. We crossed to the far side near the
railings of the park. At the end of the square the others
wanted to remain with me in case I was held up, but I walked
on by myself.

'You're very excited,' said Kay Brady when I went into
Harry McAuley's house in Fitzwilliam Square. 'Is there anything wrong with you?'

Two days later I received a despatch from Joe O'Connor
about the attack. The OC Third had seen an armoured car
under Westland Row railway bridge as he made a last-
minute reconnaissance. Its guns were trained on Oriel House
and he decided to call the job off as it created a doubt in his
mind that the enemy might be ready inside waiting for something. He met one of his company captains at the street
corner and told him to call off the operation. While the OC
Third hurried to Lombard Street to find the captain of 'G'
company, the car moved slowly off towards Merrion Square.
In the meantime OC 'G' made an attempt on Oriel House.

The plans went awry because the guard, instead of being surprised, were shot at in the hall. The first men to enter had found three men on the door, three behind a desk, and some men on the stairs, and they fired through excitement, or because the guard had not put up their hands quickly. The men in the hall surrendered, but one of the CID on the stairs tried to draw a gun and was killed, and another was wounded. Our men outside retreated instead of immediately following up. None of them had been captured.

There was no question of the information being a plant, as far as I could see. The following day I was told that Brunswick Street police station had been asked before the attack if there was any activity in their vicinity and had replied that everything was quiet there. The armoured car probably came as a result of men being noticed in the neighbourhood. Paddy Mannion had got as far as Mount Street bridge where he was halted by the Staters, put up against the bridge parapet, and wounded. As he lay on the ground he was killed by their rifle fire. At his inquest a verdict of wilful murder was returned against the military.

The Command Director of Publicity had at last printed a paper, *An Phoblacht*, 'The Republic'. Before it came we used cartoons drawn by Countess Markievicz pasted on letter-boxes and lamp-posts; handbills, and small mimeographed typewritten sheets sent around by hand. The CID raided vigorously for the printing press; it had to be moved frequently. The printers were often captured, but daily *An Phoblacht* was sold on the streets of Dublin by newsboys or copies were pasted on the walls, despite all efforts to locate it. Cumann na mBan and young boys painted with whitewash and tar the walls of Trinity College, the pavements, the walls of the Mansion House, any dead wall space they could find. News of the fighting in the south, accounts of ill-treatment of prisoners and the names of the officers concerned, appeared. —————— CALL OFF THE MURDER GANG. And ..., THEY HAVE MURDERED PRISONERS. UP THE REPUBLIC. My brothers were nearly captured bill-posting.

Robert Brennan was in charge of our publicity and was ably seconded by Frank Gallagher whom I met on the south side a few times. Frank had a small room cut off from a larger one, and bookcases in place of a door concealed the opening. Here he kept his papers; here if a raid took place he would retire. After our meetings I would generally remain the night with him. We listened to our snipers sending an occasional shot at the sentries in Portobello, and the increasing volume of reply as machine-guns stuttered and sprayed. We planned impossible plans and laughed at their absurdity, talked of books or discussed literature. That was a welcome break. In Munster, Erskine Childers had published his daily paper in the mountains, but after the hasty evacuation of our GHQ near Glengariff the paper had been discontinued. I had written to him. He did not complain, but I knew how isolated he felt in the south.

Jails were being filled. Soon barracks housed prisoners and internment camps had to be prepared. If all active Republicans were arrested, the fighting would cease. The Staters knew who to raid for, and they were able to identify our men in a round-up. Prisoners would sometimes be released if they signed a form stating they would not again take up arms against the Provisional Government. I sent instructions to all prisons in the Command that the form could not be signed by anyone.

CHAPTER TEN

SEPTEMBER—OCTOBER 1922

I FOUND another house to stay in as the activity circulating round an office of mine was sure to attract attention after a while.

I moved to Mrs. Humphreys on Ailesbury Road. The neighbourhood was sedate, leisurely, respectable and imperial, removed from fighting, arrest and sudden death. The last time I had met Mrs. Humphreys had been in 1917 when, as a volunteer in 'F' company of the first battalion of the Dublin Brigade, I had seen her pin religious medals on men who had been out in the 1916 Rising. She and Miss O'Rahilly, who lived with her, were sisters of The O'Rahilly who had been killed in a charge on Moore Street in Easter Week 1916. The house was so frankly Republican that I thought it would not be suspect. Cathal Brugha and others of the Headquarters Staff had stayed there during the Tan fight. Surely the Staters would never think that we would have the hardihood to use such a well-known house again.

I was kept awake for successive nights by a sniper. By the sound he must have been using the roof of the house next door, but what was he firing at? Beggar's Bush, the nearest post, was a good mile away. The moon, then, was his only target, unless there was some kind of a Kentucky mountain feud being carried on between my respectable neighbours.

I worked in a study off the breakfast room in the front of the house. Madge Clifford came every morning and she worked till seven o'clock or often late into the night. She had been a typist at 23 Suffolk Street and was fairly well known. She had her hair bobbed and she tried to change her appearance frequently. I was known as Mr. Ryan to the maids in the house for fear of any leakage through talk. At night-time I slept in a concealed room at the end of a corridor; if there was a raid during the day I could go up there with my papers. The room door had been changed to a cupboard in which clothes hung, but by pulling a wire connected to a powerful spring the cupboard swung open. It had been built in the Tan time by Batt O'Connor, a great admirer of Michael Collins, and he was now on the other side.

We joined the family at the Rosary in Irish, then they were off to bed by ten o'clock. Mrs. Humphreys, her son, Dick, and her daughter, Sheila, as well as Miss O'Rahilly, spoke Irish fluently; at meals *bearla* was seldom used, save when I could not follow the conversation and that was often enough. My Irish was poor. I was talked to by Mrs. Humphreys with gentle severity on the incongruity of an Assistant Chief of Staff of the IRA who had to have his own language translated for him.

At times I would see myself through their respectful eyes; then I would realize how unfitted I was for the responsibility of command. I was admonished about my hours. 'You should go to bed early,' Mrs. Humphreys often told me. 'It's bad for your health to stay up late, you'll ruin your eyesight, and I feel sure you keep dreadfully late hours.' Evidently they saw nothing abnormal about our life. I crept upstairs, always after one, often between three and four; then I read for a while to clear my mind of this undue demand of war on its time. My crime was not discovered until I had knocked over a small clock one night. Next morning at breakfast the clock which had stopped near three o'clock was shown as evidence of guilt.

The Director of Operations and his assistant came every day. It was difficult to avoid attention as members of the staff visited rather frequently. Couriers brought and collected 'the post' as the despatches were called, many times a day. During the day I cycled around to visit the offices of the Director of Communications, Adjutant, Quartermaster; held staff meetings; and met journalists, messengers or officers from remote districts in the Command. Writing notes meant more work for couriers; it would never have the same result as a personal contact. The chief danger was in being 'tailed' from place to place. That would endanger the staff, their papers and couriers. A single unimportant routine form forwarded by hand might result in the capture of our entire staff. Papers were a worry, but files had to be kept for those who would take our places. The Command was not effective, operations were not planned and carried out in proportion to our armament and the opportunities presented. However efficient the staff might be on paper, the result would rest with flying columns and supporting units. There was the danger of over-organization in staff work, a tendency to work out beautiful paper schemes with every man in his place, to draw up delightful forms which would give accurate, intensive information, to receive reports under varied headings with perky satisfaction. Men get drawn into the organization scheme; they become efficient, self-satisfied automatons. The objects to be aimed at were intelligence, operations, training and administration, in their order of importance. Our senior officers were mainly satisfied with administration, and organization gnawed at itself. It would have been better results if they had taken command of flying columns. That would strengthen morale and give an example of the handling of men, of courage and of capacity for leadership. Tod Andrews, the Assistant DO, was lanky, his stilted legs could not be mistaken. He often dropped in for a chat. He was one of the few active organizers we had to visit distant commands and came to report whenever in town. The DO could see no end to the fight; his battalion had been badly disorganized when the attack on the Courts began, and he had seen the Dublin Brigade lose its officers in successive raids. His records of areas were on a sliding scale as weakly-held areas were often nearly eliminated, but again recruited and re-organized.

In the evenings we stopped work for half an hour to play tennis. The DO objected at first, it was too silly and too risky, but eventually he was glad to take a racquet for doubles with Tod and Sheila Humphreys and I, or we played singles. Tennis kept us fit; we forgot the risk in the game. It was necessary to keep physically fit and tennis with its intensity gave us an opportunity to unlimber muscles and minds daily. We could see the adjoining houses from the court at the back, and as our household had no contact with its neighbours, that made it additionally secure. If troops appeared during the game, I had a ball in my pocket which I intended to hit into the next garden, then climb over the wall and disappear amongst the fruit trees. Often I thought of the lads on the hills in the hostile areas. They had little food, no comforts, while we could have regular meals, the only regular meals I had had for five years, and even play tennis.

Workshops were prepared by the Directors of Chemicals and Munitions. Jim O'Donovan and Sean Russell had also been in charge of those departments during the Tan fight but machines were now with the Staters. The Quartermaster-General in the south evidently did not see the necessity for concentrating on Dublin and consequently did not forward explosives when requested; we would have to wait until the Chief of Staff reached us.

The Provisional Government met at Leinster House on 27 September and an Act was rushed through, setting up secret military courts and thereby giving the officers commanding districts power to inflict the death penalty on our men captured with arms. I was anxious that a fitting reply should be made and had ordered all units in the Command to plan a successive series of attacks to take place the night after the Bill was passed, but the attacks did not materialize; instead posts were merely sniped at the same night.

However, a proclamation was being prepared, outlawing the Provisional Government and declaring them traitors to the Irish Republic.

Six or seven miles outside of Dublin the mountains begin. For thirty miles they are twelve to eighteen miles in breadth, running south to join the higher ranges beyond the Wicklow border and stretching to the sea beyond the Bray river. Few roads followed the valley running east. The winding road built by the British after 1798 crossed the length of the chain. Bogland; heather; gaping, useless land, nearly impassable in winter; no forest, timber only along the lowering eastern slopes of the pleasant valleys. Very few houses save in the glens, Glenmalure, Glendasan, Glenmacnass; the western edge unpeopled. Food dumps would have to be made, and dug-outs for shelter. Using the mountains as a base, columns could attack posts in the neighbourhood of Dublin and inter-

rupt communications. Small wireless sets would be needed to
keep touch between columns. We had few men in Wicklow
and adjacent Kildare; the work should fall on South County
Dublin, but the scheme was never developed.

Sean Lehane, in charge of Donegal, was hard pressed and
was instructed to attempt to make his way to the midlands, to
Meath or Westmeath. His column started off, harried and
weakened.

The column in South County Dublin suffered heavily yet it
had to be replenished and when we sent men there we knew
they would not last long. Boys were sent out from the city
when it was difficult for them to find houses to sleep in. When
a boy left us he had a slim chance. The area in a circle around
Dublin had never been properly organized in the Tan fight; it
was late to begin now when there was little support, but it
could have been done. Well-led columns of city and country
men would have given work to men on the run and have
drawn off Dublin garrisons. But the people as a whole were
hostile, and hostility was on the increase as the southern 'line'
was broken and Free State victories, doctored as carefully as
the old British reports, appeared in the press.

Dundalk was to be attacked by our men under Frank Aiken
commanding the Fourth Northern Division, the greater part
of which was in Ulster. Undecided up to the attack on the
Courts, he had protested in person to Mulcahy, who sent
him back with promises. Later, Mulcahy's men came as
friends to Dundalk and captured Aiken's barracks through a
breach of faith, and he and his officers were arrested and
imprisoned in Dundalk jail, but the jail wall was blown in
and he and many others escaped. He attacked and recaptured
the barracks, blowing up the lower portions of the building
with mines. In fifteen minutes the well-timed operation had
resulted in the capture of the entire garrison of three hundred,
and of rifles for some four hundred men. Shortly afterwards
the IRA evacuated Dundalk, which was then reoccupied by
Free State troops, and our present operation was to rescue
our prisoners again in Dundalk jail.

I left Dublin to inspect divisions in the north. A girl drove
me in her car. Twenty miles from Carrickmacross she ran

into the shafts of an ass-drawn cart. The radiator was a wreck. I obtained buckets of water from cottages along the roadside and filled up frequently. Our trail was a watery one. Coming out of a house with a bucket of water I saw two armed Staters approach the car, but they passed it without comment. Beyond Crossmaglen, across what was now known as 'the border', I met some of our officers. They were not doing anything, just moving about carrying rifles. I discussed operations and outlined plans for the area; then hurried towards Dundalk. I had heard that posts were to be attacked by our men there that night.

Outside Dundalk I met Frank Aiken and Paddy Quinn, his quartermaster, and other members of his staff. It was the intention to attack various positions in the town as well as to rescue prisoners. The officers for each specific operation were present, most of them young boys. Frank Aiken puffed slowly at his pipe. His quiet brown eyes glanced over operations maps; he held up a finger to emphasize points. The officers received instructions, asked questions, made suggestions, then outlined their plan of action. They seemed well trained, eager, capable of responsibility without much supervision. That alone was cheering, and a change to Dublin where we had clerked away without much prospect of seeing plans realized.

Aiken, Paddy Quinn and I made our way across country to the outskirts of the town. We waited for the noise of the first explosion which would be the signal to move up to action headquarters. Rain drizzled for hours, soon we were wet through. After two hours standing in the shelter of a wall we felt that the prisoners had not been able to co-operate; yet the attack might still take place, or the Staters might locate some of our small parties.

'I wish we could dry ourselves,' I said. 'I'm wet through.'

'There's no friendly house near here that I know of,' said Aiken.

'Let's try that one,' I said, pointing to a house with a garden, on the far side of the muddy lane. A gravel path led through flowers strongly scented after the rain.

'We're Staters,' said Aiken, as he tapped the knocker.

There were lights in the upper rooms. After a little delay, a man, in shirt and trousers, opened the door slowly. 'Hello; is there anything wrong?'

'We're officers from the barracks,' I said. 'We'd like to shelter if we may.'

'Certainly; you're welcome. Come in and hang up your coats. What brings you out on a night like this?'

'Snipers; they've been bothering our sentries.'

We sat down near the embers of the fire. He blew the coals with a brass-bound bellows. 'Yes, we've heard them often enough; they keep us awake at nights.' He called to his wife. She came downstairs, a pleasing fair-haired woman. 'You must be hungry,' she said.

'Well, we are,' said Aiken, 'to tell you the truth.'

She prepared a good cold supper for us. We were very hungry and we ate thankfully while our host talked to us. He was an engineer on the railway; the talk veered towards railways, the destruction of communications. He told us of bridges blown up, and of the armoured train in Dundalk; he drew diagrams.

'Are you a stranger here?' he asked.

'Yes,' I replied, 'I'm not long in Dundalk.'

Later they went to bed, but said we could remain at the fire as long as we wished, to be sure to close the door when we left. We thanked them for their hospitality.

'Do you think he believes we're Staters, Frank?' I asked.

He drew on his pipe; he slowly puffed out a thin length of smoke. 'I think he does.'

'I'm sure he doesn't,' said Paddy Quinn, 'but he won't attempt to leave the house.'

We sat and talked until morning. Our men, Frank said, frequently sniped from across the border when hard pressed by the Staters. The people on the other side were more friendly. The border was patrolled on that side by the Royal Ulster Constabulary. The Staters co-operated with the Ulster police to round up Republicans; there was a mutual exchange of prisoners. At dawn we closed the door and left the house. We were crossing a road outside the town when Paddy Quinn said: 'Drop down quick—Staters.' We lay down. 'Where?' I asked. 'Around that bend,' he said; 'I don't think they saw us.' They had probably heard our men moving to and fro in the night-time and had thrown out picquets to cut off stragglers. There was little cover; we had revolvers only. We crossed a large field, but though we saw the picquet, six men, they did not see us.

I found that the division as centred around Monaghan was not doing anything, but as I was due to attend a meeting of the Executive to be held near the Knockmealdown mountains on the Cork border, I had little time to spend there.

I obtained a car and a driver, and plotted our route on my maps to avoid all the Free State posts I knew of; I was not sure of the areas outside the Command but we could always avoid towns by taking the by-roads. A boy of seventeen, the son of a Dundalk lawyer, who wanted to join a South Dublin column, came with me; he had a .32 automatic with six rounds. I had a .45 revolver. The driver was unarmed. The Dundalk boy was slovenly in appearance as if he was attempting to break away from home by a disorganized, dirty exterior. He had read widely. His vocabulary was as lengthy and abstruse as his browsing amongst books; Latin words rumbled sonorously. We talked of books and school life whilst our eyes strayed to either side of the road, but it remained mostly with the driver to watch for troops. We passed through Co. Cavan into Westmeath without meeting any enemy. At the entrance to a village near the foot of the Slieve Bloom mountains we saw two lorry loads of Free State soldiers approaching. Just then we saw a rough lane which had not been marked on the map. We turned slowly up the lane, increased the speed of the car, crossed the ford of a river, and by a series of by-paths reached the main road again beyond the village. I knew the by-roads from Offaly onwards, through the mountains of north Tipp where I had often cycled, till we could see the straight height of the Galtees rising massive from what looked like plains, and the Comeraghs joining the sky on the south-east. The enemy did not seem to be active around south Tipperary and the people whom we met were as staunch as ever.

My dog Moss was the first to scent me as I crossed the fields to Tincurry. He pawed me and wagged his tail till I feared it would fall off. Mrs. Tobin and Eva came out at his wild barking. 'And how is every inch of you?' Mrs. Tobin

asked, shaking hands. 'Sure we never doubted but that we'd
see you again.'

It was pleasant to munch sweet apples in the orchard and
to look up old nooks with Eva. Rhododendron bushes were all
around; Mrs. Tobin had stories about individual trees. 'We
knew you'd get through,' she said, 'but we thought you'd
never come.' Fighting always seemed a distant interlude in
the peace of Tincurry.

We moved down to the Knockmealdown mountains for the
Executive meeting. Liam Deasy in charge of the First
Southern, Seamus Robinson of the Second, were in a house
further down beyond a bend of the Suir. Between them they
controlled more than the province of Munster: that area was
still intact as a fighting force. I was ragged about Dublin and
the poor area I had. Here our men could move around at
their ease. The Staters had penetrated the south, some of the
towns, but the mountains were still ours.

Liam Lynch, Chief of Staff, came in; his face looked bonier
than usual. 'I wish you had kept your information about the
Staters' encircling move,' he said. 'We broke up our headquarters over it.' He had had a secure area in the mountains
of Ballyvourney; I had received information from an officer at
Stater Headquarters about an intended sweep of that area.
General Murphy was to be in charge: he had planned his
encircling advance carefully on a $\frac{1}{2}''$ map, but I knew his
troops would never be able to advance in that rugged country
as easily as he could on a map. I sent a special messenger to
Ballyvourney with the detailed plan for the round-up, expecting that GHQ would be able to resist enemy penetration,
particularly as they would know of the exact disposition of the
forces pitted against them. Instead there had been a hurried
evacuation of the entire area on the arrival of my notes.
'Besides, the Staters didn't carry out the round-up,' said
Deasy.

Joe O'Connor from Dublin wore a hard hat. The hat
seemed funny to us in the mountains. The Connacht men
had not arrived. Frank Barrett came from Clare, mud
splashed to his hips, as the meeting began after six o'clock.
Communications were bad: GHQ seemed more out of touch
with Connacht than we were with our isolated fragments in

Donegal. It was decided to send a staff officer to the west to co-ordinate activity there. Clare was in a bad state, or according to Frank Barrett; he made a poor mouth, I thought. His men had to dump their rifles in some battalions as they had no ammunition. Joe O'Connor and I laughed when some of the officers furnished their reports. The Northern and Eastern Command existed more on paper than in any other way; the Fourth Northern was the only division that had any cohesion. We had little ammunition, practically no explosives, but there was a slow improvement: areas had begun to wake up, yet areas with twenty times our resources in men and arms were complaining and more pessimistic.

Billy Pilkington arrived from Sligo next day. His area had done a good share of fighting; he seemed confident and assured. He gave me more hope than any of the others.

The south was to disband its large columns. We suggested the southern men should equip motor columns and mop up posts in the midlands, or co-operate in sudden raids and surprise attacks there, but that was not accepted.

A long haze of talk was brought up by a motion to ask Eamon de Valera to form a government. We had acted without consulting the political party; now, in difficulties, we were again to give allegiance. Civil government could function in the south and west, so the officers representing those areas stated, and that would give a necessary background of support. It was agreed after a long discussion that the army should proffer allegiance to de Valera, who would select a Cabinet.

We each nominated two successors to take our places in case of our arrest or our death so that the Executive Council would be kept up to strength.

A question we were anxious to discuss, what to do when the Free State began to execute our men, was not considered; it was thought too remote a possibility.

We sat around a blazing turf-fire in the kitchen, in the night-time, talking. Officers told of narrow escapes and mishaps; we related humorous incidents of the fighting, with a laugh often to end our own drawbacks and defeats. We discussed officers and men. Great numbers of prisoners captured had to be released; it would be too great an expense to feed them. They immediately rejoined their units and fought again.

Liam Lynch motioned to me, during a pause in the talk, to move into another room, off the kitchen. We sat at a table, in 'the room' of the house; two candles gave us light.

'I'm thinking of moving to Dublin,' he said.

'It's about time; then you can fall back on the resources of the south.'

I told him what headquarters in Dublin would be like. 'Can you arrange for a headquarters for me?' he asked. 'I will bring a number of staff officers with me.'

'I'll do that, but if you remain together, you can't move around much,' I said. 'It's best to have only your adjutant with you.'

'That can't be helped. I'll be there soon. You make all the arrangements, then I'll send you to Connacht.'

'That will be a relief. I'm tired of being a spare fountain pen.'

'Do you remember North Cork,' he said, 'and the old column? That was a good time and we didn't know it.'

Joe O'Connor and I left the Cahir valley and arrived in the old South Tipp Brigade centre at Rosegreen. The Davins were expecting us; many of my old friends gathered around the fire in their kitchen. After we had drunk the inevitable 'drop of tay', they recalled incidents from the Tan fight, trivial happenings, what we did or said, doings and sayings we had long since forgotten, a trick of speech, a sudden anger and a humorous jest in a tight corner. 'Musha, do you remember,' someone would begin; then a roar of laughter from the others. Bill Quirke had captured a 'ghost train' the previous week near Cashel. A ghost train was an armoured car on railway tracks, driven by a noiseless engine, to protect the line. Bill had commandeered it. 'Then he brought the prisoners down here for a few pints apiece.' It was good to be back here again.

We slept in another house a few fields away and returned in the morning. Joe O'Connor, an elderly married man, had been promised slips of plants and trees in Rosegreen for his city garden. He had already collected slips from Tincurry, wrapped them in folds of paper at the back of the car, and talked of them proudly. With a splash of holy water on our foreheads, accompanied by many blessings, we started off. We planned a return route and reached Dublin without having to pass an enemy post. This could be utilized in future for special messengers, I thought.

The meeting had shown me that there was no unified operation plan for the whole of Ireland. No concerted action would be taken, and the Staters would recruit and train an army in the meantime. It looked as if we would be worn down piecemeal, but men seemed to think that we could carry out much the same tactics as we had used against the British. During the first month no definite operations orders had been issued and in many instances Republicans awaited attack. The offensive spirit was negatived and in areas where men had carried through a minor campaign of guerilla warfare against the British, and were now capable of developing a system of semi-open warfare, their potentialities were ignored. Slowly the resistance retrogressed back from some semi-open fighting to disintegrated guerilla war in which smaller and smaller columns and groups took part. Ireland would have been more partial to us if we had been defeated after heavy fighting, but this scattering of energy, this indefiniteness, this decentralization of action potentialities, meant that control became increasingly difficult and that co-ordinated action was impossible. To the country at large a fight was being waged by bands of men who might be worn down little by little, or their morale lessened by executions. Continual guerilla warfare, with its oft-repeated instructions to safeguard one's line of retreat, had worn down an offensive spirit and undoubtedly it affected the outlook. Once in a while a sustained fight was needed to reassure ourselves.

Raids became more frequent in Dublin, as did hold-ups on the streets. The CID, with women searchers, were fond of that peculiar form of raid known as the 'sit-down raid' in which they entered a house quietly, unknown even to the neighbours. They locked all the family in a room at the back; then they sat down inside for a day or two, enjoying the freedom of the house as regards food, drink and souvenirs. All callers were arrested, searched and put in with the family. That type of raid was hard to guard against, though we did attempt a series of warning signals that would tell us if the house was being occupied, such as a front-room blind at a certain angle, but it was not often successful.

The Catholic Bishops issued a pastoral from Maynooth in October and instructed the clergy to read it from their pulpits. It crystallized the random fulminations of the great majority of the priests who were in favour of the treaty. Sunday after Sunday their sermons had degenerated into essays of political abuse. Now Republicans who continued to carry and use arms against the State were deprived of the Sacraments. This had little or no effect on the men but it undoubtedly affected public opinion. Those people who supported the Republican movement resented the abuse of clerical power to suit political ends, but Republicans already had their minds made up, and despite the clergy, the press, and the Provisional Government, their views remained unchanged.

Arrests continued, upsetting attempts at organization, but fresh officers stepped into the vacant places. Isolated groups of our men had been rounded up by the Free State in Dublin and neighbourhood, and individuals were murdered. This continued. We had the names of the Free State officers responsible for the murders but we were unable to catch them. It had become increasingly difficult to move around Dublin, yet we had to hold staff meetings, interview officers from the country, and visit each others' headquarters.

Sean Dowling, our Director of Operations, was also Director of Organization and Jail Escapes. He still came to Humphreys every day as it saved couriers for communication purposes. Specific operations could not be easily planned by a Command officer as none of our units were certainly capable of carrying them out. I had to meet officers from the country, as personal contact was essential, and then I could outline operations which might be carried out. Dowling was trying to control despatches and letters for jails. Everyone who had a relative or friend in prison was anxious to send in news in a surreptitious note, but this meant that the few soldiers or military police who were friendly were over-burdened with notes. He tried to arrange that only letters bearing certain marks would be taken by friendly soldiers but his efforts were being frustrated as quickly as he built up a reliable system. For a time letters to be delivered were sent to him, and his remarks as he read them, to cut down the in-going post, were piquant enough.

One of our principal objectives should have been an attack on Mountjoy prison, as the Four Courts garrison, Rory O'Connor, Liam Mellows, Andy Cooney, the Plunketts, and many of the staff were there, together with a number of other experienced officers; and men arrested in the Dublin Brigade area some time after the fighting in O'Connell Street had ended.

We handed the problem of Mountjoy over to the engineering department. We wanted large supplies of explosives, a few simultaneous breaches in the surrounding walls, and some storming parties to cover escaping prisoners in the exercise yards and to hold the Staters in the Joy. A delicate timing from inside and outside, with good transport to get the prisoners away, would be needed. The Dublin Brigade was very short of explosives, and our GHQ in Cork had not sent us on supplies, nor had we been able to get them from our dumps in the Fourth Northern.

Already there had been an attempt at escape from inside the Joy. Some guns had been smuggled in. They were not taking any chances of a leakage; I had not been told about the plan. But at the last moment something unforeseen had occurred. The rush was made, some of the guards were killed and wounded, but the heavy gates of 'C' wing swung back. Our men were driven to cells by rifle fire, and Peadar Breslin was killed, Peadar who had remained behind with me in the Courts to set fire to the rifle stocks and the piled heap of our arms. Andy Cooney undertook full responsibility for the escape attempt and it seemed that the Governor, Phil Cosgrave, brother of the Staters' Willie Cosgrave, stopped the troops from firing on the prisoners. They were marched into the yard, surrounded by machine-guns and riflemen, but the Governor walked up and down between troops and prisoners until quiet was restored.

Our engineers began to tunnel into the jail from one of a

row of small houses close to the walls. The work was slow, fatiguing, as there could be little or no relief for the men engaged on the task. Girls brought them food daily, but the neighbourhood was actively hostile. From inside the jail other tunnels were sunk to meet the incoming diggers.

Sheila Humphreys was a very active member of Cumann na mBan. Before dawn she often started off with her paint brushes to join companions who decorated the dead wall space of the city with slogans in coloured paints. Dressed in uniform she attended burials of our boys at the Republican plot in Glasnevin. She looked after our wounded, moving them from place to place; found safe houses for our men to sleep in; guided strangers through the city, and carried despatches. That was routine Cumann na mBan activity. One morning we heard that she had been arrested. Madge and I quickly parcelled up our papers and I was ready to move at once in case of a raid. Late in the evening Sheila came home, bubbling over with joy. She had been arrested with other girls that morning while they had been painting their favourite site for our exterior decorations, the boundary wall of Trinity College. Troops in an armoured car surprised and arrested them. A girl had painted the inside of the car before they reached Portobello, the Staters' headquarters. They were locked into a large whitewashed room, but two girls had managed to hide their paint and brushes. Here was a grand chance. A room in the enemy's headquarters. They worked quickly and soon the walls jumped with green paint: CALL OFF THE MURDER GANGS, ———— FIGHT FAIR. DON'T TORTURE OUR PRISONERS. THE IRISH REPUBLIC LIVES. Hours later some officers came into the room. The girls had evidently been forgotten. 'Why, what brought you here?' one of the officers asked in surprise. 'If you look at the walls you'll soon find out,' said a girl. They were released, and Sheila brought back some cartridges which she had stripped from the feed to the Vickers gun whilst inside the armoured car.

I received a report which had come from a friendly source in one of the Staters' barracks. Sheila and other Cumann na mBan girls had tried to remove a wounded prisoner from a city hospital. They had been too late, however, as the Staters had already taken the man to jail. The girls had been armed with revolvers, and Sheila was mentioned by name in the report.

I spoke to her about this with diffidence as I did not consider myself of importance, but my knowledge of men in the by-ways of the Command was peculiar to myself; all I possessed, then, was an experienced staff officer's knowledge, and maybe a certain influence with good men, and if I became a casualty that information which could not be added to paper would be lost. Documents had to be kept for my successor, and there were others which had to be referred to continually, yet I had the habit, I knew, of keeping too many documents. I was reluctant to destroy our files. Whether that was due to a collector's instinct or not, I do not know, but when I went through my papers with the intention of destroying them, I found a great number to excuse their continued existence.

One night late I was working in the study when there was a loud sharp knock at the door. I took my gun from beside my pen on the table and listened. The knock was repeated. Sheila ran downstairs quickly. 'I'll open,' she said. 'It must be the Staters.'

'No, I'll go myself,' I said.

I cocked the hammer of the Webley, unlocked the door, threw it open, and waited to one side in the darkness of the hall. A figure walked in, brushed beside me and laughed.

'I frightened you,' she said. It was Mary Comerford, with a despatch from the north. I was frightened for I had intended to fire, when she laughed.

Newspapers wrote romance about 'fierce battles' in which there were often no wounded or no objectives gained.

I had been instructed by Liam Lynch to capture and execute the editors of the *Irish Independent* and the *Irish Times,* but I did not carry out his order. Undoubtedly they were doing the enemy's work by their misinterpretation of events and by their wilful perversion of facts. They were inflaming public opinion and ignoring the more brutal side of the Free State methods: the murder of prisoners, the work of their murder gangs, and the consistent ill-treatment and torture of prisoners to extract information. Yet I considered that the Free State Cabinet should be first dealt with.

Why not the Cabinet or a few bishops? They were more nearly responsible for the direction of the offensive against us. When I first came to Dublin I was willing to have the Cabinet shot; I would have gone on the job myself with a few officers, but Liam Lynch had interfered. We could have wiped out the Free State Cabinet but it would not be worth while beginning anything like that unless we could see it through. Now that the Staters had built up an army it would not have the same effect. We would stand over any shooting and accept responsibility. The fight, such as it was now, would then turn into a hunt for individuals; the other side would shoot prisoners of lesser rank and it would degenerate into gang war. In the Command we had decided on one line of action. I had sent out orders that any Stater officer who was responsible for the torture or murder of a prisoner should be captured, tried and executed; if unable to be captured he was liable to be shot on sight. I obtained the lists of such officers from the different areas, with statements of the offences. Their names and sentences were to be printed and circulated at once and painted on the walls of the city so that the people should be prepared for the executions that would follow and understand why they had been incurred. We had the movements of the Cabinet under observation and intended to arrest two of them.

The newspapers had been consistently hostile. In effect there was a strict censorship, but in the majority of cases no additional pressure was required. Our intelligence department intercepted and forwarded me a communication which was sent out to censors and the editors of papers:

MILITARY CENSORSHIP
GENERAL INSTRUCTIONS

1. The Army must always be referred to as the "Irish Army", the "National Army", "National Troops", or simply "troops".
2. The Irregulars must not be referred to as the "Executive Forces", nor described as "forces" or "troops". They are to be called "bands" or "bodies of men.

3. Irregular leaders are not to be referred to as of any rank, such as "Commandant", etc., or are not to be called officers.

4. No news as to movements of troops may be published.

5. No news may be published as to movements of newly enrolled members of the army, movements of foodstuffs, or trains, or transports of equipment for army purposes.

6. Description of a military operation must not be published while the operation is still incomplete, for instance, an encircling movement.

7. Articles or letters as to treatment of the Irregular prisoners may not be published.

8. The Censors are not to insert words of their own in any article submitted to them. Their business is to cancel what is objected to. They may, however, propose to substitute words or phrases, such as "Irregulars" for "Republicans", "fired at" for "attacked", "seized" for "commandeered", "kidnapped" for "arrested", "enrolled" for "enlisted".

9. Letters, news or articles dealing with proposals for peace, or negotiations with the Irregulars, should not be passed without submitting them to the Chief Censor.

10. The term "Provisional Government" should not be used. The correct term is "Irish Government", or simply "the Government".

11. All G.H.Q. Bulletins from here should bear the date and time of issue.

12. Escapes of prisoners must not be published.

> By Order
> Army Publicity Department
> Beggar's Bush, Dublin

I forwarded notices to the Dublin newspapers giving them the option of handing their papers over to the Stater Military Council, or of printing at the head of their articles or news: 'As passed or directed by Censor'. Also they were instructed that for every use of the word 'Irregulars' instead of Republicans, they would be fined five pounds, the bill to be

forwarded weekly and collected whenever we thought necessary. Replies were forthcoming from two editors asking what
they were to do, as they said they were compelled to publish
the information as issued from Portobello barracks, but the
correspondence was interrupted by another event.

CHAPTER ELEVEN

NOVEMBER—DECEMBER 1922

I HAD been six weeks in Humphreys, and that was a long time as time was valued by us. Madge had been looking for another house for me but it was difficult to find a really suitable place which fulfilled our many demands. When I was away on a tour of inspection in the north the house was raided, but my bedroom was not touched. That blind spot reassured Mrs. Humphreys; she thought the Staters did not know of the room and her mind was at ease about it. However, I was sceptical; yet I tried to think that the room was safe when she talked about it to me, but my instinct fought against being boxed up during a raid as I was determined to fight it out.

Liam Lynch sent word that he would come to Dublin within a few days and bring some staff officers with him. He then intended to send me to the west of Ireland to co-ordinate the activities of the four divisions in Connacht. I was glad of this because I was tired of acting in the capacity of a third-class clerk issuing orders which would not be carried out. In the west, at any rate, I could have an opportunity of taking part in operations. I also received a note from Erskine Childers, who should have been in charge of publicity in Dublin, to say he would soon leave for the city to assist Eamon de Valera, and was looking forward to the change. Co. Cork away at the south of the island was no place for a headquarters. Our men had more actual control there, but communications with the rest of the country was not good. The GHQ Staff would be more inclined to think in terms of the southern divisions.

Mrs. Humphreys had been severe about my clothes, in a gracious way. 'They're unbecoming to an Assistant Chief of Staff,' she said to me a few times, 'and I hope you will permit me, dear boy, to get you a suit.'

Three or four members of our staff were not drawing any salary, though others were being paid regularly. Money had no value now that I could see, save to buy cigarettes or books, but I had very little time to read and no other expenses beyond the departmental. Eventually I was persuaded to inspect suit patterns and to visit Lehane's for a fitting.

I had agreed to sleep away from the house so that I could arrange about the suit, but I had first to attend a meeting of some Dublin battalion officers beyond Clontarf Park and was able to talk to them about their difficulties and mine. They did not complain, I noticed, although their units were being hard pressed, and I tried to read their reflections of my eagerness to get planned specific operations in Dublin. They were a good crowd of men, I could sense, and whatever they felt about the shortcomings of myself and our staff they hid under a friendly comradeship. I returned late that night to Humphreys, although I was to have stayed the night in another house so as to have a fitting next day.

The entrance door to the room where I slept at the end of a passage was concealed so that the passage appeared to terminate at the clothes rack. Chintz hangings covered the rack entrance; coats, scarfs and furs hung from hooks; my door was opened by pressing a hidden spring.

At about half past seven next morning, 4 November, Sheila tapped hard at my door. I was awake at once as my habit was when anything unusual was to happen.

'Earnan, the house is surrounded; the Staters are coming in the gate. Mama saw them outside as she was coming back from Mass. Are you all right?'

Excitement was mounting in her voice but she was able to control it.

'Thank you, Sheila, I'm all right. It's come at last.'

'*Beannacht De leat anois*, Earnan,' she said.

I shielded a match with my hand for I did not want a light to show at the back of the house through the sepia blind, while I placed my Smith and Wesson and a hand-grenade near my safety razor on the dressing-table. I heard heavy knocks at the front door and the sound of feet going downstairs, whilst I dressed in the darkness, putting my trousers and coat over pyjamas. My hand was shaking but my mind was clear as I moved the .45 cartridges in rows of six on the table beside the bed. Then I put a cardboard file of my most important papers on a chair. I would bring them with me if I broke through, or burn them in a bucket which I kept in the room for that purpose. I knelt on one knee to pray for courage; then I sat on the end of the bed, revolver in my hand, listening in the darkness.

Why the *Tain* should come into my mind I don't know; maybe the preparation for fight evoked a memory, but I was trying to remember what Ferdia wore on the last day of the fight at the Ford.

Outside of his brown-leathern, well-sewed kilt he put a huge goodly flagstone, the size of a millstone, the shallow stone of adamant which he had brought from Africa. He put his solid, very deep iron kilt of twice-molten iron over the huge goodly flagstone. On his left side he hung his curved battle sword, which would cut a hair against the stream with its keenness and sharpness. On the arch-slope of his back he hung his massive, fine buffalo shield whereon were fifty bosses.

And when Cuchulain saw the feats Ferdia had performed, he said to Laeg his charioteer: 'If defeat be my lot this day, do thou prick me on and taunt me and speak evil to me, so that the more my spirit and anger shall rise in me.'

There was nothing very splendid about a Smith and Wesson, yet I was fond of it as a good piece of mechanism, and my one grenade was not very warlike to look at, but it was the most effective weapon against a crowd of men, especially when they were bunched together.

I could hear voices in the distance that were so dim that it might be imagination as I tried to keep my breathing quiet. Voices, footsteps coming upstairs. Rooms were searched. Men came to Dick's room, then Sheila's, the bathroom, and they were in Miss O'Rahilly's where the corridor turned at right angles in my direction. I followed the sounds along the far corridor. There was now no such thing as time, for the tension of my mind neglected it and my feelings closed in and out as on a melodion. I was unsure now of myself. I did not know if I could draw on a reserve of courage, but my will to fight seemed to me intact. This trapped feeling and my use of the room made me feel unreal to myself, and therefore uneasy.

They were in Mrs. Humphrey's room, now, at the end of the corridor. There was a blurred sound of talk. I could hear her voice but could not make out the words. Men came down the corridor, tapping walls with the butt ends of rifles, as if they were searching for recesses; by this time search parties must have been aware that many houses held concealed rooms and dumps for papers. Perhaps that banging was routine now on a search. Would they notice the door? I should have padded my room, I thought; I had suggested it often to myself but had neglected to do anything further. Why didn't I have it padded to deaden a blow?

I heard Mrs. Humphreys say: 'Oh, that's a clothes press,' as the curtains were drawn back.

A rifle butt crashed against the wooden partition.

A man's voice said: 'It's hollow.'

My heart beats were now so loud in the darkness that I felt they must be heard outside, and I pressed one hand hard against my heart to keep it quiet, but it seemed to be now on top of my tongue. I had moved to one side of the door to avoid bullets, and had already shifted the dressing table to make a slight barricade.

Rifle butts crashed in shattering echoes; a panel began to give way, a portion of another splintered, showing a little light; a piece of wood fell into my room. I thought of firing through the door, releasing the spring and rushing out, but Mrs. Humphreys might be behind the Staters. Another panel was smashed in, but those outside could not see anything yet in the darkness. They had not located the hidden spring. I heard the men breathing hard as they struck in the narrow corridor. I would have to fire. I could not wait for a grenade to be thrown in. A heavy crash; the door swung open and a hand appeared. I fired twice; once at the hand, then below and to the right at what might have been the body, and there was a cry of pain. I heard a rush of feet, but I was afraid to fire again as some of the family might be in my way.

As I came out of the room I saw the attackers scrambling

out of the hall like frightened sheep. I saw a chin edged out
from a door. Another of them, I thought as I fired. There was
a thud. I fired again close to the corner and rushed forward.
Miss O'Rahilly lay on the floor, blood on either side of her
cheeks. She was pale but she did not moan. I had shot her
through the chin.

'O my God, I've shot you; that's terrible,' I said. 'I thought
I'd got a Stater and it's you.'

Mrs. Humphreys helped Miss O'Rahilly into her room.

'Never mind her now,' Mrs. Humphreys said to me as I
remained near the bed, feeling helpless and distressed. 'She's
not badly hurt. Think of yourself,' and she smiled. Mrs.
Humphreys was as calm and as sweet faced as when pouring
out tea at breakfast. Miss O'Rahilly tried to smile also.

That unnerved and worried me as I passed up and down
the corridor, thinking of her wound, cursing myself for snap-
ping so quickly and for the momentary pleasure that I had in
hitting a mark. That was a bad beginning, to have one
casualty already in the family, and through my fault. It was
terrible that such a thing should happen. The sharp tinkle of
bullets splintering glass in the top rooms made me think of
the situation. Firing had been going on for some time past,
with fire directed at the house from all sides.

Sheila was standing at her door. 'You hit one,' she said,
'but you fired too low. They're brave, aren't they? And you
should have seen them run away.'

I heard a noise of men downstairs and a confused shouting
of orders. I put the gun in my coat pocket and gripped the
serrations of the Mills hand-grenade. As I went down the
stairs I could see the Staters had crowded into the hall, and as
they opened fire I pulled the pin, held the grenade whilst I
counted, and lobbed it into them, and then flung myself on
the stairs to avoid splinters of metal. There was a stampede
and a rush for the front door. Men huddled, crouching as
they ran. I did not fire as they were too frightened, but I
watched their panic in a strange kind of detached wonder-
ment. Soon the hall was empty, only the unexploded grenade
remained below in the centre of the floor. Evidently the cap
was defective; my most effective weapon had failed me.

On the stairs I picked up a rifle someone had dropped.

There were ten cartridges, one in the breech. I went into Sheila's room.

'They're hiding behind the walls outside,' she said, 'and some must be in the houses opposite.'

Her bronze-gold hair was plaited round the back of her head. Her blue eyes shone with excitement; they matched the colour of her dress with its foamy white collar.

The house was about thirty feet from the front gate and two storeys high. Behind were flower beds, a rock garden, the tennis court and fruit trees. A wall over six feet high surrounded the grounds. Beyond the wall to the right were houses, three-storeyed, red-brick houses. To the left was an open field with bushes close to the wall. I looked through the windows but could not see anyone. I opened a window and leaned out.

'Mind,' she said; 'don't lean out too far, they'll hit you.'

Suddenly a bunch of men rushed through the front gate and across the lawn, as covering fire was opened up from different sides, but the only result was the sound of glass being drilled and smashed, the cracking of glass and the thud as bullets hit off the walls. I heard men shout 'Surrender!'

As I fired I shouted: 'No surrender here!'

This was not going to be another Four Courts. I was an individual soldier again, responsible for myself, and there was no Headquarters Staff to make decisions. I fired quickly with my rifle. On the lawn a man lay wriggling and twitching; his comrades dashed back through the gate. The wounded man lay still.

'He's done for, I think, poor devil,' I said to Sheila.

Now that it was under fire the house seemed to be full of windows, and as I searched around for the best place to keep the women safe, one room seemed as safe as another. The high front wall masked the ground floor windows and though I should have liked to repel attackers from downstairs, I had to use the upper floor for observation. I went in to see Miss O'Rahilly. She must have been in pain and her swollen mouth did not allow her to talk, but she did not complain. Her eyes followed me as I watched her but I could not see any reproach in them.

'I've telephoned for the ambulance,' said Mrs. Humphreys,

'but I don't know if they will let it through or not. Now we're all right here, so don't worry about us.'

The noise outside might have been typewriters clicking. The very presence of Mrs. Humphreys seemed to banish rifle fire; one could sit down and drink tea slowly in such an atmosphere. Mrs. Humphreys had normally a preoccupied air as she went about her daily tasks; she was probably praying, I had often thought. Now she was more business-like as she had a patient to look after. Bullets seemed a minor matter in the amenities of this household; no one appeared to be disturbed by what was now happening, and an immediate future of storming parties was faced with resolute but utterly unemphasized courage so that I would be left free to make a fighting decision. I thought of this serene firm strength as I went downstairs.

I was going out to fight in the open as the women were endangered by my presence, and it was not fair remaining in the house. I went through the rooms downstairs trying to see where the enemy were. I stripped the hand-grenade in the hall; there was a slight dinge in the cap, that meant something wrong with the nitroglycerine. The grenade was useless. On the waxed floor of a passage I found a revolver; two cartridges had been fired. I reloaded and put it in my trousers' pocket. My armament was slowly increasing, and as I searched for further weapons I met Mrs. Humphreys on the stairs. She was quietly indignant.

'I tried to get to the gate for an ambulance,' she said, 'but they fired on me; most vicious the bullets were, most vicious, and I had to roll over and over to get back to the door.'

'You shouldn't have done that,' I said. 'Now you are taking unnecessary risks, after all your good advice to me.'

Outside the drawing room window I saw three soldiers crouching against the wall. I rechecked the rifle, examined my Smith and Wesson, put the hand-grenade in my pocket as it might again serve to break a charge, and got ready to go out. I slung the rifle over my shoulder and carried my revolver in my right hand. If the Staters would not allow a woman to walk to the gate, there was less chance of any respect being shown to them as the attack progressed, for by this time reinforcements must have arrived. There was no reason why I should remain in the house. I opened the back door and ran quickly round by the trellis-work where the rose trees clung.

'Put them up, you bastards,' I shouted.

The green coats faced me, swinging round in surprise with their rifles as I pressed my revolver trigger. A man's peaked cap spun off; then all three ran around the corner making for the gate. I did not fire at them again. This running away was disconcerting, as they were no longer an enemy or a danger to me once they showed their bent backs.

Suddenly I thought of Miss O'Rahilly's precious lawn. She had trowelled assiduously at daisy roots and it was a grave offence to cross it; couriers and my visitors had been commented on adversely for an unnecessary short cut. By now the soft green had been torn and badly pocked by men stampeding over it. I laughed, thinking of what she would say under other circumstances at the abuse of the sacred lawn. Bullets whizzed around as I stood on the grass looking for a mark to fire at. It was annoying, I could not see anyone, but I used the rifle and fired back at what might be the sources of these wasp sounds.

A heavy rock struck me full force in the back.

I felt a cold twinge in my stomach and my knees bent forward, but I did not fall. I must not let them know I have been hit, I thought, as I tried to straighten myself. I walked towards the next house beyond the garden wall, firing with the rifle held against my thigh.

I was hit again, in the right shoulder with a sledge hammer, and I fell on the grass. The pain was great. That must be bone pain, I said to myself, and it's a right bad smack. I must try to make it appear that I stumbled. I fired from my left shoulder, but my rifle hand was becoming numb, the fingers seemed thick and slow to move on to the trigger. I was hit again in the back. I found myself on my knees; my legs were very shaky when I stood up. My back felt wet. Blood was glueing my right hand to the rifle stock. All my bodily movements were slowed down as if I was listening to messages being sent to muscles which could no longer obey. I clung for support to the rifle strap over my left shoulder as if it would draw up my knees and straighten me, but it weighed me down.

I tried to run for the back door through a burst of fire. Something struck the rifle and my back at the same time. I saw red flashes before my eyes as I fell against the wall. The pain made me moan. Then I was inside trying to smash a window to stick the rifle through, but I couldn't break the glass and I was whimpering at my own futility.

I called: 'Sheila' . . . no reply . . . 'Sheila.'

'Yes, Earnan, I'm coming.' She was trying to cut away my jacket as she said: 'A great big hole in your back and blood all over you.'

Her face became a haze as I lay on the floor. It felt like a harrow. I was lying on spear points and my lips were numb. I was trying hard to tell her that my back hurt, and to destroy my papers, but I could not speak.

Later I heard her say: 'Here come the Staters. They certainly took their time.'

I could see green uniforms around me. One soldier took up the rifle which lay beside me. He ejected an empty cartridge case and pointed the muzzle at my body, and then, very slowly to me, I saw the bolt move forward and heard the snap as he turned down the bolt. It was as though I were looking at carp through a glass tank, the slow swish of tail, the dignified vacuous mouth and the blurred outline. Another soldier pushed the muzzle towards the ceiling and snatched the rifle from him.

'That's O'Malley,' he said, 'and you'd better leave him alone while I'm here.'

He stood, rifle in hand, astride my legs whilst more green coats crowded in.

Mrs. Humphreys came and put her arms under my head. That was good; it took the weight off my back and eased the pain.

A doctor with a large bag came in; he looked rather fussy. 'Has there been a burglary?' he asked, but no one answered him. He worked on my back and shoulders and I felt sleepily at ease. A priest arrived and asked for cotton wool and candles; candles that had previously been blessed on Candlemas for such an occasion were lighted. He gave me Holy Communion and he anointed my five senses: my eyes, my nose, my lips, my ears, my hands; and wiped away the sacred oil with wool. I must have been given whiskey for as I talked I heard Sheila say: 'You're certainly the most lively wounded man I've ever seen.' Then came an argument in which she centred as she had dumped the two revolvers, determined that the small arms would be available for some of our men in the future, but the insistent invaders led her away.

Sheila and Mrs. Humphreys were ordered to put on their coats as they were under arrest, and it was all my fault. Mrs. Humphreys wanted me removed to a hospital and I heard them both argue with the Stater officers about bringing me to Vincent's. 'He must be brought to Vincent's. Goodness knows what would happen to him in a military hospital.' The officers refused. They had instructions to bring me to Portobello barracks, their general headquarters.

I was in the air on a stretcher and Mrs. Humphreys was tucking a large lion-skin rug over my blanket. 'Goodbye now, dear boy,' she said, *'agus beannacht De ort.'* I tried to thank her but I wasn't able.

The Pembroke ambulance was outside. I was lifted into it on the stretcher; the escort climbed into their lorries. Far away I heard a voice say: 'Go very slowly with the ambulance, very slowly.'

After a time the ambulance halted in a barracks and I was taken out.

'Where am I?' I asked a stretcher-bearer.

'Wellington,' he replied.

Why Wellington, I thought; had not the officer said Portobello? I was carried into a room and placed on a table. A man in uniform trousers, but no tunic, looked at my bandages.

'Still bleeding,' he said. 'Are you in great pain?' His eyes were kind as he bent over me. Suddenly I was able to talk.

'I'm all right, thanks,' I said.

He rolled up my sleeve and punctured my arm.

'What's that?' I asked.

'Morphia, it will ease the pain.'

I felt very numb but I was conscious. I was carried out on the stretcher. At the main gate where I was being placed in the ambulance, two soldiers came up. 'That's him,' said one, and they raised their rifles to their shoulders as if they were a firing squad.

'Shoot away,' I said, 'and waste lead,' but the Red Cross men put me on the ground and stood between them and their target.

The eyes of one of the ambulance men looked sympathetic so I asked him to make a dash for it if he could without danger to himself. He nodded and did not reply.

I heard mention of a name, Portobello, and so I was in the enemy headquarters at last.

I was in Portobello and a fog came, everything had hazy outlines except pain. I could not lie on my back or on my right side, and when my dressings were changed my back seemed to be torn open. One day I listened to a conference of surgeons around the bed that seemed to slip in and out of reality, whose voices came in and out of a vague distance. I thought I recognized a face, that of Charlie McAuley, and I tried hard to take part in the discussion, to speak to him. How did he get in here; he was one of the few who were now willing to take risks for our wounded and he was staunch. It must be a dream, for Charlie would hardly be allowed in to see me. I was lifted up in the bed. Then the precise voice of Surgeon Barniville, who bent over me; a voice I remembered from its dry concision at anatomy lectures in Cecilia Street. 'The case is hopeless,' I heard another say. Then a pleasant voice: 'Hopeless', which I was able to identify from its deep resonance and to track down between cross-sections of hearing it hum 'The Wearing of the Green' as the owner operated in Vincent's, and a jaunty tale of a mishap to a jarvey at a race meeting. That was Johnny Mac. Then someone said: 'He'll live,' but who it was I could not make out.

A hospital orderly sat near my bed one night. 'I've an evening paper that I kept for you. Would you like me to read it?' It was a 'stop press' that had announced my death some days ago. 'It's not often you can read out an account of a man's death to him,' he said, laughing.

One morning there was evidently an attack on Portobello, as excited soldiers armed with rifles rushed into our ward, but they withdrew when occupants objected to their presence.

One night I felt an orderly working at my wrist. He was trying to take off my gold wristlet watch. He had a mean face. 'I want to keep it safe for you,' he said, when I opened my eyes suddenly on him, but I motioned him to leave the watch alone; already my leather boots and my wallet had disappeared in the same kind way.

A figure in uniform stood at the end of my bed and looked at me for a long time. His face was in a dim haze. I could not recognize the features. Later, one of the orderlies said in respectful awe: 'The Chief of Staff, General MacMahon, came in this evening to see you, and he said: "I hope he won't die." '

The day never ended and the night was worse. Why, when there was no sense of time with me, one part of twenty-four hours should be more of a strain than another, I could not then work out. Snatches of poetry sang in my mind as I tried to rebuild entire verses; at times I was successful, more often I filled in gaps with lines of my own. It was an achievement when at last I was able to reconstruct

> Who will go drive with Fergus now
> And pierce the deep wood's woven shade

but my great triumph came when I could remember Villon's

> Dame du ciel, regente terrienne
> Emperiere des infernaux palus

My thoughts drifted slowly during the long days. At first I thought darkness would never come, but the days passed. I tried to make poems of things I had loved: mountains, rivers, trees, books and people. I found myself mingling my lines with those in a poem by Rupert Brooke, 'the rough male kiss of blankets', and one of Padraig Pearse.

I tried to trace the development of Italian painting. Into drifting thought moved images like the slow shuffling of a card pack with an emphasis on some, as when the unskilled dealer fumbled: Giotto, Masaccio, Andrea del Castagno, Mantegna, Piero della Francesca, for I had known them for a

longer time. Masaccio and della Francesca were my fav-
ourites. They had a classic formalism, a ceremonial grace
which enhanced their figures, to stress, whatever their
subject, the human dignity and mystery of man. I could
almost reconstruct the colouring of some and the form of a
few, but line I could remember best, the scientific and
experimental line of the Florentines, but Holbein would
intrude, with Cézanne and the glowing flame of Van Gogh,
or the vigorous direct touch of Albrecht Dürer. The imaginative, visionary line of William Blake flowed in and out in
sinuous grace. Had I not carried a volume of Blake, Dürer
and della Francesca around with me during the hard years; I
had studied them in many a strange background of mountain
or bog, and my mixed portfolio of reproductions, cut to fit my
pockets, had become frayed and crinkled, worn glossy
surfaces stuck with rain and sweat. I had met few people in
my wanderings who were interested in painting, and I expect
through dearth of discussion I was a jumble of unrelated facts
based on emotional values.

Free State wounded were in the ward, in the beds near to
mine; some of them moaned and cried. One boy kept crying
throughout the nights: 'Oh mother, mother.' Night seemed to
be the worst time for the wounded, but I had to bite hard on
my wounds for I was in enemy hands and that meant no
giving in to pain and no sense of complaint.

Stretches of country came into my mind. A cone-shaped
mountain with a white burnished top, glistening; irregular
boulders on its slopes, heather below, and steel-grey lakes and
a brown haze of bog; in the distance a mountain with steep
sides and a long ridge. Where could that be: Croagh Patrick
over Clew Bay, or Douce under snow? Slowly I solved the
problem: it was Errigal in winter in Co. Donegal, with
Muckish in the background. Rich country, with a narrow
wooded glen, mountains in the distance, some of them faint
under a deep green sky. The mountains showed up more
clearly, they changed from cobalt-blue to mauve, they bulked
closer to the eye. It was raining; earth-breaths of clouds
puffed about their tops and hovered, and one of the hills had
a piece missing. That was the Devil's Bit in Co. Tipperary,
seen from Templemore. The Old Boy had once grabbed a

piece of those hills but had dropped it some twenty miles away in the plain where it became the Rock of Cashel, Cashel of the Kings. Cliffs shattered with coloured light on varied rock: Slieve League, Bloody Foreland, or Arranmore at sunset. More difficult country would come, with features not prominent, harder to make out and to track down. I would run down in my mind lengths of wall, a copse, or small wood, glimpses of sea and river, and the subtle colour of budding trees; then full summer-leaf strength, or lonely bogland with its fugitive bird life. The days were no longer dark and lengthy when I could visit Ireland, area by area, remembering places that I thought I had forgotten. When I had recognized a place it faded away slowly as if pleased that I had been able to remember it, nor did it come again. I followed long streaks of grey or reddish mud-roads, puzzled over turns and the country on either side, flat country with long white roads seemingly never ending, hilly country with twisting brown roads winding up and down. I was physically tired when I followed the roads, tracing them out of my knowledge of the country. It was as if I had actually walked them, and I would fall asleep, tired out.

Some of the wounded were sympathetic and offered to help me in any way they could; many of them were soldiers of the World War, a few were young boys. In the next bed was an ex-Connaught Ranger. He talked of his officers, some of whom I knew by name because the Connaughts were once largely recruited from their own province in the west of Ireland where I was born. To talk to a country-bred Irishman about his townland was like being moved by a woman's beauty and telling her of it. We talked of lakes and mountains and soldiering in India. He had belonged to the battalion that mutinied in India and he told me the story.

I had kept a copy of Shakespeare's Sonnets in my trousers' pocket and as we got to be friends I asked him to read them to me. He was shy and nervous as he read, and at times really embarrassed, but he saw the reading meant a good deal to me, so he screwed himself up resolutely. He read in such a soft voice, so low at times that I had to strain my body towards him.

'Can't you raise your voice a little?' I asked once, 'for it's hard on the wounds.'

He looked shyly at me. 'You know,' he said, 'the other lads think I'm reading a prayer book to you and they call me a sky-pilot.' And Shakespeare continued to be murmured in the condoned guise of religion.

Erskine Childers had been captured, with David Robinson, on their way to Dublin, in his cousin Bob Barton's house at Annamoe, where he had spent many young years. He was a prisoner in the Portobello barracks, and I listened to men who came into the ward talk of him as that damned reactionary spy of an Englishman. They hated him, many of these ex-soldiers from British regiments, yet they knew nothing about him, except what their officers told them, and what propaganda directed by Piaras Beaslai they had read in the papers, and through the bitterness of his opponents in their parliament. He was 'for it', they said, meaning that he would be executed. I told them about Childers, his gradual change which went in hand with the integrity of his mind; of the gun-running at Howth in 1914, how his yacht had carried the 'Howth rifles', as the long Mausers were afterwards called, to Ireland; and his work on publicity during the Tan war to interest outsiders in our cause. Then, members of their present Provisional Government were very anxious and willing to have his advice and judgement, and to use his psychological knowledge of the British bureaucratic caste. They refused to listen to me. He was a damned English spy and he had always been a spy. Arthur Griffith's bitter words had carried weight, coming from a man who seldom stooped to abuse. Winston Churchill, in a speech the day after the capture of Childers had: 'seen with satisfaction that the mischief-making murderous renegade, Erskine Childers, has been captured. No man has done more harm or shown more genuine malice, or endeavoured to bring a greater curse upon the common people of Ireland than this strange being, . . .' Churchill could have gone closer home if he were really looking for a rogues' gallery of those who had been a curse to what was now his benevolent concern, 'the common people of Ireland'.

The way had been prepared; he, a staff captain attached to

Publicity, had been blamed for destruction of railways and roads and held responsible for our successful operations. Formerly our separatist people as a whole would have suspected the meaning of any English pronouncement, and would have at once looked for the hidden motives, but now, in division, I heard men in the ward quoting Churchill.

In Munster, Childers had not taken any part in activities but had moved about, often amongst men who were rather hostile, as he could not get official reports from our units for the paper which he was responsible for printing. Dilatory correspondence was a national weakness; for an efficient staff officer like Childers to deal with its devious by-ways of delay and the consequent queries to despatch carriers meant a temperament philosophically attuned to resigned sainthood, or energetic nerve-fretting irascibility, and he had to eschew the latter. He had suffered much in his isolation, that I knew from his letters before I had been hit, and I could read between the lines, as he would not complain; he had felt the publicity of his opponents which had filtered through and influenced some of our people. Secret Free State reports had tried to place him as an insistently active force, as against de Valera who was anxious to end warfare. His English accent was against him; his whole mental build was not understood by men who were now directing their energies into a formless kind of guerilla warfare; his Anglo-Irish heritage raised a subconscious barrier which could bristle with history, being cross-memoried by Cromwellian troopers, merciless aggression, confiscation, and the determined killing of Irish brains. It was hard that a man like him should, when intentions were sincere, meet this deep-buried race feeling at the turn of a phrase or the intonation of a voice. A medical orderly told me that Childers was trying to get a note to me from his prison in the barracks, and in return, with the help of the Connaught, I had written a letter to him but could not get it through for he was watched too carefully. He found it hard to sit down, I was told, because he had been severely kicked. I had met him on several occasions before and during the truce and had learned in a small way to appreciate his worth. Kindly, courteous, chivalrous, aesthetic-looking, his body consumed by the fire of his spirit, he had at all times been willing and ready to help in any and every capacity. He knew the mentality of the British ruling class better than anybody amongst Republicans, and so British publicity had endeavoured in every possible way to portray him as a sinister figure.

On the morning of Childers's trial, 17 November, four of our prisoners were executed, and Kevin O'Higgins, Minister for Home Affairs, spoke that day in the Provisional Parliament and indicated why they had been shot: 'This particular punishment was not vindictive. If these were merely average cases it might perhaps have been because it were better at the first to take cases which had no particular facts about them to distinguish them from the cases of thousands all over the country who were bleeding the nation to death. If they took as their first case some man who was outstandingly active and outstandingly wicked in his activities, the unfortunate dupes throughout the country might say that he was killed because he was a leader, because he was an Englishman, or because he combined with others to commit raids.' That to my mind was the ignoble crime, to shoot four young boys because they were unknown and were not yet in folklore, to prepare the way for getting rid of a man whose brains would have been of use to this nation. He must have known about the young lads who had been executed as an excuse, and their deaths must have saddened his last days. One week later he was brought to Beggar's Bush barracks, where he was shot.

The Connaught Ranger brought in a Webley and put it under his mattress. 'That's for you when you're able to use it.' He had been in charge of a sentry post, which might be a means of getting me through to the outside, he thought. 'I've been talking quietly, feeling my way with a few of the men, and I think I'll be able to square the guard.'

'But you can't remain here any longer in hospital,' I said in wonder.

'Oh can't I? I haven't been an old soldier for nothing, and there's nothing I don't know about swinging the lead, for that's the most important part of a man's training.'

He carried out my messages; people outside were doubtful about him, as he drank, but he brought back replies.

The chaplain, a young priest, visited me by request. Previously, after I had first come, he had administered Holy Communion, but had not since been to see me. I asked him to give me Communion in the morning. He said: 'Have you read the bishops' pastoral?'

'Yes, I have.'

'Do you agree with it?'

'Certainly not. I take my orders from my Chief of Staff, and he's not a bishop. You wouldn't like to take your orders from him, I know.'

He turned quickly towards the door. 'Then I cannot hear your confession.' I told him I did not need confession. 'I want to receive only.'

'So long as you intend to wage war against the existing lawful government, I cannot give you the Sacraments.'

'But you attended to me when I first came here; you have already administered Holy Communion, and you did not question me about the pastoral, for I would have answered you as I now answer you.'

'Yes, you were in danger of death.'

'But I'm always in danger of death. Can you guarantee that I will be alive this time tomorrow?'

'No, but you are not dying now.' His lips pursed. He did not care for the conversation in an open ward with an attentive audience of sick and wounded. I did not then know that a Catholic has the right to select the confessor that suits him and that by Canon Law this must be complied with. Not one of our men whom I later met knew this law, nor were they ever informed of it.

'How can a badly wounded man wage war, and anyhow you know I will be shot as soon as they think I've recovered sufficiently.'

'I must carry out the orders of my bishop,' he said tightly.

'All right, then, you refuse. If you have an *Imitation,* you might lend it to me.' He did not come back, but he sent me in *The Imitation of Christ* which had been last in the hands of Erskine Childers.

A soldier laughed as he turned towards my bed. 'You'll hear no more of Rory O'Connor from this on.'

What did that mean? Perhaps there had been another

attempt to escape from the Joy and he had been killed. An orderly read the evening paper to me. Rory O'Connor, Liam Mellows, Joe McKelvey and Dick Barrett had been executed that morning, 8 December, without trial as an official reprisal for the death and wounding the previous day of two Free State members of parliament. Sean Hales of Cork, whose brother was fighting with Liam Lynch, had been shot dead by our men in Dublin; Padraig O'Maille had been seriously wounded.

The news was a great shock to me. I felt as if I had again been wounded, the same swift disappearance of my innards, an icy chill where they had been, and a trembling in my legs. The four had been imprisoned since the fall of the Four Courts on 30 June, and we had grown accustomed to think that prisoners in jails were safe unless they had been captured in arms after the Free State's secret military courts began to function from 15 October. A sudden murder, or death in action, we were accustomed to. When I was outside I thought there was no surety of life, that death for some of us was as inevitable as daybreak, but inside were some good men who were safe; they could carry on when all this fighting was over. The absence of a trial did not mean anything, just a legal formula. McKelvey and Barrett I knew only since the occupation of the Courts, and then I met them in an official way in the manner of GHQ officers. I could not see why McKelvey had been appointed to the Staff save that he was a northerner and he represented the Ulster point of view. Rory was the sole member of the old Headquarters Staff that I could talk to of things outside of staff work, but that kind of talk, though friendly, did nothing to explore a deeper self. He was droll and laconic, with a strong reserve. He had been made a target by the Staters at which to hurl abuse. It had served their purpose better to refer to us as 'Rory O'Connor's men', than to admit that we were organized on the same lines as themselves, that we had a Headquarters Staff, and he as Director of Engineering filled the same post as he had done on the old Staff during the Tan scrap. Neither Liam nor Rory had any sense of side; they never tried to swing their weight that I could see.

Liam's death affected me most. He was our greatest loss.

One thought of him as a clear flame, steadfast, burning of its own strength. Cheerful, chivalrous, clear in intellect, possessing political intuition, no bitterness in his outlook and no warping of his fine qualities by hatred of opponents. In him, as in some of the young men who had come through the fire, old Irish habits of thought, speech and mind were recognizable: a crystal hardness without harshness, an intense love of nature and of the earth, a simplicity that made the flippant earnest; direct, serious, restrained, unemotional in speech, gay in company, with personal aloofness. Well the Free State knew his mind, his influence and his strength. Founded deep in the Gaelic tradition, loving its song and story, its high endeavours, realizing its importance, capable of interpreting its every nuance of thought and feeling, one of the soldiers of the spirit was gone. One instinctively placed him with Pearse and Sean MacDermott; and he was against the surrender of the Courts.

I was moved into a small room where I was by myself. The large ward had been noisy but I had found a few friends there. My Connaught had tried every trick in his bag but he could not malinger any longer and had to leave at last.

'I'll come in to see you whenever I get a chance, and I'll keep my eyes open to get you out. A Connacht man has leave to speak twice and to poke the fire, and he has the right to stand by his friends.'

I had been thinking hard about escape but that was more my feeling about captivity than anything else. I could hardly sit up in bed, and I certainly could not put weight on a foot, yet constantly escape was on my mind, even if I died on the pavement outside their barracks. There was no desire to escape a firing squad as such. Yet I did not like to be shot to the orders of men who I had once fought with as friends.

A friendly Red Cross orderly from another part of the barracks slipped in a few times to see me. He was elderly, there were silver-grey streaks in his hair, and he talked as if escape for me was the most natural subject in the world, which, in truth, it was.

'We'll try to take you out of here some night on a stretcher, through the window. I have two men. If only I could get another.'

I told him about my Connaught Ranger.

'I wonder can we trust him,' he said. 'It's a great risk for a man the likes of him.'

'He has no loyalty to this crowd, he doesn't like them, but it's a job for him and he was out of work. Anyhow he has a strange loyalty to this country and once he was willing to face death for it.' I told him the epic of the Connaughts in India. He sat on the edge of my bed and ran his fingers through his hair. He was worried, for there were few he could trust; he could not see a solution to some of the minor difficulties and he felt responsible for the whole operation. He could trust the driver of an ambulance, and said that he could work a pass to allow it through the barracks' gate; when the job was finished it could return.

One night late, he came in, cursing softly. 'Blast their souls, blast them, but I'm being moved tomorrow. Maybe they've spotted me, for you know they watch you close. I'm for Athlone, I think, and I must get hold of that Connaught sergeant and have you shifted tonight.'

'Take it easy,' I warned, 'and don't be rushed into any false moves, for I'm responsible for the lives of the men on this job, and nobody is going to be shot for me if I can help it.'

'We don't mind,' he said simply, 'and if there's a scrap we can all die together. A man you know can't do much less.'

Escape on a stretcher could be normally looked upon as sheer idiocy. A chief of the O'Donnells had once been carried into battle on the necks of his men against his inveterate enemies, the O'Neills, and here was I preparing myself for a similar excursion. The O'Donnell had died before the fight was finished, so maybe that was an omen.

Early before dawn he came back into my room. He walked up and down for a while, unable to speak, twisting one hand hard in the other.

'What's wrong now?' I asked. 'And don't worry; you've done more than your share for me.'

'I can't find the Connaught anywhere, and I've searched the barracks twice for him. Now I'll have to move off myself in a few hours' time.'

I was fed on milk from a feeding cup, but the sameness of

taste was making it difficult for me to take anything except
when I was very hungry. Utensils were dirty and uncared for,
cups unwashed; there was a general feeling of improvisation,
anything would serve, and the less washing there was the
better in this service. I had to watch the orderlies when they
dressed my wounds, make them take ordinary antiseptic
precautions, and inspect bandages and dressings and anti-
septics, as I had found them willing to use a wrong bottle, an
infected pad or unsterilized instrument to save trouble. Most
of them had served in the British Army but with one
exception they were slovenly and untidy, due to improper
supervision and little discipline, and though there was a
doctor there from the west of Ireland who chatted and smiled,
yet he never endeavoured to improve conditions.

An orderly was rubbing my wound granulations with
copper sulphate as he said: 'I'm afraid it's healing too
quickly, and I wish it was not, for they intend to shoot you as
soon as we have patched you up.'

I sent for books but they were not forwarded. I had money
smuggled in and bought some books through an orderly: *The
Wallet of Kai-Lung* which I re-read several times, with some
volumes of Yeats. I was able to read slowly now, but the chief
trouble was in trying to angle my head to see the page.
Gradually I solved the difficulty of posture, but the physical
strain wore my body down. Yet I could browse over a book,
fall asleep and wake up at leisure for another read.

At dusk on Christmas Eve I was moved on to a stretcher.

'What's up now?' I asked an officer.

He looked at me but did not answer.

'Maybe you're Santa Claus and you're going to put me in
a sleigh with reindeer in front. Anyhow I want my fur rug,'
for my lion-skin backed with fur had not been added to the
blankets.

One of the orderlies was crying as he helped to carry me
out. 'You're for it,' he said. 'They're taking you to the Joy to
shoot you. Oh, why are they doing this to you?'

The guard outside the hospital saluted, as if I was to
receive a last courtesy before the final farewell. So this was the
end, I was thinking, as the stretcher bumped with the
irregular march of the hospital attendants. I was to be shot

sometime during the morning, maybe with polite regards, for the barrack or jail elimination makes for a kind of rigid, but nostalgic, courtesy.

Outside the ambulance an officer bent over me as he pulled back the blankets.

'I am sorry to do this, but I have to do it.'

He put handcuffs on my wrists and snapped the lock-clasp into position.

'You are doing your duty, I expect, so why should you apologise? The last men to handcuff me were Auxiliaries, and they did not apologise.'

The frozen air made breathing difficult, but above me were the timeless stars, and the sharp clearness of an unhurried night sky.

CHAPTER TWELVE

DECEMBER 1922—APRIL 1923

THE opening and shutting of gates; questions asked, a scrutiny by officers who looked in at me as I lay on the stretcher. I was in Mountjoy jail. The prison doctor had me brought over to the hospital.

It was dark; a glimpse of great gaunt buildings in faded grey, barbed wire in twisted masses, many sentries. Inside the hospital gloomy corridors ran into cold blackness, with stone stairs and a clang of metal under the boots of the stretcher-bearers; iron rails, dull white walls above, dull from lack of light. I had somehow the same feeling as when I was brought to Kilmainham jail in 1921: walls stretching to infinity, of height that seemed to reach the sky, of footsteps of a brazen clay, and cold stone without colour. Monotony without relief, a crushing weight in the mass of the structure and a sense of being trapped. It was as if the guards had smiled with teethed joy and had said: 'Now we have you, me boyho.'

I was carried into a cell, but removed to another where was a prisoner who could look after me, and the hospital orderlies placed me in bed. The cell was larger than the usual prison cell. A boy with long hair and a thin white face lay on another bed which almost touched mine.

'You're welcome,' he said. 'My name is Brennan. What's the idea of sending you here on a stretcher? Even the hospital is crowded.'

I shook my head.

'It looks like a firing squad. How are the wounds?'

'Pretty bad,' I said.

'You'd have been with Rory and Liam if you hadn't escaped from the Courts. Well, they'll hardly do anything to you till the new year.' He dressed slowly. 'I'll get you a cup of tea.'

From shelves made from boxes he took down fruit and

bread. His suitcase covered with old newspapers was the table. 'That will be low enough for you,' he said.

In Mountjoy a firing squad seemed to be accepted as part of my lot. The offer of a cup of tea made me feel at home immediately.

'My stomach is bad,' he said; 'prison food. Parcels are often stopped.'

That explained his colour and the drawn look of his face.

'Bob Barton is next door. I'll get him for you.' He knocked hard on the wall behind me. Robert Barton walked in, smiling. 'The Staters' Christmas gift,' he said. Bob was recovering from pleurisy. He looked thin and sick. 'David and I are making arrangements for tomorrow's dinner. Can you eat?' And he rolled off a long list of delicacies. 'Have you enough blankets?'

'No, I feel cold.'

'We'll see to that at once,' he said.

I was cold despite the rough sheets, three brown army blankets and my heavy lion-skin rug. In a few minutes two boys carried in a heap of blankets; I was given three more. They were heavy on my legs.

'We'll make a cage out of a bit of a box. That'll take the weight off you.'

Bob sat and talked in his quiet, gentle voice, a mellow Oxford accent. David Robinson, tall, thin, and still worn from his European war wounds, came briskly in. He had managed to get a transfer from one of the wings on some slight pretext so that he could be near to Bob in hospital. He was planning Christmas dinners with great care and thoroughness. I could not talk much, a few sentences, then my head swirled. Bob Barton, always considerate, said: 'You're tired.' Then both of them went away.

David later told us of the Cork and Kerry fighting. He had been adjutant to a cavalry company raised in the south, but it did not last long. He had been a major in the Tank Corps; had been severely wounded in France, and had the viewpoint of the regular army officer. Our type of fighting did not recommend itself to him. The inevitable 'drop of tay', and the often repeated cry of 'They're coming! They're coming!' in rousing a bunch of armed men, were seen again through his tales. The climax for him was an attack in which the men had to advance in stockinged feet in the wet morning. He also told vividly of trench warfare, attacks by tanks, and the flaming sunset of a heavy barrage at dawn.

The hospital consisted of a large ward and outside in the corridor a row of cells. The ward was crowded. I was carried in to see Joe MacDonagh, TD, in a bed inside the door: a brother of Thomas who had been executed after the 1916 Rising. He had a severe attack of appendicitis and was in great agony. He would be removed to the Mater Misericordia hospital opposite the jail for operation if he signed the form, but he refused to sign. His face was twisted in agony when we met, but he managed to smile between spasms and to crack his little joke. There was a new arrival in the ward, a Galway man with a rather bald head. Joe was also bald. 'Who's the man who wears his hair like mine?' he asked. In jail, books were seldom returned when once borrowed, and his books he re-read. When asked for a good book by some of the boys he always offered *The Brothers Karamazoff* or *The Idiot*. 'That's a good book, you'll like it,' knowing that it would be a task. The borrower would not get through more than twenty or thirty pages and keep it for a time, as Joe would inquire how it was being enjoyed. The reader would not admit that he could not make any sense of the book. Later the book would be returned and the borrower, dreading another ordeal, would never ask him for another. A day or two later Joe was taken to the Mater where he died.

Bob Barton taught me chess and we played a game each day, then I was tired out from the effort. Bob worked over chess problems hour after hour, or played with David in my cell. Soon I was able to get the stimulating heightened sense that a piece of good play gave. Bob read to me and talked of literature and art. We discovered that we had interests in common. The bare dirty walls took on another texture. A friendship was able to change their grimness. He had been a landowner and a member of the Kildare Street Club. During the 1916 Rising, as officer in charge of prisoners, he had been influenced. He resigned from the army; later was a friend of Collins and Minister of Agriculture under the Republican Dail. He had been imprisoned by the British but escaped from Mountjoy; then was recaptured and sentenced to penal servitude in the English prisons. He told me of the proposed revolt of the Irish in Portsmouth prison and the plans to seize the arms there and to fight. It had not come off.

We were allowed to write a letter a week, but might receive as many as were forwarded to us. Letters were heavily censored, passages scored out with a puce pencil or cut with scissors. My rank was carefully removed from parcels and letters. Frequently reprisals on the part of the prison staff deprived us of letters, parcels, books, laundry and cigarettes. That was due to an increase in activity of our men outside, or to some peculiar kink in the mentality of the Free State Cabinet. It seemed especially mean to deprive prisoners of privileges on account of action taken by our men outside the jail walls. We had underground communication with the four wings of the prison; with the women prisoners in Mountjoy; with different internment camps, and with our own General Headquarters. In the women's prison, in the female hospital wing close by, Mary Comerford and Sheila Humphreys had been on hunger-strike; concessions had been granted them. They had made several attempts to escape. Copies of *An Phoblacht,* and general orders and instructions from our GHQ, were smuggled in regularly. I read orders to the men in the hospital. The daily paper was forbidden but we always managed to obtain a copy and endeavoured to read between the lines. New arrivals supplemented what information we already possessed so that we were enabled to keep in touch with events. Extracts from the *Morning Post,* the English Tory paper, forbidden entry to the Free State for its jocular remarks, were sent in to me. We read and enjoyed the reports and descriptions of ourselves and of the Free Staters, and I am sure the editor would have been amused to see how much we looked forward to his notes on Ireland. They were more welcome than the comic supplement, the funnies of American Sunday papers.

Sentries fired at birds and pigeons perched on roofs, eaves and walls, and this intermittent shooting went on jerkily during the days. My nerves were bad now. I jumped when a soldier in the hospital grounds fired a shot. Guards fired at prisoners who waved to relatives and friends on the canal banks which were overlooked by end windows of a wing. The men were satisfied if they could see a vague outline of a wife, son, sweetheart or friend. Such an appointment had been prepared weeks ahead; a note would be sent out surreptitiously in laundry and replied to within pie crust, soap or tobacco. Some of the boys provoked the sentries by a jack-in-the-box appearance at a cell window. They ducked when the sentry swung his rifle to shoulder, and came up again with a taunt after the bullet had hit off the wall or had smashed the glass. At night imaginary attacks were beaten off with rifle and machine-gun fire from sentry posts.

The Catholic chaplain, Father MacMahon, visited me by request of Bob Barton. Bob was not a Catholic and was, I presume, considered a possible convert. The chaplain came neatly dressed, silk hat in hand, and partly hesitant when he stood inside my door. A bird-like appearance; something perky in his look, bright in the eyes, and the jerk of his double-quickstep movement.

He was not anxious to remain with me. I asked him to recommend me a course of spiritual reading. He would not sit down. He nodded his head and withdrew after a few words. He did not return. Mr. Greer, the Protestant minister, we liked. He was a Christian, not a Catholic, we agreed. He came to see us; chatted of things in general, and then, unasked, sometimes visited our people and told them how we were. Visits were forbidden, even before execution; anxiety was increased when our letters were stopped as a reprisal. People outside read between the lines of our official letters, or gleaned some information from scanty notes forwarded through by-channels.

Phil Cosgrave, brother of the Free State's President, was Governor of the Joy, nominally so, for his deputy, Paudeen O'Keeffe, controlled the prison.

Cosgrave came to my cell one day, opened the door and stood hesitatingly in the entrance. He was heavily built, stout and flabby. There were deep-wrinkled pouches under his eyes. He drank hard, I had been told, and had become morose, so prisoners said, since the execution of Rory O'Connor and the three others. His green uniform puckered on his waist; he would find it hard to be a soldier. I had never met him before.

'Are you all right, Ernie?' he asked.

'Yes,' I replied.

He walked over on heavy feet to my bed and looked down at me.

'Would you like anything?'

'That's for you to decide. I will not ask for anything.'

He held out a fat-fingered hand, slowly, as if he were afraid of a rebuff. 'Will you shake hands with me?' We shook hands. 'Thank you, Ernie,' he said.

Slowly he turned and walked away. That evening, parcels of books and laundry which had been lying in the office for some time were delivered to me. Next day a box of apples came, carefully packed. I knew that they had come from a good Tory orchard. The apples had each been cut in four and then been left to rot.

Again he came and asked if he could be of any assistance to me. 'I'll do anything I can,' he said. I told him that I wanted to send out some personal letters and would expect a reply enclosed in a letter addressed to him. He said he would deliver the letters when they arrived. Three times he carried my mail, handed it to me, and then left quickly as if he was afraid he would be found out.

O'Keeffe, the Deputy Governor, or Paudeen, as he was called, was well known to all prisoners. 'Paudeen!' would be yelled by a young boy, and his reply would come in an unsteady stream. He had a vocabulary of obscene words which he used on every possible occasion, but he was not brutal. He threatened, but never to my knowledge did he beat up prisoners himself; however, he allowed others to do so. Fresh prisoners were consigned to the basement cells, dirty, oozy, ill-ventilated, where they were ill-treated by officers and lashed about by men of the garrison or by the CID. As secretary of Sinn Fein, working zealously in holes and corners of Dublin, O'Keeffe had distinguished himself during the Tan war by an interview. An English journalist visited Sinn Fein headquarters at 6 Harcourt Street to interrogate him. After some conversation he asked: 'What is the policy of Sinn Fein, Mr. O'Keeffe?' O'Keeffe leapt to his feet and pounded his desk as he roared: 'Revenge, be jaysus, Revenge!' Nobody could take O'Keeffe seriously as a soldier. He had enough shrewd common sense to mingle it with dry humour which made him almost tolerant. Paudeen's sayings were repeated and had become wing folklore. His strong Cork accent was mimicked before his face and in the telling of stories. 'Nothin' escapes here but ghas, be jaysus,' he frequently observed, which was true enough as our gas-joints were made of soap. Once in 'A' wing he was particularly incensed about an article which appeared in an outside paper, evidently based on information supplied by a prisoner. He waved his gun in the air. Someone called him a coward. He pulled off his great coat, handed his gun to Andy MacDonnell who was OC of the wing, and offered to fight the owner of the voice. Often, revolver in hand, he ordered men to their cells. When they told him to go to hell, with his eyes shut and head turned to one side, he fired shots at the roof.

In the evening, at count, each wing paraded on the ground floor. O'Keeffe, accompanied by our OC of the wing, checked the number of men. Often his count was inaccurate. A heavy smell of liquor and a slight roll would betray the cause; then would come a noisy slanging match with adjectives increasing in strength between the OC Wing and himself. Prisoners one night were making poteen in a cell; it smelled strongly. O'Keeffe suddenly walked into the cell, smelling more strongly. He jibed at the men, then stood over the large pan which looked like a night bucket. He sniffed. 'Oh the hard po,' he said and walked out.

If Free State stamps were affixed upside down by prisoners, he would have the letters sent back from the office; he was not going to have the Free State insulted. He came to my cell to hand me letters. Once he asked me why I did not write.

'You should write,' he said, but I told him I wrote when it pleased me to do so and not when it pleased the deputy governor.

I knew then that he was trying to think of the source by which my letters went out, as I did not write my weekly letter through the prison office. He often opened the iron slot through which at one time food was pushed in to prisoners, or stood to look in at me through the peephole, but I had the slot tied with a string and the glass of the spyhole soaped so that it would be harder for him to surprise me writing, or reading the paper.

CID came to my cell, stood inside the door and looked at me fixedly, sometimes for long periods. They did not speak. I returned their look with the same vehement intensity, or turned to the wall to sleep and pulled the fur rug over my face.

There was a young sister de Bon Secour who came to look after the sick. She harried the unwilling hospital orderlies and tried to improve the food. Sister Angela, our lady of the angels, we called her. She was gentle and sweet; she moved around with her finger-tips joined as if she walked in another world. She brought another world to us. We could forget the drabness of jail when we heard her speak or watched her face. She was well trained and capable, and her presence would be shown by an extra regard the men had for their appearances instead of their general carelessness. We were cases, evidently, when she first came, but shortly afterwards she would whisk a newspaper from under the folds of her habit and leave it on my bed. She would forage for it in the officers' mess of the garrison. She brought me candles from the Mother Superior, for the light was bad in my cell, but candles were strictly forbidden. They would be of use in the digging of tunnels. The gift of the Reverend Mother assisted some of the tunnellers in the wings.

Jimmy Mooney, a young Dublin volunteer, seventeen years old, was moved into my cell when Brennan went back to his wing, and Jimmy looked after my dressings and food when the sister went home at dusk.

The prison doctor visited me one morning.

'There have been inquiries every day from Portobello barracks about your condition,' he said. 'They seem very interested in you.'

I knew what that meant.

He looked worried and said: 'Your lips are blue. You spit up blood, you sweat,' and he continued with a list of symptoms.

I was white from the loss of blood, and I took strychnine, but I had not all the symptoms he described and I said so. 'I'm weak, but I'll be ready for them whenever they want me.'

'Well, they may send somebody else to inspect you. I wanted to tell you how often they ring up to ask about you.

And they may send another doctor who will ask you questions.'

A few days later an officer whom I had been at school with, Captain Casey, came into the cell. He had served in France.

'Hello,' I said, 'what do you want here?'

He took a bundle of papers from his tunic pocket and handed them to me. 'I'm on the staff of the Judge Advocate-General. These are the papers for your trial.'

The Judge Advocate-General was a son of Michael Davitt, I remembered. I sat up and tried to read the charge sheet, but my hands trembled. Here came the end at last when I was not expecting it. I was accused of waging war, of killing a Free State soldier, and of some other, technical offences. The evidence accused me of fighting from behind Sheila Humphreys.

'You will be tried in three days' time. I am to act as prosecuting counsel.'

The trial meant death, which I had faced often enough in my mind in the abstract, but here it was now as close as it would be the morning after my trial, four days away.

I looked at Casey. I could remember him now in the fifth school at the Christian Brothers. Now there were deep lines on his forehead. He was looking at the rusty window-bars. He must have noticed me as I read. Then I thought what if he does? Why should I feel ashamed of being afraid of death? Most of us fear it even when we think of it. The tremor of mind passed slowly as I read the typed sheets.

'Do you want a solicitor to act for you?'

'No, I don't recognize the jurisdiction of your court martial and the trial is a farce. You people are in a hell of a hurry to shoot me. You have already given me the sentence.'

'The officers will judge the case on its merits,' he said stiffly.

'Well, it seems strange to subject a sick man to trial.' I knew that I could not physically stand the trial, that I would probably faint from weakness, and that the court martial might be sufficiently mean to imply cowardice.

'Can I not be tried *in absentia?* My sentence has already been decided.'

'No, you will get a fair trial.'

'I'll write a statement to show how brave your troops were. I think the witnesses should withdraw the charge of cowardice on my part. You'll have to try me in bed, anyhow.'

I changed the conversation and asked him about his service in France. He talked of the war. 'Where's your brother, Frank, now?' he asked.

'He died in East Africa. He was in the King's African Rifles.'

'I'm sorry,' he said, as if he felt he should not have spoken.

'Sit down,' I said. 'Let's forget all this and talk about school.'

He sat down on a chair at the end of the bed and we chatted of teachers, of boys we had once known, some dead, others scattered over the world. He apologised for smoking in the cell for he recollected cigarettes had been forbidden prisoners. After a time he stood up suddenly.

'I have to go now. I'll see you again.'

I had expected that I would be tried, yet the realization came as a shock. I pulled a small mirror off a nail in the wall and looked at my face. Yes, it did look pale, but perhaps it was not much whiter than usual for that was due to loss of blood.

Bob Barton came in when I tapped on the cell wall.

'You should write at once to Liam Lynch and tell him.'

'I don't see the use,' I said.

I wrote a note to the Chief of Staff saying goodbye to him and to my comrades as I expected to be shot the day after the court martial. At the end I wrote: 'Another bit of lead won't do me any harm.' A note generally took some time to go from the hospital, but as I had finished writing, a cheery face above a Free State uniform looked around the door. It was my messenger. I told him to have the message delivered to Liam Lynch in Dublin that evening. That night Lynch sent a letter to the editor of the *Irish Independent* and enclosed my own letter. Both of them, to our surprise, were published in the paper the following morning.

My family knew little or nothing of where I had been for the past five years, and at home I had been looked upon as a black sheep. I began to write of what had happened to me since 1918. I wished that some record should be kept, especially for my brothers, but not for publication. I had broken the traditions of the family and I wanted that the elder members should at least know the extent of my folly. It was fatiguing to use a pen for long, but after the first day I began to feel an interest in the writing. I wrote with zest. It was exciting, it seemed to give me extra strength, and I hoped that I would have time to finish the story. Men and incidents which I had forgotten came back, often over-crowding my memory.

I sent out for a photograph of the commission forwarded me by Cathal Brugha as Minister for Defence, confirming me as Officer Commanding the Second Southern Division, to hand it in at my trial, but I was unable to obtain it. I sent a note to Sheila Humphreys, in the female hospital, for an account of the fight that morning when I had been wounded; I was anxious to refute the allegations of cowardice. Her reply came back from the women's prison. After I was taken away from Ailesbury Road, one of the soldiers had been found under the bed in Dick's room; another had wedged himself behind the front door.

The Chief of Staff said he would send in a solicitor to see me, but I did not intend to use his services. I had a suit which I had seldom used sent in. Jimmy Mooney brushed it carefully every day. He called it my shooting suit. Up to this month, January, nearly thirty of our men had been executed.

Casey came back during the week for the court-martial papers he had given me, and laughed when we talked about our efficient communications system. His headquarters was badly chagrined, he said. 'They were wild in Portobello when they saw your letter in the paper next morning.'

'I suppose they wanted to shoot me quietly.'

Father MacMahon was told of my impending trial. He came to see me but did not offer any suggestions or give spiritual advice.

'It's a shooting job,' I said. 'You know that.'

'Oh no, it's not.'

'I suppose you don't wish to face such an ugly fact, but I have to. I want some advice from you about preparing for death.' He moved away nervously. Perhaps he did not like to drag up the pastoral of the bishops. Assuring me that the trial did not mean anything, he left my cell and did not come back.

I had learned to pray while in jail. Suddenly I realized that I had never really known or meant much by the prayers I had always been accustomed to say. They were a pattern, somewhat of a routine, and evidently the matter and not the spirit had engaged my attention. Until one day I had really prayed. Words and individual phrasings took on new meanings and values; there was a spirit in them that I had not sensed before, as I got ready for death in my own way. The excitement of writing was calmed down by the exaltation of my prayer. I wondered what it would feel like, the physical aspect. What would the officers on the court martial feel? What should I say at the trial? I would not recognize the jurisdiction of the court. I would tell them they had no authority or right, save that of naked force. Would I be permitted to address the court, not in my defence but to state my position? What would I think the night before the execution? Would my courage hold out? Should I write letters, or just send a farewell letter to my men? I would write to the men only; they were always a cause of joy, a solace. What way would I face a firing squad in the cold of dawn? It would be good to face their rifles without a bandage, as I would like to meet death with my eyes open, and I thought they might grant this last request. Whenever I was unsure of myself, I thought of the others whom I knew who had been hanged or shot; of the three English officers we had sent to their death in the early morning. When such a death came near there was a strengthening; men and boys of different ways of life were able to face it. A week ago I had heard of four of our young boys who walked out to the wall in Kilmainham jail. One had a butt of a cigarette; he took a few puffs, then handed it to his friends, who in turn took a few jerks. 'Shoot away, now,' said the first, when the others had taken their smoke.

I felt pity for the Staters moving in a vicious circle, as I saw them, being driven themselves by their own acts in the course of empire, helped perhaps by our propaganda and abuse, to depart further and further from their ideals. The whole situation looked more like a Greek tragedy. I could dissociate myself now as a player and look on others without passion.

Always I had, so I thought, fought impersonally without hatred. I had given allegiance to a certain ideal of freedom as personified by the Irish Republic. It had not been realized except in the mind. I had fought against the British Empire in defence of that Republic, against Irishmen in the RIC, Englishmen in the British Army, and Irishmen in the Free State Army. To me they meant the same system which had stifled the spiritual expression of nationhood and had retarded our development; which had dammed back strength, vigour and imagination needed in solving our problems in our own way. The spirit of the race was warped until it could express its type of genius. Lying in bed, I had doubts about our course of action in resisting the attack of the Staters on the Four Courts; I wondered if any other solution could have been reached. Doubts did not last. Whatever alliance could have been made with Collins, civil or military, some section of the country would possibly have fought, and I knew that I would have joined them.

Men and boys from the hospital came in to talk to me; a few brought autograph albums. They would talk about their homeland shyly, or ask me questions about their brigades. Really they came to say goodbye. The weekend approached and I had not received any notification.

Sister Angela said: 'You won't be shot, I know that. I've made a novena for you.'

She turned the picture of Saint Francis of Assisi, which she had given me, face to the wall. 'You like him best,' she said, 'and yet he let them send you the charge sheet. He'd better look out or he'll stay like that for punishment.'

Sometime afterwards sisters were not allowed to enter the prison hospitals.

I expected to hear further about my trial but no word came. My execution was nearly hastened by my friends. Men from the Dublin Brigade had held up a meeting of county councils in Dublin. They called out four names, but the four were absent. 'We hear that Ernie O'Malley was shot this morning, and those four are going to go west for him.'

The girls were still in the female hospital. Their numbers increased; there were about fifty of them close by. In England

the British had rounded up Irish Republicans, many of them
girls; they had been handed over to the Free State and were
now imprisoned in Ireland. We could hear the girls singing
'We'll hang Dick Mulcahy on a sour apple tree.' Tales of
their escapades were reported by the medical orderlies or by
note. There was a turret manned by a sentry in the angle
between the division wall of our two jails. If I could disarm
the sentry, I would have a few hours in which to get over the
wall. Boys in the hospital would tie up the military policeman
there, and I would dress in his uniform and go up to the
turret. The report of a revolver, if it was necessary to shoot
the sentry, would not be noticed as there was much firing at
night. Some of the girls sent me a good plan of the grounds
and they offered to get out of their cells and help to send me
over the wall. Before I had left home in 1918 I had planned a
raid for two German Mausers which were in a house in Eccles
Street; my return journey home would have brought me past
the Joy, across the canal, down an iron ladder on to the
railway cutting, and up another ladder on the far side. Now
that short cut would save my strength. But I had not enough
strength, I found. I rapidly became weak when I practised
walking up and down my cell. I was too weak, too helpless,
and would have endangered the others, so I had to remain in
bed to read and play chess.

Father MacMahon had been asking a man in the ward,
who was in great pain from rheumatic fever, to sign the form,
then he would give the Sacraments to him, but the man
refused and asked the other men in the ward to prevent the
priest annoying him. I left instructions that if the chaplain
interfered again he was to be told to leave the ward; if he
refused he was to be put out; if they were afraid they were to
send for me. Next day there came a string of protests from the
men, and Jimmy tugging at his coat-tails made the chaplain
leave. On Sundays at Mass he preached political sermons
against Republicanism to men who, inwardly seething,
listened not to words of spiritual consolation but to a bitter
attack on their sacred ideals and beliefs. As a disciplinary
measure they were ordered by their wing commandants to
remain quietly in their seats. They resented the order.
Perhaps the chaplain carried out the instructions of his

authorities, but it seemed cowardly to attack prisoners who were incapable of carrying on active hostilities, knowing that the only way he could do so was by abuse from the pulpit. The men suffered in silence, but often I heard them say they would cheerfully wring his neck if ever they caught him outside the gates of the Joy.

One day he tapped at my cell door and came in. Had I seen the morning paper, Mr. O'Malley; very interesting news today, very interesting.

I told him papers were forbidden and that he must be aware of prison regulations. I had already seen the paper. Liam Deasy, our Deputy Chief of Staff, had been captured. The night before his intended execution he had issued an appeal to our command areas for the cessation of hostilities and the surrender of arms, but had not met with any real success.

The chaplain handed me the paper. I re-read it.

'Would you like to write a statement?' he asked.

'I would.'

He smiled. 'That's right, Mr. O'Malley.'

'Will you promise me that you will have it published?'

'Why, certainly.'

'Here it is verbally. I'll write it later. I would like to point out to our men how gallantly boys of eighteen have walked out to their firing squads. Life was precious to them, but they did not falter. I wish that their example might again be brought to the memory of all our officers. The men without rank have shown the way to die; it is our duty to follow their good lead.'

He stepped back in his nervous two-step from the bed. He looked startled.

'I cannot have anything to do with such a message.'

'You said you were willing to take one from me.'

Then I told him what I thought of his conduct; he who had not helped me to prepare for death, dared to come to my cell and for the first time had brought a paper to me. It had bad news and I was badly wounded.

'What would you think if you were ill and I came in with the news that the Archbishop of Dublin had gone over to the Protestant Church that morning?'

He had expected me to condone what I considered the abuse of authority by an officer of high rank in a time of mental stress. The letter would perhaps weaken our resistance, but would only embitter the fight and perhaps prolong it. Then I asked him to leave the room.

Prisoners from all over Ireland were in the jail. Patients from the hospital were sent back to the wings, and new arrivals told us tales of fighting outside, or affairs in the different counties, or of life in other jails and camps. I was told of a tunnel's progress by word of mouth through a newcomer to the hospital; those of us who knew suppressed our excitement, although I would probably not be able to escape. I would have to get to one of the wings, but I could walk only slowly and with pain.

Paudeen O'Keeffe came to my cell. 'How are you?' he asked.

'All right.'

'But you're not all right, I know that. Wouldn't you like to go to Mass? The chapel's not far away; it's only a few hundred yards, and you can go next Sunday if you like.'

'I can't walk much,' I said.

'But you'll be able to walk that far.'

'O'Keeffe, if you want me to be fit for trial, feed me well. I'll walk when it suits myself, not when it suits a firing squad. You can use the stretcher for that.'

It would seem that the Staters wanted to shoot me, but did not like to shoot me on a stretcher. Why there should be a convention about patching up a wounded man before a squad shot the life out of him was not clear to me.

Prisoners were transferred from internment camps, amongst them Paddy Fleming whom I had been with in Wexford. He had been sent up from the Curragh with other senior officers and came to the hospital. Life in the huts of camps was more open, shared in common, and noisier than jail life. Paddy told me of escape attempts and of tunnel digging. Men who were captured in arms and were awaiting trial often went on the run in camp before their trial came up, or men would change places in other huts to make it more difficult for a particular man to be found. Paddy Ryan Lacken of North Tipp had his head shaved, his face made-up from a box of theatrical paints; his own friends often did not know him, and he was not picked out by the CID. Free State intelligence officers tried to hunt down men, but they were seldom identified or recaptured. Sentenced men who were not well known signed the form in the name of other prisoners who were expecting release and were set at liberty. It was rumoured that executions were pending, and that was given by some as the reason for the transfer of senior officers, but perhaps the enemy were attempting to smash our organization in camps by removing camp officials and outstanding men. Raids and arrests continued, and in camps, barracks and jails there must have been close on twelve thousand prisoners. Anybody opposed to the Free State was liable to imprisonment. As well, each jail and camp had a quota of men arrested on criminal charges and a number of touts and spies.

A bearded man named Byrne was brought to the hospital. He was a Methodist, a pacifist and a Republican, and had gone on solitary hunger-strike for release. He was a staunch character, not the slightest trace of self-pity. He walked around and talked volubly, or sat on his bed and discussed an endless variety of subjects. He had few friends who would interfere, little or no publicity, even from our papers outside, yet he was determined to fight his lone battle. Day by day we saw him getting thinner and weaker, but his spirit was as strong as ever and we felt ourselves powerless, watching him and listening to his talk. After twenty-six days or more he was released unconditionally.

Late one night, just before lights-out, military police tramped along our corridor shouting out names. 'Barton, Robert C. Barton. Fleming, Patrick Fleming. Pack up at once. Pack up.' One of the police said they were going back to their wings. What was on, Jimmy Mooney and I asked each other, but we guessed what we did not say aloud. Now I thought of what had been said by those who did not object to the executions: 'One day we'll take a hundred or more of you out, and that will make the rest think.' It was what we had expected. Bob Barton and Paddy came in to say goodbye. Both were sick; the crossing to the wings could only mean the one thing. Bob sat on my bed; he talked quietly. He looked content, so did Paddy. Bob talked on. It would breed more hatred; he would wish that those who had once fought with us for the Republic would not stain their hands further. He had nursed and cared for me, chatted and read. I was now able to play two games of chess a day, and had attempted to solve the problems which occupied so much of his time.

Paddy's susceptible lips caught the echo of his smile. He had a sensitive face; it looked wistful now, but really it was not. He had a slightly nervous trick of momentarily closing his eyes and moving his head as he spoke. 'You've cheated us,' said Paddy. 'We go first.' His large hands played with a book as we talked. 'I wonder what has happened outside,' he said. 'We must have had some successful scrapping.'

A knock on the door. *'Beannacht De leat,* Earnan. I'll see you on the other side.' He stood up, saluted and left the cell. The voice of the police outside. 'Barton. Hurry up, Barton.' A firm hand grip from Bob; his lips flickered and he was gone.

Jimmy Mooney and I did not speak for a long time afterwards. There was no bitterness or rancour in those two; Bob with gentleness and consideration; Paddy with a delicate sensitiveness, a strange spiritual sense. It seemed hard that so many of the people I admired had to die and would continue to die for the cause. Jimmy and I talked and thought of things one remembers another by, in absence; a smile, a humorous remark, an association in books. Bob's ivory chessmen and his joy in his ambushes in the end game; the problems in the *Times Literary Supplement;* a last talk on Italian primitives; fishing days on the Westmeath lakes; the time when he was to be flogged with the cat-o'-nine-tails in an English prison, and the description of the terrible shell cocoa of convicts which almost gave me indigestion to hear of. Paddy's salting of a phrase; his tale of a railway station in America where women had lined up to kiss him. For them he represented the Young Ireland, but I could not see it in that light. 'That'd take the starch out of you,' he would say.

The making of a flag in Maryborough in 1918 where Paddy was serving hard labour: when in solitary confinement he had cajoled some flowers, a needle and a thread; then he had barricaded his door and hung out a sheet with orange and green flowers from the handle of a broom. The Republican tricolour floated from the window, seen by people on the

street outside. Later, his escape from the Joy after men with
spoons in their pockets had held up the warders who thought
the spoons were revolver muzzles. As a final touch a prisoner
began to read aloud the proclamation of the 1916 Rising,
whilst other prisoners used a rope-ladder on the wall. The
warders thought another rebellion had broken out.

We tried to keep awake, but I fell asleep. Before dawn
Jimmy touched me on the shoulder. 'It'll soon be dawn,' he
whispered. It was very cold. The light came slowly through
the bars, making larger grills on the cell walls as we listened.
No sound of rifle volleys. We lay quiet for another hour.
Perhaps they had been taken away to another barracks or to
Kilmainham for the execution. Tired, we went to sleep. There
had been no executions, we learned that evening, and we
were left to puzzle at the ways of jailers.

Jimmy was a Dublin volunteer who had served in Fianna
Eireann. His legs were small; he was lightly built. He had
once hoped to become a jockey at the Curragh stables;
finally he had been apprenticed to a barber. Anyone small, in
his description, was 'two hands higher than a duck'. He had a
fierce contempt for the Staters. Their operations were subjects for his amused tolerance. They did not count; we would
win the fight. His national faith was simple, unwavering,
unconquerable, like men who had fought with us for Irish
freedom. Not specious arguments, not casuistry, but this
awe-inspiring certitude, simple and direct. People who had
lived outside of Ireland were affected by this faith and partook
of it when they shared its belief. There was no room for
cynicism or disillusionment, but a fierce exultance whose
sincerity swept everything else aside. Often enough it warped
human nature; with him it did not. This was the belief of the
people, who practically alone had nurtured the spirit of
freedom, had kept alive the passionate desire of the race. Not
amongst the intellectuals would it be found; they were not
free from forms of mental snobbery, intellectual arrogance
and pride. Not much amongst the middle classes, the barriers
to all ideals save those of comfort. But amongst the people,
deep down in the soil and with the poor of cities.

I climbed one day to a window at the rear of the hospital,
on superimposed tables from which I could look out across

the prison wall. Water in the canal glistened in the sun, the wind rippled its surface; trees were in bud along Whitworth Road; in the distance I could see sparkles of the quartz in the grey limestone Irish Romanesque church of Saint Columba. Houses of red brick were brighter than I had ever thought of them. It was like looking down on houses in a box of toys, ruddy reds and deep greens. It was hard to believe that there could be so much colour outside. Soon spring would be here. In the country young wheat would be bright green and the growing meadow-grass a strong green. There would be white blossoms on the hawthorne and a purple fur on the pliant beech before it leafed; apple buds pinkish white and fragrant. The furze would become a deeper gold and its odour stronger; finches would answer clearly, skylarks soar, the spry wheatears sing as they flew. All gayer in pairs mating, as winter flocks were broken up; and jail was as dour as parched grass. That view of the trees and the canal was a happy memory. The warm colour of the brick and the foliage remained with me later in the ugly drab cell.

Several times I had written to the C of S, as I expect had others, pointing out that prisoners were casualties who could not be considered. That had been my own attitude when I was free; it was my attitude now as a prisoner. If our lives were to be forfeit on account of the operations of our fighting men, we would have no complaint. Some of the officers were afraid, evidently, of the continuance of executions. Some feared that the prisoners who were considered of importance and who would be hard to replace would eventually be shot. In jail we held no rank, and it was well. No one should live on their reputation. Hell, it was hard to get rid of the current folklore which exalted men beyond the stature they could live up to. Outside, some of our officers were beaten; some of them from the south had already met Free State officers and had unofficially talked. That, unless our GHQ was willing to back them, was a source of weakness. Such meetings would only prolong the straggled fight and reduce it to one of attrition. Prisoners had no right to advise, I thought, yet to Liam Lynch I had protested about the destruction of communications as an end in itself. I thought the policy a fatal one, giving an excuse to men in some areas who would not

fight. If such tearing up of rails and roads was to be the
prelude to good fighting, then it was justified, otherwise not.
A campaign of destruction that did not serve any immediate
military objective, or did not grow out of a definite military
undertaking, seemed to me futile, and in a sense cowardly.
All my notes to him were written from the view of one who
would soon leave this side of things, and who thought that he
himself had not justified responsibility when one of the
fighting force. We were beaten as far as I could see. We had
been beaten for the past two or three months, if not longer.

CHAPTER THIRTEEN

APRIL—AUGUST 1923

A FEW days later I was removed to 'A' wing, though scarcely
able to walk. My removal was viewed with apprehension by
some of the officers as they thought that there might be a
sinister motive. Jimmy came with me, but he would not be
allowed inside as he had come originally from 'C' wing. He
refused to leave me.

'I'm not going to 'C' wing, I'm going to 'A' wing.' He
argued with the police but they would not let him in.

'I'm going to see the governor,' I heard him say; so despite
the military police he insisted on making his way to the office.
An hour later he came back. 'Paudeen's not so bad. He said I
could move in to your cell to look after you.'

So he was permitted to move his mattress into my cell. I
had the only bed in the Joy.

The hospital had been quiet and I had been afraid of the
change to the wing with all its noise and bustle. I had become
accustomed to the hospital's greyness; I had forgotten its
drabness. Now I had again to get used to an ordinary cell.

'A' wing had a big number of men who had been captured in
arms and were awaiting sentence, yet on the surface there
was probably little difference from other wings and not much
sense of strain; but sometimes the men would show it.
Outside news was eagerly gathered; they knew that activity in
the field would often be replied to by a diet of executions. The
shooting of prisoners by areas looked as if the Free State was
'blooding' its senior officers, and men from an area which had
not yet responded were less sure of life. Up to the middle of
March sixty-seven prisoners had faced firing squads. January
was the culminating point with thirty-four executions; in
February only one prisoner had been shot; in some instances
prisoners had been executed after the local command had

sentenced them to terms of eight and ten years, for the
ultimate decision rested with Free State GHQ. Some men
were nervous and peaked; some did not care, but at odd
moments a man might drop his covering and show his
anxiety, fear or dread. Boys and men laughed about executions and ragged one another's concealed fears. I was growing
used to the idea of death by a long apprenticeship. I was more
passive about it now. In Kilmainham with the British I would
have tried to struggle with the hangman. Here it seemed a
natural end. Any day the Staters might shoot a whole wing if
they felt inclined; yet the laughter of the race in the front of
almost certain death was steady and if it could be so
described, joyous. Death could win the last throw, but it
would win from many who accepted it as one meets a good
enemy, almost in a spirit of sad comradeship.

A group of men were in half disgrace, which wore away.
The officer commanding the wing had written about them to
me when I was in the hospital. The men had been assured
that if they signed the form before trial they would not be
executed, otherwise they had no hope. That was a question
for the men themselves, I replied, and for the Wing OC. I
held no rank. I would not sign myself in such a case; boys had
been given the same opening but they were now dead. The
men signed; their conduct was contrasted with that of the
young boys shot in Kilmainham, but we were all prisoners,
and months afterwards they repudiated their signatures.

There was noise all day. Heavy boots on iron stairs, men
tramping with healthy zest, continuous hammering on coins
to make rings or ornaments, catcalls, yells and greetings
though some had parted twenty minutes previously.

'Oh the hard Joe!'

'What's the latest?'

'Up Kerry No. One!'

From the outside came shouts from rival teams playing
football with rag balls. A chorus syncopated from a cell, or
the scrape of a reluctant fiddle. A casual observer might have
thought he was amongst a crowd of schoolboys. Classes,
elementary and advanced, were held daily on many subjects;
wood was carved, macramé work knotted, fretwork-saws
turned out designs in wood, pewter spoons were melted and

run in moulds to make Tara brooches. At one time the guards complained about the noise of ring hammering as men zealously laboured on the locks of their cells to batter out coins. Later, guards solaced themselves in the night watches by banging out rings below on the ground floor whilst prisoners shouted their lack of sleep. Cigarettes had been banned at intervals and smokers suffered. Tobacco was manufactured out of dried leaves and bay, or wisps of grass; some smoked brown paper, and a few bartered rings of copper covered with mercury to simulate silver with some of the military police who acted as our warders. There could be a brisk exchange for a quantity of cigarettes but this method did not often succeed.

The day after my arrival a plumber came to my cell. 'I'll fix your pipes,' he said. He brought with him lengths of gas tubing which he had torn down in another part of the wing. He tapped the gas main, bent piping behind the hinge of my door, and cemented joints with soap. He hammered fittings into the wall, and there was an improvised cooking range. Gas in our cells, for lighting only, was supplied from above the door. He made a bunsen and a fish-tail burner on the spot out of pieces of an empty pineapple tin. Another boy fitted up bookcases made out of boxes with the ends knocked out, then the frame was supported on the walls by pegs. The lion-skin rug which had been flung over me by Mrs. Humphreys when I lay wounded, and which I had clung on to ever since, helped at times to decorate the wall. Soon the cell was habitable.

A few cells had been papered early in the war. Simon Donnelly, who had escaped with me from Kilmainham, was very proud of his wallpaper which visitors came to admire. A week after he had completely furnished his cell he was changed to an internment camp. Photographs from illustrated magazines took from the walls' bareness and designs were worked out in patterns of coloured paper; some cells had drawings, others paintings. At one time nearly every prisoner thought that he could paint; the evidence yet remained in landscape, portrait and still life.

Cells had a window high up, and the walls were whitewashed. They had a bare, uneventful appearance. Some cells were dark; they did not catch much sun in the daytime. All

had defective gas for reading as light came from an unprotected jet, and because many windows had been broken in the
process of occupation, the light had additional flickers from
the wind. Lights were forbidden in cells after ten o'clock
when the gas at the main was shut off, except on the landings.
Candles were improvised, since they were forbidden, by
melted-fat cut from meat allowed to solidify around a piece of
string; then there was reading light. During the day it was
often difficult to read, there was so much 'ragging'. The night
was cold and quiet; all was still and we could begin to read.
Not for long, though. Someone would become exuberant,
roar at full-lung, or break out in song, to be howled down by
objectors or the chorus to be taken up by half the wing. Some
men darkened their windows with paper or erected tin
screens to conceal the light from shining through their doors.
Others were indifferent and did not trouble themselves to
hide their lights. One could hear a shout, 'PUT OUT THAT
LIGHT', the awful noise of a cartridge being rammed into a
rifle breech, an irritated 'DO YOU HEAR, PUT OUT
THAT LIGHT'. Perhaps a reply from the wing: 'Sockko'.
Then a shot. Another bolt ramming, a shot—silence. My
nerves were always on edge waiting for the shot when the
sentry was close to my window. My body stiffened at the first
shout; I listened to the noise of the bolt, then after what
seemed long ages, the shot. Exhausted, I would allow my
body to relax. Some nights I had to listen to shot after shot.
They had begun to produce the same effect as when I waited
in the room near the gates at the Four Courts for the rifle-
grenades to burst. My nerves were weak, there was not the
old control. Men often left an empty cell door partially open
so that a landing light would shine in to deceive the sentry,
and those in near-by cells taunted and jeered as he shot and
cursed.

Paddy Fleming was in the cell on one side of me. During
the night he often had heart spasms, his body grew rigid, his
speech became incoherent. If anyone would touch him during
an attack he would regain control; if not, he would feel as if
his heart was slowing. He would not be allowed a companion.
I was the only breach of that rule. Boys removed two bricks in
the wall beside my bed so that he could touch me when he felt

the attack coming on; otherwise he would lie supine for half
the following day. Imprisoned by the British in Maryborough, for many months he had fought them for political
status. He was confined in handcuffs, in strait jackets, or,
worse still, in 'muffs' which were used for dangerously
demented lunatics. He had smashed cell after cell, including
one specially built for him; he broke muff after muff, and as a
result of his excessive exertions he had damaged his heart.

One morning he walked into my cell.

'It's strange. I saw Liam Lynch last night. He walked in
through the cell door, stood for a while, smiled down at me,
and then he was gone.'

He believed in his vision; at other times he had sensed
things we do not normally feel. We were worried about Liam.
Perhaps he had been captured in arms; perhaps it did not
mean anything. Two days later we heard that he had been
killed during a round-up on the Knockmealdown mountains.

The fight had varied in intensity. In Connacht the western
divisions maintained their ground, especially Billy
Pilkington's area. Areas like Longford and portions of Meath
struggled with difficulty. South Dublin maintained its small
columns which had probably more vicissitudes than those of
any other area. Wexford continued to improve. North
Tipperary maintained its position in the mountains around
Newport; South Tipperary was still staunch and true. Kerry
fought on despite all the efforts to crush it. Our casualties had
not been heavy, but many of the best officers had been killed.
We didn't know how to fight and we didn't know how to surrender.

In the night-time in the cell it was pleasant talking to
Jimmy, listening to him. He gleaned information from many
sources. During a pause in conversation he would say: 'Have
you heard the latest?' and would recount some amusing
incident from one of the wings, or some further attempt by
the Staters to crush the resistance outside. 'Any news?' was
generally the introduction to talk, as it would be out of jail.

'It's terrible that these half-soldiers are keeping us in
prison,' Jimmy would say. He had the sturdy Dublin volunteer outlook, his unit was the best in Ireland, and the Staters
could never beat us. With him it was only a question of time

until we wore them down. His face was pale, he had a high dome of a forehead, and he swayed a little when he walked. He was self-conscious about his feelings for Ireland; he tried to conceal them. When men sang 'The Soldier's Song', he laughed as many of the others did. He baulked like a skittish horse at the singing of 'My Dark Rosaleen', but as the verses continued he would express what he felt, in that strange attachment to Ireland which was as mystical as it was practical. When men took unusual risks in jail, 'they wanted to be bould Bobby Emmets'. Yet he talked of 'the Cause' as if it had been the Quest for the Holy Grail, even as we in 'F' company, before the fighting began again after Easter Week, looked forward to and discussed 'the Day'.

From concerts held on the landings, Jimmy learned ballads of the Tan war, or the Trouble, as it was now called: 'All around my hat I'll wear a Tri-colour ribbon-O', or 'The Foggy Dew'; but they could always be roused to a marching song: 'Steady, boys, and step together' and 'Twenty Men from Dublin Town', or the humorous parodies: 'King George met Joe Devlin a short time ago, . . . And "begorra" says Joe, I don't mind if I do.'

So he would sing in the night-time an old satirical song:

> Soon we will all be civilized,
> Neat and clean and well advised,
>
> O won't Mother England be surprised,
> Whack fol the diddle fol the dido day.
>
> From the GPO to Boland's Mill,
> We made poor England weep her fill,
> But ould Britannia loves us still,
> Whack fol the diddle fol the dido day.

The old songs from the Irish he did not know, but he learned them and was helped out by voices from the neighbouring cells when we kept our doors open. 'The Castle of Dromore', a crooning lullaby, 'I know my love by his way of walking', or *Sean O Dwyer a Gleanna,* we were worsted in the game.' He could recite Pearse's oration at the grave of O'Donovan Rossa and his short sketch of him:

He jested when he was before his judges; he
jested when he was tortured by his jailers;
sometimes he startled the silence of the
prison corridors by laughing aloud and by
singing Irish songs in his cell: they thought
he was going mad, but he was only trying to
keep himself sane.

Liam Deasy, formerly the Deputy Chief of Staff, came to 'A'
wing. I told him what I thought of his conduct when he had
issued his appeal to all Republicans to surrender, so that
there would be no false footing between us. He felt his
position in the prison. His letter written the night before his
threatened execution had not resulted in the surrender of
arms, and Liam Lynch and the rest of his staff had con-
demned Deasy's action.

He had held his views for a time before his arrest, he said.

It was a matter for his Chief of Staff, I told him.

We were all prisoners, anyhow, and we did our best to live
jail life without friction. He had found the diary of a convict,
written on toilet paper hidden in a ventilator. After reading it,
he had burnt the story.

'Couldn't you have sent it out?' I asked.

'No, some of it was not fit to read.'

'But you read it, and I've never heard what a man felt like,
reviewing his past in jail.' And so another human document
was destroyed.

On 30 April, an order to suspend operations was issued by
Frank Aiken, the new Chief of Staff, and on 24 May a 'cease
fire' order and 'dump arms' instructions were forwarded to all
units of the IRA.

Arrests continued with renewed vigour. The Free State
Army was about fifty-five thousand strong. Areas never before
visited, now swarmed with troops and round-ups took place
in mountainy areas where troops had found it difficult or
impossible to get through before. Our men who wished to
avoid capture were hunted like foxes. They could not offer
any resistance, and if they went home they were arrested and
suffered very often at the hands of their captors. 'On the run'
was now no misnomer. Some of them who were put amongst

us said they had never travelled so fast, or so long, before, with their 'caps in their fisths', as they said. The 'cap in the fisth' was always afterwards associated with the ferreting out after the cease fire.

Below in basement cells were the newcomers, and the following dialogue was recounted as being the typical conversation of a young Kerry boy who was able to talk to the new prisoners through their cell doors.

'Hello . . . Hello there.'

'Are you from Kerry wan or two?'

'Did they bate you up much?'

'Were oo caught with a gun?'

'Faith, that's too bad.'

A few more discreet expressions of sympathy, and then the inevitable demand which had prompted the conversation. 'Have oo ere a butt?'

In jail you learn to do without anything. We were up against jailers who had themselves been prisoners, and who knew the ropes. The days were difficult. Anyone could catcall, yell or sing when the humour seized him. The destructive spirit could be seen in the broken cell windows which had not been repaired. In the winter time many must have cursed the former occupants who had smashed the glass for want of something better to do. By degrees I became somewhat accustomed to noise. Tin cans kicked on the floor of 'A' wing, carpenters hammering, and the exuberance of windy lungs. I read steadily, relieving history with fiction, drama with poetry, travel or philosophy, but the light was bad. In strong sun the dull yellow-white walls glared; at night the gas jet jumped and stuttered. At the back of my mind was the thought that if I was not shot I might always be an invalid. It was better to read, to prevent thinking of oneself.

I found it very difficult to walk; my muscles were flaccid from loss of tone, and my body, through nerves, was easily tensed; I could not speak when I was tired. Generally I was able to remain up for an hour or two daily. I could talk but little as talking exhausted me. The hospital cell had made me a recluse; one had been driven in too much on oneself, now was the time to go out again, to eddy round. That was

difficult, I found. Sometimes I would get tired at the voice of a
visitor. To some people I could chat, but with others I could
only utter a few sentences when the tired feeling came. It was
easier, I often found, to listen to men who had natural school-
ing, who had no pretension to learning or science. They were
natural; sometimes the others seemed sophisticated, jutting
out from themselves, and unreal.

Jimmy had learned to know my 'grey days' as we called
them, when I could not leave my bed or speak. He had
learned my idiosyncrasies, he knew the people who adversely
affected me, and would endeavour after a time to get them out
of the cell.

Sometimes we were able to borrow a small box-gramo-
phone which had some fairly good records. In the silent dark
we listened to violin solos or symphonies. We felt our souls
being slowly drawn out of our bodies; we became sound, a
feeling in sound, rising, falling, sadness, joy, memory and
unrealized desire. The warm richness and joy of the sublime
Beethoven, tempered with a fear for the record, for there were
few of his. A cracked Bach, rising in clarity and concise
strength above the needle rasp on the break. Kreisler made us
one with rhythm, swaying, beating, pulsing; or we visualized
Anitra's Dance from *Peer Gynt,* when through shut eyes we
saw a figure flash in silver light, flitting as softly as a moon-
beam till the end of the round. That was the right way to hear
music, in the dark, when everything was quiet.

I read aloud aided by a beef-fat candle until I was tired.
Paddy's voice came through the chinks in the wall: 'Good,
boy, keep it up, that's fine; try it again.' Tagore's *The Gardener*
read thus, my voice endeavouring to interpret the feeling,
grasping its sense of continuity, its fluidity. Reading prose or
poems I liked gave an added beat to the heart; feeling welled
up slowly till it reached the inflections of the voice and I had
to stop. We embroidered fantastic stories or imaginary tales
of people we both knew. I would strive hard to keep up the
adventures which gradually became real, until Paddy's voice
would break in. 'Whoa, man. That's all,' as I roved out of a
story. A rifle shot, or the spatter of a machine-gun, might
break in on the reading.

We played mental chess; it became a night-time occupation. We rapped on cell walls, then called out our moves. 'King's bishop to queen's castle four', and the reply would come back. 'Queen's knight to king six.' We studied the relationship of the imaginary chess board, the next moves were made, the game became slower as the moves developed. In the end there would be a shout of protest. 'I'm there. I have a knight there. Get off my square,' and the game would stop unfinished. Down the passage, through my half-open door, I could hear loud argumentative disputes about previous moves.

I read to Jimmy. *Don Quixote* in a huge volume with Doré illustrations, his own book; a special reading-rest was made for it. There was Sancho's advice, which I had underlined in my pocket edition: 'Let us run away now for there is no one to see us running.' Most of all he liked the *Odyssey*, as I myself did. It had more continuity and cohesion as a story than the *Iliad*, it was more interesting, more imaginative. The episode of Polyphemus he liked best.

A Greek class was held in my cell. A Tralee boy, Eamon Enright, a civil engineer, taught us. He was brilliant at science, a classical student and a linguist. We spent many interesting hours discussing, talking, working. He read Aristophanes for us in Greek, or quoted the long rolling passages of Homer. We read Aristophanes in translation, Frere's; and Sophocles, Euripides, and jumped from them to the Elizabethans. There was always the surprise of certain men in jail eager for knowledge of painting or general knowledge. My attempts through music and painting were not successful; they wanted a literary approach, every picture must tell a story. I persuaded boys to read Balzac because he was anti-British. I myself was reading Chaucer and Shakespeare to a tune of reproach. There was consolation in our lack of fight when I read Motley's *Wars of the Dutch Republic*.

Men who had been sentenced for civilian offences were also sent to Mountjoy; they added to the known touts and pigeons amongst us. A few non-political prisoners had been placed in our wing. Probably it was a prelude to treating us as criminals.

Going down stairs to a bath, very slowly, in pyjamas, sitting down at intervals, I met an old man on the ground floor. He had been sentenced for cattle driving. He always wore his brown-green hat, which had once been black. He had a long thin face, with a silver-grey scrub of beard; his shoulders were bent, but his body was straight. His neck had deep creases in the red skin.

Jimmy was carrying my towels, as he intended to give me a shampoo and massage.

'I've watched you coming down for baths,' the old man said. 'Why man alive, you'll catch your death of cold from them. Now look on me. I had ne'er a bath in my life and I'm past sixty-five.'

Attempts to escape were always being planned and tunnels were ever under way. Most prisoners had private ideas of their own on the subject. Some tunnels had been found by the Staters, filled in, and blocked with barbed wire. Often an old tunnel was used again, side-tunnels branching off from its point of stoppage. Poison gas and grenades were placed in some by the Staters but no casualties ensued. Dummy tunnels were made to act as blinds to the real one. Picked men were selected for the work; prominent men could not be chosen as they were too closely watched. Bearings for direction were taken with a prismatic compass but sometimes the reckoning was wrong. Some were too short; one was too near the surface, a sentry stepped through into it. Workers wore overalls; they had to work in muddy water yet be clean for paradecount in the evening. The earth had to be carefully removed and distributed, and the tunnel in many cases was supported by props made from cell boards or boxes. Lightning raids by police might turn men suddenly out of the wings and a count would prove that there was underground work. In one instance men were stuck in the mud before count and the Staters had to be informed of their predicament as the other prisoners were unable to extricate them. Planning escape kept some men busy. Their days were less barren. From continuous practice a few had become expert in tunnelling and in avoiding attention. They had to avoid the prying eyes of the military police, the prisoner touts, the notice of our men who did not know of the work and might be inclined to talk.

Legend said that Michael Price, who had been in command of the First Eastern when I was free, had driven a
tunnel in one of the camps, equipped it with electric lights,
and provided trucks to take away earth and sidings into
which men could fit while the debris was moved down the
passage. The story grew, soon it equalled in detail
Scheherazade's tales. I had often been told by men who had
been sent to the hospital or to 'A' wing from other jails of
proposed escape plans, as a whispered secret. I hoped that
Mick Price's tunnel had not been found as a result of talk.

He came himself to 'A' wing. He was a prisoner in
Wellington barracks when I had been wounded, and, believ-
ing the evening paper which said that I had died of wounds,
he had held a memorial service for me. Other prisoners
recited the Rosary. Then he gave an oration. I had learned
part of it by heart, and I recited it when I met him in 'A'
wing.

'You'll be well buried before any of us will ever attempt
another hymn of praise for you,' he said.

He came to my cell to chat and told me of his camp
experiences and the punishment ordeal of the 'glass-house' at
the Curragh, where the military confine their own delin-
quents. It was a survival from the British occupation. He and
three others were removed from camp and sentenced for their
suspected part in tunnel-planning. In the glass-house, so
called because of its roof, prisoners had to do everything at
the double and were harried by sergeants who seemed to take
a delight in barking orders, and in giving vent to their
parade-ground voice in narrow cells. Unnecessary, meaning-
less tasks were thought out for them and at night their sleep
was interrupted by numerous counts. Price and his companions had been tied up with outstretched hands to beams
so that the tips of their toes barely touched the ground. They
were kept in this position for long periods as they refused to
submit to the impositions of the loud-voiced ones. The other
unfortunate military prisoners submitted and other punish-
ments were meted out to them. Such institutions existed in
different parts of the British glass-house empire.

During late July and the first week of August, 'A' wing was
practically emptied, and we were distributed between 'C'
and 'D' wings. With most of the others, I went into 'C'.

A carnival in the wing was arranged. Plays were rehearsed; there was an air of mystery about as groups gathered into cells to discuss their schemes.

The great day arrived. Cells and landings were decorated and costumes improvised. I was helped downstairs but was able to walk slowly to the exercise ring. That was my first day in the ring, and my first real view of Mountjoy. The prison proper contained four blocks or wings of harsh grey stone, radiating like the spokes of half a wheel, the hub forming what was known as the circle, shut off from the wings by high iron gates. The walls on the outside showed three layers of cells; there were four, but one could not see the cells of the basements. The small barred openings were the windows. They seemed smaller than ever from the outside. Each wing had its exercise ring rounded with iron bars. Tall polygonal chimneys stood high from the roofs. The earth was bare; it had been trodden into surface dust and hardened by feet. Cinders gave a touch of rawness. In the angles between wings long shadows were thrown; cells there had very little light. The prison architects must have studied hard to evolve a soulless building. No touch of warmth of earth or stone; nature was barren here, only the ruthless strength of men who built such walls to crush, to teach a lesson, rather than to cure men, to make the grey stones eat into grey souls.

A procession was formed, led by a bishop with a large crozier, and his attendants. Representatives from the British Empire and other uncivilized countries followed, whilst the civilized communities—mostly coloured—brought up the rear. Fortune tellers, gamblers, strong men of the loop, side-shows, thimble-riggers with their vanishing peas, plied their trades. Pickpockets and robbers moved around, but a force of detectives scattered through the crowd made many arrests. Tribes of Red Indians appeared, under a coat of brown-red boot polish, and various coloured races wandered about; some, it seemed, would belong to the particular race they had selected for many a day, as it would apparently be very difficult to remove their paint. Disguised Ku Kluxers raided and carried off struggling victims, mostly touts, who were summarily dealt with. Plays were performed in the open, tables side by side forming a stage. 'In the Shadow of the

Soup', and 'The Mist that does be on the Bog', were staged,
the dialogue in many scenes being simple but effective.

'God save all here.'

'May God save you, kindly stranger.'

'It's a fine night.'

'It's a fine night, surely.'

'Musha, it's a quare world that's in it, avic.'

'Did ye see any men whest of the cross?'

'No, woman of the house, nor east of the cross, sorra wan.'

In the evening there was a dance on the ground floor, the
'girls' wearing handkerchiefs on their heads or on their arms.
From the landings, which acted as balconies, rice, confetti
and streamers showered down on the dancing couples, and
the day was voted a pleasant memory by all. We were sorry
when lights-out came.

One day Jimmy Mooney fell on the first landing, after per-
forming some trick gymnastics. He was carried into the cell
and suddenly developed epilepsy. I managed to insert a spoon
between his teeth, and he lay there shivering in violent per-
spiration. He was taken away to the hospital and died four
days later.

My cell was lonely then. I missed his cheery direct
optimism. I had envied his courage and intrepid spirit, and
admired his humorous lack of bitterness. He typified the best
of the Dublin Volunteers, and that would suffice for an
epitaph.

Sean Lemass, who escaped with me after the Four Courts,
and had later been in charge of communications when I was
responsible for the Northern and Eastern Command, moved
in. He read aloud Carlyle's explosive sentences; quoted
Kropotkin; sketched with enthusiasm the plots of Upton
Sinclair's novels, and recited Kipling's spattered word
rhymes, the latter possibly because he thought they would
annoy me.

CHAPTER FOURTEEN

AUGUST—OCTOBER 1923

A GENERAL election took place outside. Many of the prisoners were nominated, and I was put forward as a candidate for North Dublin city. I protested against my selection, but my protests were unheard. Sinn Fein had decided that I should be nominated, and nominated I was. It did not matter if we had no ability or political bent. We might be honest, anyhow we might gather votes.

In Mountjoy, elections were held to test and teach knowledge of electoral organization, and to study the complicated system of PR, proportional representation. Meetings were addressed from landing-rails or empty butter-boxes in the exercise rings; waves of oratory flowed to and fro on rocks of interruption and hecklings. Business men, farmers, imperialists, separatists, educationalists, spoke seriously or in mock parody. Rival candidates offered jail utopias for votes. Paragraphs from the daily press and diatribes of bishops and parish priests were used against the 'irregulars'. Polling day was a frenzy, a principal difficulty the prevention of impersonation. We discussed the making of box kites carrying election slogans which could be flown from the wings and the strings cut before the Staters could seize them. The kites might have amused the city electors but they were never made.

De Valera had been arrested in Ennis, Co. Clare, his old constituency. He had given the Free State notice that he would address his voters on a certain day. The meeting was broken up by shooting and the threat of bayonets; people on the platform close to de Valera had been wounded.

The result of the general election was a surprise. Some had expected that ten or twelve Republican candidates would be returned, but in jails and camps, alone, eighteen Sinn Fein TDs were elected, with a total of forty-four. I was elected, and was now a TD for North Dublin; the second preference votes of the Free State Minister for Defence, Dick Mulcahy, had given me my quota. How could one arrive at the point of view which gave him first preference and myself second? Perhaps it was as the people once said when they talked of our marching and drilling as play-acting. 'Musha, God help them. They haven't much sense, the creatures.'

I was met with mock gravity and deference now, increased when they knew how I hated to be a TD. Long testimonials from my constituents in jail were sent to me, which set forth grievances, asked for my respectful assistance, and held hints of desirable vacancies in departments of government.

I received a notice from the Clerk of the Dail to attend a meeting of Dail Eireann, but first I should apply in person at Leinster House to comply with a certain article in the Constitution: which meant that I was to take the oath of allegiance. The notice was sent to my home address, then forwarded by my mother to Mountjoy. It would not be correct to admit that a TD was in prison. I told my people to return any further notice to Leinster House and inform the Clerk that I was a prisoner. Afterwards I thought of what I might have done. Apply for permission to go to Leinster House as invited, then refuse to take the oath when I met the Clerk. It would be amusing to have to go under escort, a public representative in handcuffs, but I expect I would not have been given permission.

Cosgrave, the Governor, died, and O'Keeffe was replaced by Dermott MacManus who proceeded to strengthen defences; barbed wire was festooned, and increased sentry posts were prepared on platforms. MacManus came to visit my cell, sat on the end of my bed and talked of the Tan war, of the truce, and the attack on the Four Courts. He had been in our divisional camp on the Galtees, and later I had seen his torn uniform and white teeth grinning through a blackened face as he talked while we lined up along the Liffey bank after the Four Courts surrender. He had a thick underlip that jutted out, his face was swarthy, he said 'By Jove', and his garrison accent remained from service in the British Army. He came again with a tall officer who had, so he said, met me during the Tan war, but I had no remembrance of him.

After they left, I was told that the Kerry men in the wing were very indignant because I had spoken to the tall officer. 'Why did you talk to that murderer?' they asked, he who had shot a prisoner dead on the roadside.

One of the Kerry men tried to speak quietly, but missing all through his story was the restraint of clarity. He forgot often, his story would begin to get out of control, and then the muscles of his high-boned face tightened, his eyes widened, and words shot out supported by strong curses. 'Aeroplane' Lyons was his friend; the rocks had smashed Lyons's body when the Staters cut the rope by which he was being hauled up the cliffs near Clashmealcon on the north Kerry coast, a prisoner.

Kerry was strongly Republican and a very determined attempt had been made by the Free State to subjugate it since their landing at Fenit in August 1922, just over a year ago. It was not until the back of the resistance had been broken in other counties that special attention had been directed to the Kingdom of Kerry. General Paddy Daly and his Dublin Guards were there and were given a free hand. Up to February 1923, ten Kerry men had been murdered while in custody, but during the month of March twenty-five prisoners were murdered, in three instances by a new form of execution. On 7 March, nine prisoners were brought from Tralee to Ballyseedy Cross near the Killarney and Castleisland roads; they were tied arm to arm on either side of a log and a mine was set off under them. One man, Stephen Fuller, escaped uninjured but pieces of the others were scattered on the roadside and on the branches of trees, and the crows had their pickings of them. That same day five more prisoners were brought to the Countess Bridge in Killarney; three were killed with mines and grenades, one by machine-guns, but another, Tadhg Coffey, ran to freedom. Five days later, on 12 March, five prisoners were blown to bits outside of Cahirciveen. Large crowds came to the funerals; there were protests, but not in the press, from people of different views; many Free State sympathisers had expressed their indignation. The sequel, with its implications, came with the publication of an official order from Free State Army General Headquarters:

Prisoners who die whilst in military custody
in the Kerry command shall be interred by the
troops in the area in which the death has
taken place.

The thundering pulpits were strangely silent about what
crows ate in Kerry. During the recent election campaign,
William Cosgrave had addressed a meeting in the county,
and mourning mothers, some with black shawls over their
heads, had knelt in the street in his sight and had solemnly
cursed him.

'And not long ago, Jer O'Leary was shot at till he died at
the gates of the barracks in Castleisland. Maybe you think
now we like you to be talking to men the likes of that
murderer?'

Barbed wire and platforms were the beginning of a campaign. MacManus attempted to deal with individual
prisoners only, and commandants in charge of the wings and
prisoners' jail organization were to be ignored. Paddy
Coughlan, our wing OC, addressed a letter to the Governor.
His note was returned with sarcastic comments appended in
red ink. His next letter referred to the Governor's bad man-
ners, and police came to the wing to arrest Coughlan, but he
could not be found. He slept on different landings, changed
his appearance and clothing, grew a moustache, and went 'on
the run'. He dealt with the routine work of 'C' wing, held his
Spanish class regularly, then disappeared at night to sleep in
the next wing, with which we had a means of communication.
He was caught and imprisoned in the basement of another
wing. Men in the cell above broke through the floor, hauled
him up by roped blankets, and he was again at liberty in jail.

Mick Price now became OC of our wing, and the minor
war inside the Joy developed. An Act was passed through the
Free State parliament authorizing the Staters to intern
prisoners for a stated length of time; the internment order
had to be served on each prisoner in person. We were ordered
not to answer to our names. At nights cells were raided by
CID and officers who attempted to identify our men, but as
they had changed their cells it was difficult to locate
individuals. We were awakened at night by men crowding
into our cells; lights flashed on our faces, and when ques-

tioned as to our names, we replied that we did not know them. Eventually, I think, most of the internment orders were served.

As a reprisal, the gas fittings in the cells were torn down by the military police while the men were at exercise. Warned, I hid mine under the blankets. Another raiding party found them, but as I was in bed they did not take them away. A further supply of piping was obtained by us; walls were channelled, the lead buried, joints soaped, cavities filled in with bread softened between the fingers, moistened in the whitewash that was scraped from off the walls of empty cells. The opening was hidden by hanging a coat or a photograph on a nail in front. A detachable tin jet that could screw into the opening, and a detachable stand to rest tin cans or saucepans on, completed the fittings. To the casual observer a cell did not contain gas pipes.

A ladder was left one day standing against a new sentry platform on the outer jail wall. I saw the ladder from the main window. That's a chance, I thought, but there's a hell of a drop on the far side.

George Gilmore, a boy from South Dublin, quiet faced, slow to speak, of a good fighting record, looked through the window. We were always anxious when Gilmore went to Mr. Greer to hear Service in the library; he would stuff his pockets with books from the shelves and he might be found out.

'There's a chance,' he remarked casually. 'The drop is worse than the sentries.'

He walked downstairs into the exercise ring, climbed the railings, ran hard towards the ladder. A few of us watched him. He was climbing the ladder; he had almost reached the top before the astonished sentries opened fire. The sharp lash of a rifle bullet; other shots. He held on to the top of the wall by his hands, then the hands went out of sight. Firing continued. Military police followed by the prison staff rushed into the wings to search. Men changed their cells to keep them guessing: they evidently thought that some whom they looked upon as important had escaped. After count in the evening they found out who it was, and next day, to our relief, we heard that he had not been wounded or retaken. O'Keeffe with his common sense had defeated all attempts at escape,

and now MacManus's military efficiency had meant the
escape of a prisoner. Wherever he was, O'Keeffe must have
laughed and slapped his unsoldierly thigh, as he emphasized
in singing Corkese: 'Nothin' escapes here but ghas.'

New locks were placed on all our cells and doors were put
in order. Our men were shut out in the exercise ring, then
brought in by twos and locked up in their cells. The intention
was to treat us as criminals. By night-time we were all locked
in.

Through the hole I talked with Paddy Fleming and we
decided to bore through to other cells and wait for orders
from the wing commandant. Paddy told me how to smash an
open door by swinging the hinge sharply back on a hard
bulky object. He had generally used his Bible in the British
jails. The door would then remain open until taken down and
new hinges put on it.

There was less noise than usual during the night, and no
taunting of sentries; the men knew that a crisis of some kind
was coming. Each in his own cell must have thought of how
to defeat the new scheme, or have felt the blankness that
comes when a prison door locks with a smash. Free State
Ministers had talked of putting us on trial. We would be
selected and sentenced to terms of imprisonment, and when a
number of others had been released from the camps and jails
there would be room in the prisons for those whom the
Staters intended to keep.

In the morning doors were opened in turn. Military police
doled out breakfast cell by cell; the sloppy tea was cold. Men
went to the latrine in the company of an armed guard. By
midday some locks were smashed and doors sprung out of
their hinges and the men who were free, in spite of police,
helped to smash other locks. Soon all doors hung at awkward
angles. Some of the military and CID drew guns. Men
rushed them, disarmed them and chased them out of the
gates of the wings. Their weapons were thrown out into the
circle. Men armed with door bolts, legs of tables, lumps of
wood and sections of gas piping, asked their officers to charge
the gate when the police next opened it and to get through to
the circle. They bayed wildly, shouting, asking to be led. The

worm had turned at last. The men showed that they had not
been cowed by long imprisonment. They were persuaded to
leave their makeshift weapons in their cells and wait for
instructions. Some of them chatted in groups and wondered
what would happen. The wing became quiet, as if not sure of
itself. Later, military police arrived in the circle, and Lewis guns
guns were placed in positions commanding the wings.

'We're for it now,' said Paddy Brennan, a youngster from
the north; 'we'll get it in the neck.'

We heard the noise of a heavy car in the yard. Sean Lemass
climbed on the table and looked through the cell bars.

'An armoured car beyond the exercise yard,' he said, 'and
extra sentries on the walls.'

A sound of marching men. Soldiers with fixed bayonets
tramped into our wing; their heavy boots rattled on the stone
floor. I put a blanket over my pyjamas and stood near my
landing railings, looking down on to the floor below. The
wing was rectangular. One end looked into the circle, round
which were built the other wings. The opposite end faced the
yard; a large window high up gave plenty of light. The cells
were arranged on the remaining sides, opposite each other in
three rows. The second and third landings were of wood,
protected by iron railings; formerly a wire-netting stretched
across between the balconies so that prisoners could not
commit suicide. Below, men stood at their cell doors, or
walked around talking. Above, men leant over the balconies,
watching.

'GET TO YOUR CELLS,' the officer in charge of the
party roared. Nobody appeared to hear him. 'GET TO
YOUR CELLS AT ONCE.'

His voice boomed up through the wing. My nerves jumped
suddenly.

No one went into their cells.

The officer gave the order. 'Prepare to fire.'

The soldiers took a half-right turn and brought the rifles to
their shoulders, sighting along the barrels at the men who
stood in front of them.

'Fire!'

The volley went high.

Our wing commandant leaned over the balcony of the

second landing. 'To your cells,' he ordered. His voice reached
to the end of the wing. The men quickly obeyed. From the
other wings came the sound of shooting and of cheering.

What were they going to do now? Close the doors of the
cells and put on new locks, or remove us to other jails? I
heard a whistle blown and a voice shouted: 'Outside to the
exercise yard!'

Paddy Brennan looked out the door. 'It's only the Staters.'
He came in again.

The officer was left to blow his whistle and shout.

'They want us outside now,' I said. 'What's the idea?'

'I don't know,' said Paddy. 'Perhaps they don't know
themselves. They came here to find a mutiny, now they have
to make one.'

We laughed. Instructions came from our OC that we were
to resist removal, passively.

The Free State officers and police were on the lower landing, trying to make the men leave their cells. I heard a voice
shouting 'If you don't, I'll shoot', and the reply, 'Go to hell',
but no shot came. Another party of police arrived wearing
their green-glazed peaked caps. Men were carried from their
cells, struggling and twisting whilst they were hustled and
struck by the police, but they did not hit back. This was going
to take some time. Hoses were brought on to the three landings. Streams of water at high pressure were turned on the
cells and the prisoners, but they remained within as long as
they could. Our adjutant marked the doors of sick men with a
large white cross and the police were notified. On the top
landing the jet was weak; there was not sufficient pressure.
The nozzle was placed down the backs of our men while the
police held their arms; they should have a taste of the water,
too. I heard a group on my landing shout: 'Now, boys,
ready!', and saw them rush forward, seize the hose pipe and
slash at it with knives. The nozzle was out of action, but the
holes served as a watering-can to drench anybody near at
hand.

Water swished, swirled and flowed down the landing.
Police found the work more difficult on the second and third
landings as men clung to doors, to the iron railings and to the
narrow, circular winding stairway which had room for one at

a time. On the ground floor cells were now vacant. I saw the attackers turn the hoses into empty cells. They tore down shelves and fixtures, which floated out mixed with books and clothing. The police became more excited. They kicked and struck the men, they shouted and cursed. Some used the butts of revolvers and rifles on the heads and clinging hands. The police on the ground floor roared approval. 'Plug the bastard.' 'Knock him stiff.' 'Use your bloody bayonet.' At the door leading to the exercise yard our men had to run the gauntlet. Some of them lost their tempers and hit back. They told the officers and police what they thought of them, and threw a new light on their ancestry. I got back to bed as I was cold standing in the wet.

I placed a basin of dirty water near the head of my bed, intending to throw it at the first officer or NCO who entered my cell in charge of a raiding party. A few of the sick men had had their cells hosed already.

An officer came into my cell. Police stood at the door.

'What's your name?' he asked.

I did not reply. We had been ordered not to answer any questions.

'Get out of bed. There's nothing wrong with you.'

'No, I won't.'

He took hold of the fur rug and tugged. I raised the basin. 'If you don't let that rug alone, I'll give you a wash.'

He let go the rug. One of the police came near the bed. 'It's O'Malley. Nobody is going to touch him while we are here.'

The officer turned quickly and walked out. The policeman who had spoken linked arms with the others and they stood outside the door. One of them called out and three more linked on and would not permit anybody to enter.

I could hear the noise of our men being removed. Some were dragged along the floor of the landing. I saw between the legs of my police guard our OC, Mick Price, pass along, his lips tightened, clutching at the legs of those who tried to carry him and at the railings. Hours later the last man had reached the yard. The prisoners were told they would be given food if they came in one by one, but they refused to eat unless their own food orderlies gave it out. It was a hard cold day. Men were outside in thin, worn, wet clothes. Catcalls, yells and song came up from the yard. A boy who was sick came into my cell. He moved over the table beneath the small window, stood on it and looked out through the bars.

'They're walking round the ring, and running to keep warm, and the armoured car is slouching about. Some of the sentries have Lewis guns pointed at our lads. I wouldn't put it past them to shoot.'

We gathered blankets from near-by cells and dropped them through a broken window. I stood on the table. Some of the iron bars ringing the circular exercise enclosure had been pulled up. Beyond that, the high stone wall, about twenty feet high, covered with barbed wire. Sentries stood on platforms erected on high poles. The neighbouring wing ran in at an angle to join the end of ours. Some of the men were sitting down; they looked very wet and scrawny with misery. A few had blankets wrapped around them; others walked, played leap-frog, chased each other, or sang loudly. A number were delicate; they would find the night hard. We collected fruit from the cells. We dropped oranges and apples down to them but were told to cease; there would not be enough to go round.

Night came. It was cold enough in my cell, though I had a pile of brown army blankets under the rug. Searchlights brightened up the yard; the mild purr of the armoured car would be heard. A noise of crackling wood and a glare. Men must have broken through the iron railings to raid a supply of building timber in the basement. Whenever I woke up I could hear men singing during the night, and the hiss of burning wood; when I looked out they were walking or taking turns by the fire.

Next day the prisoners still refused to eat. Even the acknowledged touts and spies who were present in each wing threw in their lot with us. The songs and yells came at more frequent intervals. Police came to my cell from time to time; some handed me packets of cigarettes. 'Give them to the lads outside,' they said, then slipped away quickly as if afraid they would be noticed. I threw out the cigarettes and men went through the railings for them; they were received with cheers. Small pieces were handed around and puffed with enjoyment. A milk cart and a bread cart passed by on the way to the kitchen, and men scrambled over or through the railings and captured the supplies. The noise increased after the food had been doled out. The fires were burning low; a group got through the railings with the intention of raiding the basement for more wood. Some of the sentries on the walls shouted: 'Go ahead, we won't fire,' and heavy lengths of timber were carried out and added to the glowing embers. I heard a 'ma-aa, ma-a-a, ma-a-a' outside. They were imitating the bleat of a goat. There was a pet goat well known to all of us and friendly to some. Now friendship was forgotten, but the goat must have guessed. He kept away from all four exercise rings.

Late that evening, MacManus, the extra-military governor, had to admit defeat. The hungry prisoners marched in, singing; some making music out of combs covered with thin paper. We were hungry ourselves for we had not been given food whilst the others remained outside. On the first day the Deputy Governor Fitzpatrick came over to my cell with a pot of tea. I had met him on parade in Co. Fermanagh in 1919, when I had spent half the night with a small company in a deserted house. I drank the tea, but told him I could not accept any more food until our men were brought in. There were no hospital cases from the continued exposure. Men seemed to lose thought of the body, of themselves, in such a resistance. Boys came to my cell and told little humorous incidents of the lock-out. All were heartened and cheered, but what would come next, we wondered.

Parcels and letters would not be delivered to our orderlies; individual prisoners would have to come to the gate. Men were ordered to cells several hours earlier than was usual.

Mick Price tried to set an example by scrubbing out his cell daily, but discipline was only readily followed in what was thought a matter of principle. In the evenings, at about seven-thirty, he stood on the wire-netting of the second balcony, after military police had roared: 'To your cells.' The order was ignored. Men strolled about, or leant over the balcony to chat, until sentries fired from the centre. Price then ordered: 'C wing to your cells,' and our men obeyed. From the netting he read out general and routine orders. A shout from below. 'Get to your cell.' The voice read on. A roar. 'GET TO YOUR CELL.' Shots echoed up the wing. His figure was clear against the whitewashed wall of the landing but he continued calmly, without hurry or excitement. 'A fountain pen has been found on'—*BANG*—'the first landing; if the owner applies to the'—*BANG*—*BANG*—flakes of plastered mortar fell on the landing floor—'adjutant he can have his pen. The food orderlies for tomorrow'—*BANG*—'Get in YOU BASTARD'—'will be . . .', and the even voice went on to the end. Evening after evening I shut my teeth at the rifle noises and waited, nervously expecting him to fall to the floor below. I was limp and trembling by the time I heard him walk back to his cell on my landing. A few boys who ducked their heads out of doors were hit by splinters.

Exercise was restricted; sanitation and the cleanliness of the wing were interfered with, and gradually the attempt to ignore our prison organization under our own officers increased in intensity. It looked as if the attempt meant the beginning of a determined plan to treat us as criminals. Underground communication became more difficult, but it was still maintained and copies of *Sinn Fein* were now printed on a special onion paper for camps and jails, and orders and letters from our General Headquarters were typed on the same thin paper so that despatches would be less bulky.

Parcels, letters, books and papers were prohibited. Exercise was further limited. Men were driven to cells by rifle fire. No order was carried out save soldiers and police produced their only authority, rifle or revolver. They had to draw guns continually.

We had to make out on prison food now. Jail food was never palatable, only the milk was good. Tea was always a mystery. It might be better or worse, it might be coffee or tea, it might be anything. Soda was added to it in the kitchen to break the monotony and to help us try our ingenuity in analysing the contents. Meat which was good raw was boiled to rags; it came hard and dry. It might have made a good substitute for leather. 'Leather up!' was the shout for dinner. Soup was possible to taste if one added enough pepper to stimulate taste buds. Friday meant one good meal, boiled rice, which was invariably good, and we thanked our stars that we were yet considered to be Catholics. Luckily, I was able to get a little tea through some convicted men in the civil wings; the tea made up for the food I could not eat. The stoppage of parcels must have meant a big saving to people outside. Some women sent much more than they could afford; often they must have gone hungry to lavish luxuries on their men folk. I often wondered if some of our men realized that.

Further restrictions were imposed, and the attempt continued to break down resistance and methodically deprive us of privileges, so that eventually our captors could impose criminal status by degrees, and use its acceptance as an excuse to apply it to newly arrested prisoners. They had not learned the lesson that the British had, when numbers of our men were in prison.

Free men cannot be kept in jail, for their spirits are free, and jail for political prisoners is always a duel. We were not prisoners of war, no prisoner had been conceded political rights, and the duel went on. Positions are usually reversed, for jailers and warders have to peep and pry, to be ever on the alert, to glue their eyes to keyholes, to listen at cell doors, and to deal with what to them is an unknown quantity—the spirit of freedom.

There was a tendency to think in terms of one's immediate surroundings: food; warders, their sayings and doings, their tricks of speech and idiosyncrasies. Sometimes one would discover that a greater part of one's thoughts was taken up with the trivial happenings of the day, the doings of the little automatons that help to keep one captive. That is the danger point. In our code it is the duty of prisoners to prove that they cannot be influenced by their surroundings, or affected by the personalities of jailers. A prisoner must reverse their whole system, place them in the position of prisoners, make them concentrate on petty doings and sayings, limit their minds to the confines of prison walls. Make the enemy feel a jailer but be free himself. Prisoners have to maintain a constant fight to prevent being dominated by what is around them. Individual as well as co-ordinated action is always necessary to enable men to realize that only by such organization can they realize their strength and effectively nullify or destroy a prison system.

Sean Lemass was released. The body of his brother, Noel,

murdered by CID and missing for months, had been found on a lonely bog patch in the Dublin mountains.

There were a few courses open. To smash the prison, to attempt to fight our way out, or to hunger-strike. There were those in favour of each plan, but an order would be obeyed by practically all in the jail. In the meantime tunnels were being prepared; the shaft for them went down through the prison wall to the basement, and men worked harder than ever as officers might be sent to other jails in an attempt to destroy our organization. Fighting our way out appealed to many. Jail had weakened the men physically, and on some the strain of the past six years was beginning to show. It was thought a better thing to die fighting than to die on hunger-strike, yet this had to be ruled out. In the action, Staters would be killed, and reprisals would assuredly be taken against the unfortunate prisoners remaining.

A hunger-strike was discussed informally. I had always disliked such an idea because I was afraid of it, and also to me it was an unsoldierly way to die, or to face death.

I had been sick for over six weeks, and was confined to bed practically all day. I could eat but little of the prison fare, and I seemed to be letting go hold on life, for it had been a continuous fight to attempt to regain health under prison conditions. I had learned to doctor myself: at night, when I could not sleep, to relax all my muscles, leave my body passive, and allow my mind to rest. This seemed to compensate as much as sound sleep would. To lie quiet and let the pain flow through, not to resist it by tension and muscular activity. Learning to get rid of serious thought; avoid any unnecessary movement; never to get into an argument; to lower the pitch of the voice. Most of all it was important to control one's temper. For any expression of irritability or of ill humour meant exhaustion and prostration, so my physical condition helped to produce some form of equanimity.

Other officers opposed hunger-striking, perhaps because they were afraid of it, but more likely because we had since the death of Terence MacSwiney regarded it as an obsolete weapon. In the jail phraseology, 'it had died of wounds'. We knew what mercy we might expect from our enemy. A strike for prisoner-of-war or political treatment was one thing. A strike for unconditional release was another. Yet a cease fire order had been issued in May, and it was now October. The Free State had little excuse for still keeping large numbers of men in prison.

It was finally decided to declare a strike for unconditional release, and volunteers were asked for. It would have been better to have selected a number of really determined men, who might have been more fitted for such an ordeal than the heterogeneous complement of the four wings.

CHAPTER FIFTEEN

OCTOBER—NOVEMBER 1923

THE jail went on strike on 13 October. Practically all volunteered; some were exempted, including myself, but I refused this concession.

Any action was good, it seemed, and everyone was more cheerful when the hunger-strike began. We listened to the tales of men who had undergone previous strikes and we, who were novices, wondered what it would be like. We laughed and talked, but in the privacy of our cells some, like myself, must have thought what fools we were, and have doubted our tenacity and strength of will. I looked into the future of hunger and I quailed. I had been without food often enough; I had been sick from lack of it, but hunger itself was a gaunt thought built up by the desperate associations of other people's experiences.

What would it be like at the end of two or three days, then when a week had gone by? Hunger-striking was an unknown quantity for me; I did not approve of it; I was frankly afraid, but I could not see young boys of sixteen and eighteen take their chance whilst I could eat and be excused. The first four or five days were bad, violent headache and nausea, yet all, except those bedridden like myself, were able to walk about and keep their thoughts off food, while reading or yarning in one another's cells.

Father MacMahon came in to see me. He shook his head when he talked of the hunger-strike and wondered if any agreement could be reached, but he was surprised when he found that I was on hunger-strike also and withdrew, perturbed. A month before, men were permitted to receive the Sacraments but few did so; prisoners at any time by signing the form could have gone to Communion. Some men had become violently anti-clerical, but many thought the whole greater than the part, and that a Church should be judged by its spirit rather than by its ministers. We had learned to interpret the Catholic faith in terms of our daily life. I had told the chaplain that the men were very embittered; they would remember his sermons at Mass, and his visits to cells only when he heard they were reading the King James Bible. If he really wanted the men to go to the Sacraments and had the interests of the Church at heart, he should leave the jail and ask for a successor. He withdrew officially from the prison. I liked him for that.

We learned that other jails and camps had decided to strike out of sympathy with us, and that soon thousands of men were depriving themselves of food. This weakened our chance of success. We had not meant to make a gesture, but knowing the enemy we had counted the cost and were prepared to face death if release was not granted.

I wondered how long I could last; two weeks, I thought, since I had been sick for the past month, seldom out of bed. I had become thinner. The favourite end of an argument was my being lifted up and carried around. That made me power-less, speechless, and I had to keep quiet. Jail had been a con-stant struggle, a determined effort to recover health, a fight against the drabness, the lack of colour, the oppressive brutality of the very stones. Jail life is a slow poison even in the case of a healthy man, a poison more of the mind than the body. I had been drifting; the sense of struggle was beginning to be absent. Now, even though one thought one's death would be of use, there was no passive acceptance. It was a challenge, a fight, and again resistance was built up. The slow adjustment of the body to the new conditions was pain-ful, but the body seems to have an infinite power of adjustment.

I felt that it would not always be as it was at first. Soon the mind with its fears would begin to make its influence felt more and more. The mind would suffer more than the body. The struggle in the end would be between mind and spirit. Perhaps the suffering of the past years would now provide a reserve of strength. In our cells, we discussed these aspects; men wrapped in blankets squatting on the floor around my bed like Bedouins. There was no morbidity, no vain regrets. Often the conversation partook of a Socratic dialogue. We were like eager searchers for the truth of things.

A doctor from the outside, a heart specialist, visited the prison and examined me. He had evidently been sent in by my people. I refused to be examined at first, then permitted him to sound and percuss, for his conclusions would not interfere with my decision.

He said that I was in a very weak condition, undernourished, and that a hunger-strike would prove fatal in a very short time. I asked him not to visit prisoners again, as it would serve no useful purpose but would impose an additional strain on our relatives outside. His visit was illogical; to inform a prisoner who intended to strike that he was in poor condition, then tell his parents he would not stand much of a chance if he continued, seemed to me a stoking up of anticipatory fears.

One night, about a week after the commencement of the strike, some of us were removed to Kilmainham jail. Mick Price, our OC, and Sean MacBride escaped en route, from their ambulance.

I was back again in the jail where the British had imprisoned me in 1921, but I was put in a different wing. There were about sixty of us, mostly senior-officers; our company was good. Seoirse Plunkett, Austin Stack, Billy Pilkington, Frank Gallagher, Bob de Courcy, Peader O'Donnell, David Robinson, Mick Kilroy, Tom Derrig and Gerry Boland; we renewed our acquaintance where we had left it, and discussed events of the years or months we had been separated. I met my friends in strange places. Here were confined some of the men one would most like to associate with, if one had been given one's choice of selecting companions. The Free State had helped to bring together men who had been parted for years, or to introduce them to each other, some who had up to this been names merely. Now we could talk at leisure and learn to know each other in ways we would not have dreamt of, had we met outside prison walls.

At times the hunger was worse than at others. Then there would be a peaceful interval, to be followed by a bad attack. I was kept to my bed, my legs would not hold me, but the majority of the others were able to walk around and pay visits.

Our minds ran on food. I thought of all the houses, area by area, in Ireland where I could have had good meals if I had asked for them. I tabulated the places I could visit, if released, and make amends for my previous reticence in eating. I should tell them exactly what I liked and should have my favourite dishes cooked in the way I suggested. I was full of vain regrets about food. I analyzed menus, puzzled out the recipes from soups to caviar, and what information I lacked was supplied by some of the others, David Robinson, Frank Gallagher or Seoirse Plunkett. Seoirse discussed fricassés and omelettes, explained in detail how I could make homemade sweets and candies; David told me of vintage wines and champagne, of good food in general; Frank invented succulent delicacies which might not stand the test of actual preparation. We all invented dishes. The prison was like a chef's research laboratory. The first man to visit me in the morning learned the menu of my imaginary breakfast and then supplied his own, striving to outvie mine. We laughed and chafed each other and wondered how long we could last.

Billy Pilkington came with a *Caesar* in his hand. He was trying to learn Latin; he intended to join a religious order on release. I tried to remember my Latin, juggling the meaning of a sentence when I felt I knew every word of it. Billy often said: 'I think I know as much Latin as you do yourself.'

The hunger-strike was not approved of outside; the responsibility was left to those inside, but once it began a bureau was opened and a 'stop press' came regularly. Our publicity was active and frequently we received copies of our papers giving us an account of conditions in the other jails and camps. The information was often inaccurate enough about our own jail, Kilmainham; whoever was responsible for forwarding reports, I do not know, but they provided us with a laugh when we read of our exaggerated state, which was generally described as extremely grave. Men who were reported as dying, often came into my cell and laughed with me. Sean Buckley, an elderly man, was bad. Paddy Fleming had been released. Austin Stack and Bob de Courcy, of the compressed-air gun, were losing their memories.

We had been refused the Sacraments whilst on hunger-

strike. Church and State were united in breaking us. Then
suddenly the priests decided to administer them, and some of
us were able to receive Holy Communion every morning.
That strengthened us. I had been reported as dangerously ill,
and was given Extreme Unction by one of the chaplains.
Their demeanour had changed. They had come to visit us
with adamantine minds; were we not criminals, looters and
robbers? But the personal contact had made a difference.

I read practically all the time. My chief difficulty was to
hold a book or lie at such an angle that I could read. I
chuckled with Mark Twain and adventured with Huckleberry
Finn and Tom Sawyer; admired that splendid villain from
Ballantrae; pilgrimaged with Chaucer; followed the Dutch
people in their stubbornly heroic wars in the Low Countries,
also the indomitable Cortez and Pizarro, exploring the
downfall of Spain. I laughed with Pickwick, and thought of
the food that had built his rotund form; selected proverbs
from Sancho Panzo, and wondered how the lean knight
would have tilted a hunger-strike. In Tartary and Thibet I
followed Abbé Huc, admiring his calm acceptance of reverse
and misfortune, and his unconquerable will. Doughty in
Arabia, sick, weary, hungry, unafraid. The archaic, stilted,
difficult English bouldering the epic of harsh gutted men and
the lean mawed beauty of the desert. *Moby Dick,* epic of the
sea and of the hunt for the soul of man. *Suibhne Geilt,* madness
in beauty, and the *Tain Bo Cuailnge.* Each of us had now to
face the ford of death, to keep away the hosts of fears and
worldly cravings. Could we hope for the *gae bulga* of courage
to shatter them at the last? I re-read those books I had always
loved. The *Tain* brought up Nannie; where she had learned
the story I could not guess. Seldom our people knew of it save
through books. There was a red-covered book which I tried to
remember, *The Lost Cause;* we had read it as children. It had
backed our ideas of kingly respect, gathered from fairy tales,
and made us take sides for a Stuart king against the
Cromwellians in a losing fight. Jane Austen's books I had
read and re-read as they seemed particularly suitable for
reading in bed. They were uneventful, quiet, peaceful; she
laughs gently at the snobs she often portrays, and gradually a
section of English society emerges.

Icelandic sagas gave a grim touch, an icy breath, a stark nudity of clear incident; their lack of ornament suited the bare cell walls. Hakluyt's *Voyages*, and Conrad, took me out again to the sea I had loved. Costa made Spanish dominion laughable, but the Dutch were rid of it; perhaps we, too, could laugh in the same way at the English. Plutarch's *Lives* brought back boyhood memories of Thucydides, Cato and Brutus. Vasari told his biased, gossipy tales of Italian painters. I went back to my old friends for comfort, for ease of life, for amusement.

I could read in peace, anyhow, as one was seldom disturbed. Doctors took blood pressures and examined us occasionally. I objected, as it would serve no purpose as far as I was concerned, yet the doctors came, and eventually I did not refuse their tappings and examinations. I asked them to take notes on our condition. It might be of use in the physiology of starvation and its psychological effects, if they were interested in that side of it. The medical men were not interested; as individuals they did not want us to die.

'Why don't you smile?' one asked.

I did not see anything amusing in him, I might have replied, but he thought I was stiffening against him because he represented something hostile.

'I don't see anything to smile at,' I said.

I was given a heated water-bed; perhaps they were determined I would not die on land, but in a lukewarm way. Bed sores had to be warded off, as we were gradually getting thinner; I had become almost immune to them since I left Portobello hospital. My hip was like a board. I was almost immune to fleas.

Some days I found it hard to read. There was too much to remember; shades of meaning in an action, the many-sided implications of a situation or of a remembered state of mind, the uncertainty of one's own actions, the little things that determine those of others and the melancholy of individual living. Books could not satisfy then; frustrations, incompleteness, strivings, half shades, the fleeting perishable sense of beauty and the inevitability of death.

The general strike in the camps had broken, but in every prison and camp a nucleus remained, whose numbers were

daily being reduced. The women had gone on strike, too, and
we knew that there would be no faltering where they were
concerned. In the Joy, an officer in charge of a wing came off
strike and signed the form. He had been anxious for a strike
before it began.

Frank Aiken, the Chief of Staff, asked me to send a message to the men in other camps and jails to encourage them. I
refused to do that. I was not responsible for the hunger-strike.
I was opposed to it; I did not know if I could maintain it
myself, and I was not going to ask other men to continue the
strike. That was for the individual to decide for himself. I did
send a message to say that I was glad to be of some use again,
and that men could not be beaten unless they were beaten in
their hearts.

Hunger seemed to come in spells, but concentration on
other things such as reading and writing helped to keep our
minds away from the most important subject, that of food.
We thought we would not be released until a good number
had died. We knew the type of enemy we were fighting, and
we felt that Kilmainham with its small number of prisoners
was in a better position than other jails to maintain the strike.
Already it had lasted more than four weeks; many of the men
were still able to walk around, to come in and chat with me,
but others were confined to their cells, some because they
were ill, others because they wished to conserve their energy.
As the days wore on, I could see that it became increasingly
difficult to refrain from taking food. The orderlies suggested it
in a compassionate way, and one found one's will beginning
to weaken. Water had become disagreeable, its taste was flat,
even metallic, although salt added to heated water seemed to
improve it. In the Joy we had at first added pepper, but the
monotony was deadly, always the same taste. If people who
spoke highly of their refreshing 'ale of Father Adam' had to
partake of nothing else for over twenty-eight days, they would
soon realize how unpalatable that beverage might become.

The unimportant tissues, seemingly, are first affected; the
unimportant muscles waste, then more vital organs are
attacked, memory and sight impaired. My people sent the
family doctor in to see me. I refused at first, then consented.
He had served in the European war, and afterwards had

attended clinics in Vienna after the ending of hostilities.
There, he had been able to observe the effects of the new war,
the organized hunger-blockade by the Allies on non-
combatants. Poverty-stricken students attended clinics; often
they had two books to a whole class; they were barely able to
walk, and their legs seemed to behave more like stilts than
living tissue.

'When muscle wastes too much it cannot repair,' he said.
'Your back and thigh muscles are far gone now.'

He examined me thoroughly, muttering between instru-
ments. 'What a constitution.'

He thought more of the ruin of a good constitution than of
anything else. This attitude I liked, and sitting up I laughed.
He looked surprised but chatted away.

'I can only give professional advice, but you won't take
that. It's hard on me to have to examine you. I wouldn't like
to be a soldier in your army,' he said, as he packed his bag. 'A
man is tested there in too many ways.'

My back was painful. I lay on my sides in turn as much as
possible until my arms became numb, then I turned face
downwards. Pieces of metal in my back pressed on tender
spots, on the small nerve links. Alternatively I lay on pins or
had the ache of bad teeth in my back. It was wearying, there
was little rest. There was the sense of fatigue, which is almost
pleasant in itself, but mentally one knew there would be no
end to it. The danger was in thinking of one's body in terms
of self-pity. Sentimentality had to be fought, as well as hunger
and the strife in the mind. I could laugh at myself, anyhow,
and jeer at my body. A sense of humour, a stark grimness, to
be cultivated.

The pains and aches might relieve somebody else who was
suffering outside; the sum total of misery might be decreased.
I might attract more than my share. Courage and fear can be
transferred; why not pain? Anyhow, pains are deserved for all
our misdeeds in thought and word and act.

The adjustment between mind and body had lost its har-
mony, there was disproportion. The mind was too clear, too
active. It ran ahead of itself while the body dragged along
plaintively. I had to attempt a constant readjustment; to tone
down the velocity of the mind which sprang freshly from one

hurried thought to another, or whirled them around together.
Sometimes I could concentrate clearly on an idea, then
restlessness would cease. A clarity that made me see the
futility of much previous thought would result. This was the
time to solve problems. Then some extraneous thought would
intrude and it would battle for possession; one's sense of
space widened out with the fight, but the result would mean a
leap forward in restless nervousness.

The attitude of our jailers changed; they had become more
kindly, the strike had affected them. The prison censor was
stout. He carried in parcels of books. He would stand and
look down at me, pity on his face.

'My God, I can't eat now. Why don't they release you? I've
only known you by hearsay; why don't they release you?'

There was now no difficulty in getting notes out, and often
our mail was bulky. It is cheering when sick to receive letters,
but to be given a pocketful of long letters written on thin
paper from friends one had not seen for years, was exciting
and delightful. David Robinson was adjutant of the jail and
had much work to do. Parcels continued to pour in, and he,
provided with a long list in hand, visited cell after cell and
saw that the office delivered everything due to the individual
person. He had been invalided for some years after the
European War by reason of wounds. Normally he was thin;
the strike had told on him, perhaps, more than it had on us,
for we had regarded it more or less as a weapon, but he had
never done so. Day after day he grew thinner and tottered
more as he walked, but he carried out his duties meticulously.
Halts to check his list became longer and longer in each cell
as the days wore on. We admired him most of all for we knew
he suffered additional pain.

A few prisoners had lost their memory; some seemed somewhat crazed. We looked, and wondered when our turn would
come.

Bob de Courcy, with a haggard grey face, came to my cell.
His hair looked grey. 'It's funny, but I can't remember anything about the Tan war,' he said. He put his head between
his hands. 'Not a thing.'

I was yet able to read steadily and to think clearly during
the day, but I could not sleep. My eyes had become fixed and

staring from facing the bare gas-jet which had been turned on at full pressure. I tried to count the nights I had been without sleep, and remembered from physiology that a dog will die more quickly from lack of sleep than from lack of food. Visitors said I must sleep without knowing it.

The gas-jet danced and changed its outline. The twisting shapes were not easy on the eyes for I had been turned to face the door and the jet was above the sill. It threw shadows on the whitened walls. The shapes became coloured. They leapt forward at me; I felt I could hear them shriek, but it was the gas noise. Fantastic thought-shapes came out of that jet until I thought I was losing what reason I had left. You must not eat, I'd say to myself, then say it aloud. 'Do you hear, you must not eat.' I did not take sleeping draughts though some of the prisoners advised me to try them.

I noticed the resistance had slackened somewhat. Men had evidently become more depressed, and some, at this late moment, had begun to realize that the Free State meant to allow us to die. Some men talked to me of their wives. They should have thought of them before the strike, I felt, but it was no dishonour for a man to break strike. There would be enough, I told them, to last out. Hunger-striking was not a fair test, anyhow; it seemed to attack the spirit more than the body, and the situation in the camps had obviously affected our morale. The camps had practically all broken the strike, although a few still held out strongly, as did numbers in Mountjoy. David Robinson had been promised release if he agreed to take food. This decision had been arrived at due to pressure from some of his influential friends in England, one of whom had visited Dublin and had interviewed Mulcahy, but David was still refused release even after he had taken food.

The chaplain came to see me one day and found me reading Plato's *Republic*. He was very much distressed at the continuance of the strike.

I said to him: 'It is strange, Father, that we who suffer for our country, might not suffer for our spiritual development.'

'They are the same thing, my son.'

A Cork prisoner, Commandant Dennis Barry, died in camp whilst on hunger-strike, and Andy O'Sullivan was removed to hospital in a dying condition. Various public bodies had petitioned for the release of the prisoners, but it seemed that Barry's death had hardened the resolve of the Free State Cabinet. Barry's body was refused entry to a Cork church by Bishop Cohalan, who stated that:

Republicanism in Ireland for the last twelve months has been a wicked and insidious attack on the Church and on the souls of the faithful committed to the Church by the law of the Catholic Church.

We had been informed that the Free State officials were weakening but that this decided them to refuse any concessions at all. Another prisoner was reported dangerously ill. I was said to be in a very weak condition.

There did not seem to be any hope, but I think the greater number of us did not very much mind. We had faced death before, a quick death, now it was a lingering one, but we had time to prepare, we had our good comrades near us, we were able to receive Holy Communion daily, and we were content. All carnal thoughts seemed to disappear after the first four weeks. One could realize why the early Christians and the priests of Eastern religions fasted and mortified the body. The result seems to be a state of exultation in which one is removed from worldly thoughts and cares, where one obtains a clarity of mind difficult to realize when engaged in the ordinary course of existence.

On 23 November, the commandant of the jail, Michael Kilroy, consulted with some of the officers and decided to end the hunger-strike. Tom Derrig and David Robinson were sent to Mountjoy, to the girls in the North Dublin Union, and to the Curragh camps, to inform the other hunger-strikers of the decision.

After forty-one days the strike had collapsed without any definite promise of release. We had been defeated again, and although some wanted to continue the strike, yet they all agreed to fall in with the majority. I expect many of us spent the same miserable hours in our cells as I did, after the decision had been arrived at.

Tom Derrig after his visit to the Joy, had a story. One of

the men there, on the last day of the strike, had said to a
doctor: 'What day of the strike is this?'

'The forty-first.'

'Be cripes, we bate Christ be a day.'

We were given a little beaten-egg and brandy at intervals;
then we passed through all the feeding stages of babyhood.
Neaves food, extracts of malt, arrowroot biscuits, and milk.
One had to be very careful now, as the discipline of the first
week or more was as firm as that when on hunger-strike: the
danger lay in over-eating. Some who had exercised their will-
power during the strike, now in defeat seemed unable to
control it as parcels of food came pouring in from all quarters.
They disregarded warnings and ate lavishly. Our conversations would have delighted the members of a baby club:
discussions on the merits and demerits of predigested foods,
and of the building-up values of various types of liquid
nourishment.

CHAPTER SIXTEEN

DECEMBER 1923—MARCH 1924

CHRISTMAS was coming, and friends and relatives sent parcels and hampers of food. Hunger-strikers were to make up for their fast by an indulgence against the future.

On Christmas Day in Kilmainham cells glistened with holly, pine branches and the blood of oak; tables were taken from cells and laid end to end on the ground floor. David Robinson was busy ticking off lists of food. I could not leave my bed, or eat, but I could hear the feasting through my open door and watch the effect of bottles of wine on some of the others. This was my third Christmas in jail: the first with the Auxiliaries in Dublin Castle; the second in the hospital cell of the Joy; next Christmas where would I be? The thought of Christmas made me feel lonely.

On New Year's Day all prisoners were ordered to pack up. Police said we were going to the Curragh internment camps. Huge boxes were filled with food; Andy Cooney had a hamper of gargantuan size. He sorted and repacked it, stuffing in food, his chief worry was to wonder if it would get through the smaller doors to the main gate. The men were afraid of another spell of hunger.

I was not able to walk. The Free State officer in charge of the escort wanted to have me removed in blankets, but after a heated discussion I was left behind.

I was alone in the jail. My friends had cooked for me; now my meals were scanty. A medical orderly came near me at long intervals, but nobody cooked or heated my food.

Three days later I was handcuffed, then put on a stretcher to St. Bricin's military hospital on the heights above the river Liffey. I was kept in a private room for a short while, then placed in a large ward with our own wounded and sick.

I heard one of them say as I was brought in: 'For God's

sake, what do they want with a poor ould man like that?'

It was Peter Hegarty who spoke.

My beard had grown since the beginning of the hunger-strike, my hair was wild, unkempt, dull from lack of sun, and my cheeks were sunken. I did not recognize myself when I looked in a mirror.

One morning a French barber, in frock coat and silk hat, came into the ward. He rolled up his sleeves, and without covering his coat he began to operate and succeeded in getting rid of my beard, seemingly by main force, as he was very sparing in his use of soap. Half way through the ordeal I asked him to stop, but as he seemed insulted, I allowed him to continue. He told me, in French, that he had daily shaved Eamon de Valera, who was imprisoned on his own and guarded by CID. De Valera had been instructed by the acting President, Padraig Ruttledge, not to go on hunger-strike.

Peter Hegarty had a waxen yellow face, like old cheese in the daytime, at night under the electric light it was ivory. His hair was a sombre reddish-brown. He cursed steadily; his pain was severe. 'Be jaysus' was the emphasis, and perhaps his clarification, of every sentence. I told him his use of bad language was unscientific. The edge of his anger and its relief in cursing would be dulled, and in the end when he would really want to curse, he would not know how.

He used to lift himself on his elbows, look at me in a perky way, and say: 'Do you tell me that now?'

Wounded after surrender, his hip had been made *bruscar* of by a rifle bullet. The wound had been neglected, now recovery was thought impossible.

'Before I was hit,' he told me, 'I was that innocent I could go into a field and ate grass with the lambeens.' Evidently he thought his language depravity. In Athlone a priest had told him that his suffering in the next life was atoned for; he had suffered more than his share through the pain of wounds. 'So I can curse me fill, now,' said Peter, 'and it won't be marked agin me.'

Next bed to him was a Kerry boy, Foran. Hegarty and Foran fought like the two old friends and enemies in *The Workhouse Ward*. Peter had a quick, biting tongue. 'It'd raise blisters on ye.' Foran had sudden anger, the lines of his high cheek bones would glow, but compassion kept him quiet. He had been newly married; he read his letters often under the fire of Peter's shots.

Mulcahy, Free State Minister for Defence, had visited Peter in Bricin's. Peter told the story.

'In he comes with all his trappin's and bends over me bed.

' "What happened to you, me man?" says he, as grand as the Prince of Wales.

' "Shot with me hands up," says I, "be a bloody Stater, and his rifle not ten fate from me, be jaysus." '

We laughed.

'What did he say then?' I asked.

'Divil a word,' said Peter. 'That knocked all his grand sympathy out of him.'

In the corridor a military policeman was on duty. Two armed Free State officers were appointed to guard me; they sat in the ward, in turn, near my bed. At night the electric light in my corner was left burning, so I found it difficult to sleep. The officers had a boring time. To me they were as the scene shifters in a Chinese play, who were supposed to be invisible to the actors.

One had become so accustomed to the prison cell that it was hard to realize the nature of one's present surroundings. The ward was bright and airy, with many windows, painted frames and chairs, floor waxed till it smelt efficiently, clean sheets and blankets. The colour was gay when one remembered jail, but the food was poor. In jail we could cook our own food and give parties; here was regulation and organized cleanliness.

Peter warned me about the nurse in charge of our ward. 'She's a voice like a bull-frog, and she's gintle as a jennet.'

She had a deep hoarse voice, a heavy step, and a brisk metallic appearance. That was unfortunate; a womanly nurse would have meant a good deal in a prisoner's life. She objected to books on top of my locker; she reported me to the medical officers for insubordination, but as I did not care whether I left the hospital or not, it had no effect. I refused to be awakened at five o'clock in the morning by the nurse going off duty, to have my pulse taken and a thermometer stuck in my mouth. It might help to fill a form, but it was difficult to sleep again due to the electric light.

Operations were performed on the prisoners, and the almost continuous atmosphere of banter was then changed, as in hushed silence we listened to the moans of our friends.

Bob de Courcy, who was now the Mayor of Limerick, arrived. His memory was dim, his face still haggard.

'By golly, you mean to tell me I was on hunger-strike forty-one days? I don't know how I did that. Are you serious now?'

Slowly I led him back to the Tan war. He had forgotten much, but he remembered his compressed-air gun; in time he thought of incidents, but when I spoke of what had happened only last year, his face had a puzzled, dull look.

Later he entertained us with stories, legends and ballads of his native city; he seemed to know the very stones of it; he led us through the streets of Irishtown and told us where the remnants of the walls of the city could be yet seen. Soon we knew the beauties of the reaches of the Shannon and its tributaries, up towards Killaloe and the shores of Lough Derg; we could talk of fishing and shooting along the banks. I was able to supplement his knowledge of the river. When in Co. Roscommon, I had walked the bank from Lough Allen to Clonmacnois in Offaly, fifteen miles above Lough Derg; I was shown fords not marked on the ordnance maps, the bridge by which the French had crossed into Longford in 1798, the ford used by the Williamites before the Irish defeat at Aughrim in 1691. He told us of the method of finding dead bodies in the river, of lighted candles being floated down until they were caught in the eddies where the corpse was most likely to be found. We listened to amusing stories of land disputes, as he was an engineer and had prepared the plans of disputed territory. We heard about the faction fights in Newport and vicinity, of the Coffeys and Reaskawallahs; listened to legends of the siege of Limerick in Sarsfield's time, and eventually we knew the outstanding characters in the city. Some years ago, an officer of a Highland regiment stationed at Limerick asked about land marks long since destroyed. He had an intimate knowledge of Limerick in the seventeenth century, and later he explained that he had read

a detailed account of the siege in manuscript at his home in
Scotland, written by an ancestor of his, an engineering officer
responsible for the defences.

Bob's laugh was as hearty as ever. His toothed grin would
interrupt his own stories.

I was X-rayed and soon afterwards operated on, twice, with
local anaesthetics which did not seem to work. I tried to
remember what muscles the surgeon was cutting through,
and recalled the anatomical relations, whilst the knife seared
like a red-hot iron, and the forceps and probe produced the
sensation of a hammer hitting me hard in the back.

They were afraid to give me a general anaesthetic, and
though I did not look forward to the further operations I was
promised, yet I would have been glad to have the metal
removed, but for some reason the operations ceased.

* * * * * *

Unable to walk, I was removed to the Curragh hospital,
where the atmosphere was less depressing as the cases were
not so serious as in St. Bricin's. Tom Derrig was there, who
had been Adjutant of the Command, and then Adjutant-
General to Liam Lynch in Dublin. Tom's eye had been shot
out while he was a prisoner of the CID in Oriel House. 'The
bloody fools, they missed me,' he said. He told me of what
had happened down to his arrest. CID had increased. The
civilian intelligence department spread until there was an
agent on nearly every street. Our staff officers could move
about only after dark. Concealed rooms were made in greater
numbers; raids took place continuously; hiding-places had to
have supplies of food; often our officers remained hidden for
over twenty-four hours while the CID tapped the walls, took
measurements and dug up the floors. Noiseless typewriters
were used. It was difficult to find places to stay in; often the
children of a house did not know of the officers' presence. In
flats, the men and typists wore soft slippers so as to move
quietly. I could never have stood that slippered kind of life, I
thought. I would venture out anyhow and take my chance.

A mutiny threatening for some time in the Free State Army
had failed to make head; it was an offset from the men of the

IRB who had followed Collins and the Supreme Council of the Brotherhood. Officers and ranks had formed a secret oath-bound society and objected, so they said, to the anglicization of their army. Prominent officers had resigned, or had been forced to resign, all over the country, but they had been placed on the pension list. Fighting between the two sections was almost brought about by the action of Mulcahy, who, with the Adjutant-General, resigned after censure by the Free State parliament. The result was insecurity, and rumours of new combinations amongst our captors.

Our section of the Curragh hospital was by itself, less influenced by regulation it was gayer. There were men from Tipperary, Waterford, Cork, the midlands, Dublin, and they told stories of their townlands, legends, bitter or droll accounts of life and doings, and greed for land and money. They talked most about eccentric characters. Then the conversation would veer to the Tan war, finally to the civil war and jail.

A boy told us what they had to undergo in Kerry, and as usual relieved the grim tale by a joke. A Kerry prisoner arrived in Killarney, his face was swollen and bloody; he motioned with his hand to the departing green uniforms of his guard. 'Boys,' said he, *'the Tans are only a rumour.'*

Tadhg O'Sullivan, Brigadier of West Cork, was in the ward, and later Cooney from Tipp Three and others whom I knew arrived. Paddy Quinn from the Fourth Northern was near, very badly wounded; he had seen his brother die through neglect in the bed beside him. Tadhg O'Sullivan, who had been captured after the cease fire, related 'cap-in-the-fisth' experiences, with his men hunted in the rough mountains, and Staters everywhere as they had increased their strength for the big round-up. Tired out after an all-day tramp, in the night they would have to break through a fresh encircling cordon. He had been in one of the camps during the hunger-strike and told of the breakdown; how men, mad with hunger, armed with knives, had rushed the quartermaster's stores in the dark, slashing and hacking at raw meat and flitches of bacon, fighting to get at food. They did not wait to cook, but gorged it on the way back to their huts.

There was a prisoner from Longford who suffered from

sciatica, and when he heard a funny story he laughed immoderately, his face at times screwed up with pain as a twinge from his leg interrupted his laughter. We had learned to increase his hilarity by shouting at intervals when his voice had reached a certain pitch. Then his laugh which was dying would again revive and he would go into another spasm of laughter, interrupted by prayers and groans. By this time the ward would be nearly in a similar condition; then came a steady decline, until silence was restored and we recovered.

Cooney of Clonmel told me stories of Erskine Childers in the south, of his going to bed without dinner because men were expected to arrive during the night and he wanted to ensure that a fighting man would not go hungry. He had a good pair of boots at first, but he exchanged them for a worn pair on the feet of a column man, and repeated the process many times, until the once neat, naval lieutenant-commander walked in very torn, ragged boots.

'In the Comeragh mountains below Clonmel,' said a man from that town, 'there are parts that say you're not a Catholic if you don't believe in the banshee.'

The ward told of ghost-stories, and then lightened the eerie silence by song.

The saying:

> Ulster for a soldier,
> Connacht for a thief,
> Munster for learning,
> And Leinster for beef

was always bound to provoke controversy, and men defended their provinces at the expense of others. They were devoted to their counties, in a way I could not feel myself. Some carried a folklore memory that made them bitter about feuds of which they were hardly conscious.

One night a boy arrived from the Curragh camp, a dazed stare in his eyes. He seemed to look through and beyond the walls, his mouth opened and shut blankly as if he was repeating something to himself. He did not speak to any of us while he undressed, but got into bed. An hour later he got up, put his white shirt over his pyjamas and walking over to a window, with his palms joined and held on high, he began to conduct what was evidently a service, because we could hear scraps of Latin, and once he turned and faced us and murmured *Pax vobiscum*.

We watched him in amazement and spoke in whispers as we did not wish to disturb him. Was he sleep walking? A hospital orderly came in, and when he saw the boy at the window he put a finger to his lips as if requesting silence; then, moving over, told us that the newcomer was suffering from religious mania. He had been accustomed in his hut in the camp to say Mass, preach sermons, and hear confessions, often getting up in the middle of the night to do so. We wondered if he would read aloud any pastorals.

The new arrival, as he passed by me on the way back to his bed, winked. Then I remembered his face; he had been attached to one of the Dublin battalion staffs. In the night he got out of bed again and awakened some of us by hearing confession in a corner. We listened as he advised an imaginary penitent. 'How many times did you do it? . . . You must fight against such temptations, my child.'

Next day he talked a little, still appearing to be dazed. He sat on my bed. Had I any message to take out, he whispered; he was pretending to be mad and expected to be set free soon. That evening he was released.

A man from Paddy Quinn's northern division, who was now in the military police, had offered to help him escape but he was too badly wounded to walk. A way of escape was open for me if I was able to walk sufficiently, for a police uniform was smuggled in and hidden in the lavatory, but I was unable to utilize it as I could not walk far.

One day I had taken the uniform from its hiding-place to brush it, when the officer in charge of prisoners walked in on top of me. I sat on the floor, proceeded to take off my shoes and began to practise toe exercises, talking to him to distract his attention until I had managed to sit on the uniform.

I felt like a child's toy which had been taken to pieces and wrongly readjusted. I applied for massage treatment; soon my muscles would be too flaccid from lack of use. A masseuse tried to restore tone to my muscles, but before she had made my legs ready to bear me in an escape, I was moved to the Curragh camp.

CHAPTER SEVENTEEN

APRIL—JULY 1924

OUR medical officer sent me to the camp hospital, but some hours later I was ordered to be removed by Free State police who said that I could not remain there. The doctor protested, but I had to go to a hut; evidently the hospital was not regarded as being sufficiently safe. I had heard of camp life, of the noise and bustle, the lack of privacy, and I looked forward to it with dread.

The huts were of wood and each contained about thirty-six men. The beds were in rows against the walls, with a passage down the centre. Our hut was reasonably respectable; very few windows had any glass, its place was supplied by strands of barbed wire. There were gaps in the floor, all superfluous woodwork having been removed for firewood. During the night there was a tramp of heavy feet as the military police unlocked the hut door and counted us; often they would flash lamps on our sleeping faces, or pull down the clothes to ensure that a bed was occupied.

In the morning the doors were opened at seven o'clock. Men went outside for 'jerks' in the open and washed from running water behind a street of huts. Orderlies carried in breakfast or men prepared their own, using a tin can in which holes had been punched as a brazier; cardboard and paper supplied the fuel. Inspection of huts occurred about 10 am; huts were expected to be cleaned and tidied, beds made up and all men indoors. The men stood at ease at the foot of their beds; at the command of the hut leader they sprang to attention and numbered off, while the Free State officers checked the count. Each hut supplied orderlies for drawing food, for the cookhouse, for fatigue work, and for the sanitary squad.

Rows of huts faced each other throughout the camp, backed by the playing fields. The camp was surrounded with heavy rows of barbed wire, with sentry posts on platforms at intervals. At night powerful lamps lighted up the limits of the camp and military police prowled around. Even in daytime we could not walk within a certain distance of the barbed wire entanglements, which were placed at a considerable distance from the nearest huts, so as to lengthen the tunnels which prisoners were expected to dig.

My hut contained two touts, as suspects or spies were called; touts for the most part were criminals who instead of being sentenced were forwarded to camps where they had to supply a certain amount of information in return for not being imprisoned in jails. On my right side was a Clare farmer, 'a strong farmer', who smoked his pipe continually; even at night he awoke to light it. He told me of the wild life near his place. His eyes were far away when he described lakes and wooded country. His pipe drew curves and spirals to copy the startled flight of widgeon, woodcock and snipe.

Mostly at night we talked. He filled his pipe five or six times and I could watch the glow flaunt his face out of the darkness when he struck a match. We talked of hunting, poaching and shooting; I had never shot unless I was hungry. I could remember for him the night wait under a bridge for jack salmon. A twisted piece of bog-deal held above brightened the stream with quickly changing reflections in the yellow light. A man with an upraised grip would wait to catch the red shining eye of the jack before he fanged its belly.

As the months passed we talked in pipe glow. When I came through bogs there would be two sounds, the gurgling watery bubble of mating curlews, now less wary, and the feathery thrash of the jack-snipe as he came down in a curve with tail outspread to make his goat sound. In Irish he was the 'airy kid'. Then the mayfly gorged yellow bunting, whinchat and trout. Trout would be too full to nip the water now. In the evenings, further on, they would move out from their bank shade to rise at dusk. He knew the ways, flights and feeding grounds of birds and game as only countrymen or hunters do. When the moon came through the barbed wire he'd talk of lying out for geese. In strong wind and light they would come high. That watching I had always liked best. The moon would angle on patches of water, black clouds would furl up and be undershot, light would drift through as in an El Greco sky. Wild swan would come past in a thunderous wing-hum, darkening out the light; widgeons's long pinion-spread added to their speed. Then the gaggle and a distant heavy beat: wild geese, maybe with a black gander leading their wedge. Shot-guns would let loose; the geese would throw themselves back into the wind and soar high.

In late summer he talked of long waits behind sheaves of corn for duck. A heron might flap by with a harsh, disjointed scream, its head on its shoulder; woodcock croak like distant frogs, and redshank tube a thin, weary cry. Then at last the sharp quack as wild duck circled the stubble before settling to feed.

He had kept a pet fox which had caused some damage around about his place. The neighbours traced the fox one day and found the owner sitting behind it, with a rifle across his knees. The crowd threatened to shoot the fox. He swore to shoot the first man who fired a shot, and the crowd broke up. That happened during the truce. 'And none of the crowd were any good, anyhow,' he added. 'They spent all the time watching their skins during the fight.'

I often awoke at dawn and watched his light brown eyes shining as he looked at the greedy sparrows pick at crumbs which he had left for them beside his bed. A noisy chirp of fear, a hurried twist of the head, and a swoop. Often young sparrows clung to the barbed wires of the window opposite, squalled and squawked until their wants were satisfied. Their parents and relatives rushed for food and dropped it down the open mouths of the youngsters. Silence for a moment, then an angry, peevish scold whilst their providers hurriedly flew again for crumbs. 'The cunning little divils,' he'd remark, smiling, 'the little divils.'

On my left was an ex-soldier from Westmeath, who had served in France. He had been unspoiled by the war; he did not carry that tough, military look around with him. He had made it his business to look after my food and to cook for me.

I had not previously known anyone in my hut. I expect that was why I had been sent there. Hardly any of the men had been officers; that I liked best about them. There was a great strength in the men, if it could have been properly directed. I was told stories of myself, what I had said or done in different

places. I could not recognize myself for the legend. That was
a difficulty. The confusion between the legendary and the real
self. Time jumped a gap with us. People saw us as a myth,
which bore little relation to ourselves; and our real selves,
how could we find them? I could see the discrepancy between
myself in my own eyes, and myself through theirs. We were
expected to live up to that external evaluation; it often meant
that one had to represent a cross-section of other people's
minds. When I read Chaucer in the Joy, some had looked on
me as if I had become a deserter; I was going outside what
had been wished on me as a composite separatist. My radius
would be narrow indeed if I would only think or act as a
movement wished. If I had not been able to get outside of the
organization in the earlier Trouble, I could never have been
able to see even the fight, and now I would not be drawn too
closely by the web of a movement.

A few beds up on the opposite side was a lean, brown-faced
cow-puncher from the Argentine. His eyes were quiet and
resolute; he did not speak much; he was lithe and gentle,
dependable, I would say, in whatever he said or did. He
talked of savannas, skunks, snakes and gun fights, of life in
the cities and on the plains. Boys were restless when they
asked him questions, as some were already planning to go to
the Argentine when released.

Near him was our hut leader, a tall, well-built, serious
man, who had served in the RIC, the Irish Guards, the Civic
Guards, and who had progressed by successive stages to the
IRA. He seldom exerted his authority, but when he did he
was obeyed. He was slow enough in speech; police work had
increased his gravity.

A TGWU organizer, handsome, slightly built but hardy,
talked of the towns and districts he had worked in. He sang
for us at night, or performed gymnastic tricks.

At the far end of the hut was a one-eyed gunner from Co.
Cork, with a heavy beard. He stroked his beard. Hair was a
sign of strength, he said, and he should have been strong. The
one eye was very bright and smart. He was smart himself; he
could not be told much. He had a rough voice which quickly
deepened to a roar in argument; volume would clinch the
matter. He proudly showed the hair on his chest. It was

curly; he swung rights and lefts to it and to his resilient
abdomen with a tom-tom result. He swore strongly and with
ease. He could quickly be drawn by apparently innocent
questions about the prowess of Cork; then a burst of laughter
would show that his leg was being pulled.

It was hard to distinguish, as one walked around the camp,
the professions or occupations of the men. A doctor might
have ragged trousers and a nondescript shirt, while a labourer
might have a neat collar and tie. We were prisoners, it did not
matter about one's position or education, here all ranked
equally. Officers who had been in charge of divisions counted
no more than did the volunteer; no one was allowed to swing
his weight about. Men had been tested in the field, in jail,
and in the camps, and some had not withstood the test. In
Clare they said: 'Never trust a peeler till he is seven years
dead.' As a Republican one was evidently never sufficiently
tested until one had died in the Republican faith. A man was
judged not by his exploits in the past, but by his outlook at
the present.

Men had been taken from all that goes to build up a dis-
tinct environment and whatever tended to influence their lives
and their outlook, and here in camp they met. All super-
ficialities were stripped off, all appendages that disguised a
man's worth. Here were countrymen, townsmen, citizens,
with their different accents, the crisp, clipped, flat, even,
undulating, broad, singing. Flowing intonations of those who
had read well, the sturdy speech of the soilsman, Gaelic from
the Gaeltacht, Gaelic idiom in English, the slang of cities,
especially that of Dublin with its tongue stuttering against the
palate. There was no background into which men could
imperceptibly fit. We were particles in suspension waiting for
further tests of our properties. There was a recasting, a new
shaping of values. Some had nothing but the touch of earth in
their voice, but others carried a whole atmosphere with them,
the clay was yet on their feet. A few walked with a perpetual
sag and bewildered look; others with chins out, a 'damn
them, anyhow' expression. Often the schooled man was
stripped of his air of assurance, his dangerous little knowledge. The city man, away from factories, workshops, streets

and the excitement of movement, must have found himself lost, but he was adaptable, more so than the country man who was used to good food, and a bulk of it. Country bellies cried the most.

Listening to the talk of men whose conversation is a part of life and whose social sense is strong, one felt how little of real living there was in towns and cities, just a series of incidents strung together like their tram lines. Dublin was different to the other cities in that its men were more sturdy but I did not see much of that other Dublin that I had once sensed, with its intellectual, communal spirit, and the talking out of ideas which became an end in itself, to the loss of organized creative force. I could see how discipline, technique, and form gave way to the Irish curse of facility. But things mattered in the country. They happened and were woven into the life. As surely as the elements shaped the land and both shaped the people, so surely did the people mould the accidents, the minutiae of daily life. There was craft, cunning, caginess, a bumptious disregard of applied or conventional knowledge, often a know-all assertiveness, but there was a strong sense of life and youthful vitality to compensate. The city, with one's neighbours an enigma, a cipher, met the open book of the countryside. Not so open, either; it needed understanding, alertness and interpretation.

A simplicity that was seemingly gentle and disarming could hide a store of satire and malice. There were layers of intolerance and budding pastorship in the individual; he would watch and comment on another's soul solution. There must be a big dose of the school teacher in our race. Life was dismissed too easily in terms of morality or lack of it, but when talk stopped, there was singing. That was a definite expression; nearly everybody sang. They put into it what they would fail to convey in the speaking voice. Men who would not speak of Ireland as they would of their sweethearts, changed when they sang. Then she was Dark Rosaleen, the Dear Dark Head, *Grainne Uaile,* Silk of the Kine, and the older names, *Erin, Banba, Fodhla, Inisfail,* the Isle of Destiny.

The provinces could be distinguished. Connacht, more out of the way, less visited, more of the why and where and what was his father; neighbourly and gabby; the quickness of the sky change in them, and a hardness that was like the strange lights there that defied distance; wild blood. Ulster, quieter, with a droll humour, a swarthy anger, more men of action. Leinster, more anglicized, stabler, flatter in speech, a little introspective because of the cities, chiller in conversation, but observant. Munster, loquacious, egotistic, quicker in mind; the furthest south had remnants of the old learning, they trimmed and adorned and brought forth swift arguments. Men from the Gaeltacht had sometimes an impenetrable aloofness; their bleak-coloured lands released imagination by sense of space and the misted effects of changing light.

Ours was the country of broken tradition, a story of economic, social and mental oppression, propped up by a mythological introduction innocent of archaeological or historical interpretation. To compensate for the submerged centuries our early historical significance had been emphasized. We were a nation of saints and scholars, we had often been told, but our experience had disproved this cliché. If sainthood was intolerance, we had a great share of it. If scholarship was living on the unearned appreciation of people who wrote or taught eleven hundred years ago, and whose works were hardly known by us, then we were scholars. We did not see through either the unbroken arrogance of chiefs, or a purely literary tradition unsifted by literary criticism. We saw France and Spain through retrospective glasses, when they, to suit their ambitions, sent us expeditions that came too late, landed in the wrong place, or were destroyed by protecting English storms. The laws of aristocratic tradition were in our teeth. We favoured the royalists in the English civil war, the beaten South in America, and the Irish battalion that had fought against Italian freedom in the *Risorgimento*. Bookish fairy tales had the glamour of a feudal tradition; bright resourceful kings and lily-skinned princesses; in print they ousted the verbal folklore that dealt with heroic characters as human beings.

For Spain and France there was still a traditional friendship. England we looked at through centuries of conquest and the image of the Troubles. We expected sympathy from nations who, past the stage where a diversion of their campaigns to Ireland would help them, were now disinterested.

Cut off from scientific and intellectual eddies, we had built a world of our own, an emotional life but no philosophy or economic framework. Physically we had never had control of the land in peace, save with the Grattan ascendancy men who had made big economic changes which were then wiped out by the Union with England. As an agricultural people, we lacked scientific training. We were a ranch, sending bullocks to England, boys and girls to America. The Catholic Church, unlike the Empire, made use of both ends of the social system, the very poor as well as the rich, but civil war had given us a sense of reality about ourselves and about the nation. It had taught us how Irish history had once worked in the sixteenth and seventeenth centuries.

The people had been written about often enough by those who of the Pale looked over the fence. Why could we not have submitted hundreds of years ago? Was there not something inherent in our civilization, our experience, our outlook on life and death? We had fought a civilization which did not suit us. We had striven to give complete expression to the genius of the race, in a fight against organized imperialism, the personal against the impersonal, but our old idea of life, the stress on its human values, the awareness of natural things, needed to be renewed. We wanted to solve our problems in our way, in our own time, to release the effort that had been frustrated, to readjust our warped sense of values.

It had been difficult to accustom myself to all the members of my hut. Some made noise a virtue, others wished for quietness, some wanted to work, other to laze and play interminable games of nap or twenty-one, some to rag continually. A few wanted to make the best use they could of their time to prevent demoralization; the rest did not care, or thought little of the directions to which their time could be turned. Gradually I solved the problem of my hut in terms of the occupants. I found that the spirit of comradeship smoothed out many difficulties. I had time to study the men to find out their little idiosyncrasies, whilst they discovered mine. A spirit of good humour, of tolerance, pervaded. Most of the men were light-hearted; though there were some grousers, they did not affect the majority.

We were still not allowed to have visits from our relatives and friends. Men had been separated from feminine influence for years, the more intimate touches of living were absent, and our huts were bare, stark in the way men prefer to live when together, ornamented with the general air of comradeship. The lack of possessions was lightening. Some books, a carved chess set, a few bookshelves made from boxes; these helped to maintain an evenness in the standard of living. We had learned to cook, to wash our clothes and to sew; for the first time some of the boys learned what they had most scorned: household work. Many of the men had never made a cup of tea in their lives. Morose individuals had almost to simulate cheerfulness to avoid seemingly kindly, but really barbed, inquiries. If one asked for more than his due he was informed that he 'wanted jam on it'; if he complained of life in general, he was told: 'Cheer up, you will soon be dead.'

Everyone in the jails and camps seemed to carry around an autograph album and to be able to recite a poem or ballad, the ballad generally being 'Dangerous Dan McGrew'. A new arrival to a hut would be asked if he could recite. Yes, he could. What could he do? 'Dangerous Dan McGrew'. That would be great, a real treat to hear, and thus encouraged, the newcomer would begin, while the men sprawled around on beds or on the floor in a semi-circle. Silence at first, covert smiles, and lowing murmurs of approval. But at the lines:

> Boys, said he, you don't know me,
> And none of ye care a damn

a wild chorus would startle the reciter, and the hut would continue the verse to the end.

A boy called 'Mabel', who had been in Mountjoy, helped to entertain the camp. His name may have arisen from an indiscreet confiding of his love affairs, or from some of the songs he sang. His very walk was humorous. He wore baggy trousers which wriggled at will. He was always ready to recite, to sing, to begin with a wail.

> I want to go home to see my mama,
> I want to go home to see my ma.

Impromptu concerts in the night-time in the hut, the men
squatting on the floor or lying on their beds. Ballads, come-
all-yez, doggerel, old traditional songs, sometimes a song
which had been composed in camp, or *Sean O Dwyer a Gleanna,*
a song of the defeat of the Gael at Aughrim in 1691.

> After Aughrim's great disaster,
> When our foes in sooth were master,
> It was you who first plunged in and swam
> The Shannon's boiling flood.
> Still Sean O Dwyer a chara,
> We're worsted in the game.
>
> Long, long we kept the hillside,
> Our couch hard by the rillside,
> The sturdy knotted oaken boughs
> Our curtains overhead.
> The summer's blaze we laughed at,
> The winter's snow we scoffed at,
> And trusted to our long steel swords
> To win us daily bread.
>
> And though we part in sorrow,
> Still Sean O Dwyer a chara,
> Our prayer is: God save Ireland
> And pour blessings on her name!
> May her sons be true when needed,
> May they never feel as we did,
> For Sean O Dwyer a gleanna,
> We're worsted in the game.

Often I watched their faces around me become tense, some
men clenching their knuckles hard till the white sinews
gleamed. They were again keeping the hillside. Defeat was as
bitter in 1924 as it was in 1691. A long silence always
followed the singing of this song, to be broken by a facetious
remark or a forced laugh, but some of the men with their
knees clasped, or their hands under their heads as they lay on
the beds, remained silent till 'lights out'.

The northern men had their own ballads. They sang or recited the Orange songs with vigour. 'Dolly's Brae', 'The Protestant Boys', 'The Battle of the Boyne', and those which many ancestors of the present Orangemen had sung marching in '98 when they carried their long pikes against the red coats. Some huts would take part in a Twelfth of July procession which would have edified their northern critics, although none had learned to make drumsticks of their hands.

> King William called his officers saying:
> Gentlemen mind your station,
> And let your valour here be shown
> Before the Irish nation.
> My brazen walls let no man break
> And your subtle foe you'll scatter;
> Be sure you show them good English play
> As you go over the water.
>
> When that King William did observe
> The brave Duke Schomberg falling,
> He reined his horse with a heavy heart,
> On the Enniskillens calling:
> What will you do for me, brave lads?
> See yonder men retreating,
> Our enemy encouraged
> And Irish drums are beating.
> He says: My boys, feel no dismay
> At the losing of one commander,
> For God shall be our King this day,
> And I'll be general under.

There was a long bitter memory of King James.

> Royal Seamus he has gone to France,
> And left his crown behind.
> Ill luck be theirs, both day and night,
> Put running in his mind.

Mick Sheehan came from Tipp, a prisoner. He was now one of the Army Executive, and perhaps proud of the importance of his new dignity, he approached the cookhouse out of his turn. He made demands but was refused.

'Do you know who I am?' he asked.

'No, nor don't care,' was the reply.

'I'm a member of the Executive.'

'Oh, you are, you bastard. You're the kind that keeps the rest of us here. Get to bloody hell out of this.'

There were too many 'spare generals', as they were called, walking about the camp for the rank to impress anyone. Jail was a hard test of a man. He had to live intimately, in the physical sense, in camps. He was tested in many ways, probed at from different angles by circumstance, malice, humour and his own lack or strength of worth. We saw unexpected and unforeseen glimpses of each other, heard peculiar points of view. Some had fallen in the estimation of the men; either active service or jail had discovered faults and flaws. Often, with authority stripped from them, officers sank back and haloes became smudged.

Some men had two sets of language: one for themselves, plumbed with curses, which was on the increase. To their senior officers, or to those for whom they had respect, they spoke without decoration. Was the other language a relief? Did they think we were womanly? Were there really .two languages, that which men used to men, and the other for the rest of the world? What a man really thought, and what he said.

Educational and Irish language classes were held, elementary and advanced; dramatic and musical societies were formed, entertainments arranged and sports organized. Rival teams from the different counties played football, and soon the turf on the playing field was worn into a substance that had more of the qualities of macadam. A wooden lathe had been improvised and chessmen, amongst other articles, manufactured, as many men played chess and tournaments were constantly being held. Brush handles were sawn into sections to make draughts and heated pokers burned out squares on blocks of wood. Coloured wool provided material for the making of rugs, designs for which were forwarded from the outside or were invented. Handkerchiefs were coloured by hand; macramé work of various kinds was knotted out, and men knitted jumpers and scarfs. Ornaments were made out of bone which was dug up in the camp ground, and woodworkers tried their knives on whatever wood there was. Committees were appointed to study industrial and economic problems; officers' classes were held; plans of escape were discussed, and the inevitable tunnels were dug and discovered.

I was a philatelist; I found the earlier occupants had decorated their huts with the surcharged stamps of the Provisional Government and of the Free State by pasting them on the walls. Accompanied by a group of boys carrying tins of boiling water, I visited the huts and steamed the stamps off the walls, to the surprise and general amusement of the hut members, for we must surely be soft in the head to waste our time collecting old stamps. Time and exposure had bleached or torn most of the stamps, yet I was able to obtain a few rare specimens.

It had been very cold in winter, I was told, in the bare huts on the wind-swept, level Curragh, but in summer it was pleasant enough, although a rainy day meant muddied, dirty boots which occasioned extra work in keeping the huts clean. Firewood was not as serious a problem as it had been in the winter, yet we needed material for our braziers to cook our own food. Coal might be obtained by taunting the orderlies as they carried buckets of fuel to the ovens, as discreet invective might result in lumps of coal being fired at his tormentors by an exasperated orderly. Wood for the lathe was more difficult to obtain, but a certain type of brush issued from the store provided suitable wood so every artifice was devised to extract brushes from a reluctant quartermaster. One day a military gun-wagon entered the camp and its soldiers and officers moved to the far end of the enclosure to inspect the sewage system, which was faulty. The wagon was hauled in between two huts and our men got busy with improvised saws. A knife could be made into a saw by hacking notches in it at intervals, forward for wood, backward for metal, and soon not a trace of the wagon remained. The parts were hidden or buried, and when the escort returned, their gun-wagon had disappeared, nor could it be located. Then there was a plentiful supply of fine material for the wood-lathe.

I met men whom I had not seen for years. Boys who had scouted the road for me and at whose houses I had stayed, were now officers. I got to know men who had been names only to me. We could talk about many things and our judgements were varied, but I kept away from organized discussions. I had not made much of my own responsibility. I could not see a definite future and I could not pronounce on it. A movement was not going to get under my skin so much that I could not see life around me. The men I met were straight as far as neglect of personal gain was considered, but not clear for the future, for they were not trained in thought and were loose in their standards of action. I could not see any leadership. Our lives did not touch intimately save on the effort for political separation.

It was difficult to define even to myself what I felt. I saw a certain hardness in our idealism. It made us aloof from ordinary living, as if we were above it. There was insistence on principle, which often stood coldly out where immediate feeling was needed. And of the men I fought with I could not say I had an intimate friend, and yet we might fight again together, bound by a common spirit. If I could find an acceptance of the two lives, that of the struggle, and that of one's own development in the feeling of beauty and all its shades which I could not express—that would be an ideal.

The old discipline had broken, the last fight had shown that. Perhaps it was because the people had stampeded; it was they who had held us together in the Tan fight. Men were more critical now. That was good if they would learn to think for themselves. We discussed the breakdown of the hunger-strike, and of the change in mentality, the element of disillusion and of cynicism that was creeping in. Pooling our experiences, we examined the months during the truce and the period before the attack on the Four Courts, and in the light of our present knowledge of men and events we saw things in a different way. An incident, then seemingly unimportant, was followed by a clue. The Headquarters Staff of the Tan time, Mulcahy, Collins, O'Connell, O'Hegarty, Price, Sean MacMahon, did not compare with the Easter Week men, with Pearse, Connolly, MacDonagh, Sean

MacDermott, Plunkett. An element of intellect and spirituality was absent. What made the Irish Republican Brotherhood accept the treaty and force it through? Why should men who suffered and planned through the years break the back of their sacrifice? What did Collins mean to himself? Did Mulcahy and Cosgrave carry out his intentions?

The IRB had driven Sinn Fein under ground. Perhaps the situation would have been different if Sinn Fein had been able to develop slowly, if their main energies had not been put into the electioneering side. Driving force was there, but no vision or attempt at economic solution. There was an economic root to the fight, though many on our side would not better their position by a result in our favour. Freedom comes religious, political, economic. We were at the political stage. We had not the faculty for thinking things through sufficiently.

Some men were worn out. That was not the trouble, but either they did not recognize the fact, or else would not face up to it. Others would not again be active; they would, several years in arrears, have to make a living. A few would want to change the system of society by which empire in exploited countries kept its control and fell back on its willing allies. If there had been a definite, clearly defined objective to fight for, people could never have deceived themselves by thinking they could accept another system.

What had they fought for, I often thought, as I watched the men in my hut. They were from country, city and small town, and on the surface, all they seemed to have in common was that they resisted economic, social and clerical pressure together. It was an urge difficult to interpret, the right of a people to its own soil so long as that people would not accept domination. George Russell, who like other intellectuals had been with the people only when their agony was recognized abroad, had said:

If between myself and Heaven I had to confess
about Ireland, I would admit I know nothing
truly of its people, though I am of them. . . .
Why do they desire freedom? I think it is
because they feel in themselves a genius

which had not yet been manifested in a
civilization, as Greek, Roman and Egyptian
in the past have externalised their genius
in a society with a culture, arts and sciences
peculiar to themselves. Ireland, through Sinn
Fein, is fighting for freedom to manifest the
Irish genius.

But that was in 1921.

The padre in the camp was liked by the men but he was not
popular in the sense that he was invited to the huts for a chat.
The Protestant chaplain visited us from time to time, and we
invited him to tea and produced our best ware and food for
the occasion. He had been born near my mother's place in
Roscommon and had known some of the family. His comments on the Free State officials occasioned many a laugh as
we uncharitably listened to their incursions into Society.
Socially they had little status. Instead of building their own
background, they often tried to ape the mannerisms of the
relics of the garrison, and to develop the ambition to belong
to a class which had another social fabric to their own.

Once while standing in a row awaiting confession, I saw
written in pencil on the board outside the room which served
as a confessional:

May the gates of Hell never screech for
want of grease whilst there is marrow
in the bones of a traitor.

During the summer months men were released slowly, yet
their absence was hardly noticeable. Other camps and jails,
however, had begun to release men in batches, and there was
always hope, though some felt that the senior officers would
be interned as long as possible. In some instances officers
were released while the men were kept; we suspected that this
was to make the men discontented. Classes continued,
though there was an air of restlessness as releases increased.
A play was produced successfully, *The Singer,* by Pearse, and
an acrobatic and vaudeville troupe staged performances.

I lectured to an officers' class in one of the end huts, while scouts were posted to warn us of enemy approach. I had an engineer prepare a map of the river Shannon, which I placed on the back of a box, intending if interrupted to lecture on the river itself. Once, whilst lecturing on musketry, I looked up during a pause to find two Free State officers at the doorway. I spoke about the river, tracing its course, talking of the tributaries. The officers remained. I asked the audience if they had any questions to ask. Nobody spoke. I spoke of seventy miles of river boundary; I remembered fords I had talked about with old people, and the stretch where O'Sullivan Beare must have rafted in 1603. The officers stayed on. I developed the possibilities of communications by light steamers. The audience kept quiet when I tried to entice them to questions. I cursed them with hard sentences as I blamed the lack of transport on the river. I thought of wild birds, fisheries and game that made me talk on. The class eventually began to ask questions, but the officers remained to the hour's end. I would damn well study my auxiliary subject and prepare my notes before commencing to lecture in future. That evening I was told that one of the officers had been a school teacher and had been born near the Shannon Pot, the source of the river.

Attempts to escape were frequently plotted. I had another uniform given to me, and for many nights in succession dressed in it whilst the others slept. I lay awake waiting for my companions from another hut, but Michael Kilroy of the Fourth Western escaped by himself one night, without being able to get to me. Anyhow, I would have been a danger. I was able to walk a little, the arches of my feet had dropped and I was lame, yet I felt sure that the excitement of an attempt to escape would overcome my physical disabilities.

Extra precautions were taken. Military police now visited the huts practically every hour during the night, to count the prisoners and shine lights on the faces of a few.

The summer wore on, slowly enough for some. I was content in a way. I had been ground to quietness by wounds and bed. Irascibility and impatience had been replaced by nervous irritability, but camp life swung me back to some kind of evenness. I liked the men in my hut, and I had ample time to read and to make good my lack of books from the year 1918 onwards.

We endeavoured to induce the organizations outside to found camp libraries. Some people had industriously collected books and forwarded them, but the books were utterly useless as a means of persuading men to read and to develop themselves. The majority of us were aimless and loafing. The Staters by keeping us interned were endeavouring, consciously or unconsciously, to make us waste time, to impoverish families and dependents, to use up the money of individuals as well as that of organizations. Released prisoners crowded to the United States. It is difficult, perhaps, to conduct a political campaign, but the amount of money spent on one constituency during an election would have equipped a camp or jail with a supply of thought-provoking books and textbooks. One realized that the movement had too much of a political rather than a national bent, and that vote-snatching counted more than the building up of an independent point of view. I found that most of the men read Zane Grey or Nat Gould because they had nothing else to read. When one gave them a decent book they invariably read it and asked for another by the same author, or another on the same subject. I gave them my books. *Moby Dick* was a favourite. I had copies of it sent in to me for the men. I had re-read it many times, now I knew some of it by heart. Was not the white whale the whale of empire which devoured us, or was it the idea of freedom, which would make *brus* of us until we could improve the harpoon of a social system that would bring it alongside. The feeling of the men was instinctively for what was good in subject matter. It seemed a pity that their time was wasted. Reading, to them, was an escape from life, rather than an approach to it. It did not enhance, enrich, and enlarge their experiences of the last six or eight years.

*   *   *   *   *   *

Some of us decided to crawl from our huts one night, advance to the barbed wire, cut it, and then worm our way through. It seemed impossible, as we would have to advance very slowly and in succession, but there did not seem to be any other means of escape now. We waited for a dark night.

Suddenly the Free State decided to release prisoners. We saw a batch of tall, lithe Kerry men march away. Releases continued, but the senior officers remained; soon there were about one hundred left. Our numbers lessened daily until there were forty. Then men were released in twos.

The enemy could not be gracious, even after two years of imprisonment, and we cursed them heartily as we waited. They wanted to avoid an organized welcome to the prisoners; that could mean they were losing ground.

Sean Russell and I were the last to visit the office, and together we made our way to Kildare station, where we found Gerry Boland, Billy Pilkington, Tom Derrig and others. We laughed as we eyed our clothes; it was easy to pick out our men on the platform. People looked at us timorously. A few came to shake our hands. At last the train puffed in to the shout of 'Here she is'.

Later, our group of officers reached the Kingsbridge station, Dublin, where, after many firm hand grips, we, who had been beaten in the fight, who had withstood the jail war, parted to take up the threads of inscrutable destiny; some to begin life over again.

IRISH WORDS AND PHRASES

a chara	my friend
agus beannacht De ort	and the blessing of God on you
Beannacht De	Blessing of God
Beannacht De leat	Blessing of God with you
bearla	English language
brus	debris
bruscar	fragments
camans (*camain*)	hurleys
Cumann na mBan	the women's organization, an auxiliary of the IRA
Dail Eireann	Lower House of Irish Parliament
Dia's Muire dhuit	God and Mary with you
Fianna Eireann	Sinn Fein/IRA youth organization
gae bolga	spear of Cuchulain (mythological)
Mesca Ulad	tale from ancient Irish romantic literature
raimeish	rubbish
Sinn Fein	political wing of the IRA
Suibhne Geilt	later romantic tale of the seventh century battle of Magh Rath (Moira, in the county of Down)
Tain Bo Cuailnge	romantic tale from one of the Irish epic cycles
TD (Teachta Dala)	member of Dail Eireann

FRAMEWORK OF DATES

11 July 1921	Truce to hostilities between the British and Irish forces takes effect
11 October 1921	Formal talks begin in London between the British and Irish delegates
6 December 1921	Treaty (Articles of Agreement) signed in London shortly after 2 am
8 December 1921	Eamon de Valera publishes repudiation of Treaty after Cabinet meeting
14 December 1921	Dail Eireann commences the Treaty debates
7 January 1922	Dail agrees to Treaty by 64 votes to 57
9 January 1922	The Dail by 2-vote majority elects Arthur Griffith as President in place of Eamon de Valera. (Richard Mulcahy to succeed Cathal Brugha as Minister for Defence)
January–February 1922	2nd Southern Division (IRA) breaks away from the GHQ Dublin *and* from authority of Dail Eireann
5–11 March 1922	Limerick crisis
26 March 1922	The banned IRA convention opens in Dublin
9 April 1922	Republican Executive established and new IRA General Headquarters Staff confirmed
13 April 1922	Occupation of the Four Courts as IRA Headquarters in Dublin
20 May 1922	Election Pact announced by Michael Collins and de Valera
14 June 1922	Collins repudiates the Pact
16 June 1922	General Election in the 26 Counties

17–18 June 1922	Republicans from the Four Courts take arms and ammunition from the Civic Guard barracks in Kildare town
18 June 1922	Another IRA convention held in Dublin, and the Army splits over motion to attack the British
22 June 1922	Shooting of Sir Henry Wilson in London
26 June 1922	'Kidnapping' of General J. J. O'Connell, Assistant Chief of Staff, Provisional Government's National Army
28 June 1922	The civil war commences when troops of the Provisional Government start the bombardment of the Republicans in the Four Courts
30 June 1922	Surrender of the Four Courts by the Republican garrison
1 July 1922	Government soldiers attack Republican positions in O'Connell Street and elsewhere in Dublin
5 July 1922	Republican forces are defeated in O'Connell Street
12 August 1922	Death of Arthur Griffith (William Cosgrave to replace him as head of the Provisional Government)
22 August 1922	Death of Michael Collins in a Co. Cork ambush (Richard Mulcahy to replace him as Commander-in-Chief, Provisional Government's National Army).
10 October 1922	The Irish Bishops issue a solemn pastoral letter against the Republicans
15 October 1922	The Special Emergency Powers (martial law) granted by the Dail to the Government's National Army now take effect
16–17 October 1922	Meeting of the IRA Executive at Ballybacon near the Glen of Aherlow, Co. Tipperary, after which the Republican Army reaffirms its allegiance to the re-

	constituted Government of the Republic
17 November 1922	The first official executions
17 November 1922	The court martial of Erskine Childers (to be executed by firing squad one week later)
6 December 1922	Irish Free State established
7 December 1922	The IRA kill Sean Hales and wound Padraic O'Maille, two Dail deputies who had voted for the emergency powers
8 December 1922	The reprisal executions by the Cosgrave Government for the shooting of its deputies (above) in which Rory O'Connor, Liam Mellows, Joe McKelvey and Dick Barrett died
10 April 1923	Death of Liam Lynch after a round-up in the Knockmealdown mountains (Frank Aiken to take over as Republican Chief of Staff)
30 April 1923	Aiken's order to the IRA to suspend all offensive operations now takes effect
2 May 1923	The last official executions
24 May 1923	Aiken issues Cease Fire order to all IRA units and instructs them to dump their arms
27 August 1923	A General Election is held in the 26 Counties
13 October 1923	Hunger-strike begins in Mountjoy prison (to spread throughout other jails and internment camps)
23 November 1923	Hunger-strike ends
March 1924	A mutiny in the Free State Army
16–17 July 1924	Republican leaders released from internment

APPENDIX

A SELECTION of published and unpublished documents relevant to some of the prison chapters of *The Singing Flame*, by kind permission of Mr. Cormac K. H. O'Malley, Mr. Frank Aiken and the Trustees of the O'Malley Papers. (In 1974 Mr. Cormac O'Malley placed his father's papers in the Ernie O'Malley Trust at University College Dublin and they are now available for scholarly research.)

A diary entry made in Mountjoy in November 1922 by Frank Gallagher, and afterwards printed among 'Leaves from a Prison Diary' in the EIRE publication of September 1924:

Rory sent over the report of the Ailesbury Road fight. It was wonderful—like Cathal Brugha's tremendous daring. 'You'll get no surrender here,' Ernie shouted and I could almost hear him as I read. ... What a war it would be, a magnificent redeeming war, if all of us had this royal gift of great courage!

Extracts from a letter written to Ernie O'Malley by Thomas Gerrard [then of Monamolin, Gorey, Co. Wexford] over thirty years after his capture by the Free State, as told in Chapter XI:

The day you came into Portobello Barracks in the Pembroke ambulance I will never forget. I was a very young medical orderly and I counted about 16 or 17 wounds in your back. Your smile compelled me to say a few quiet prayers for you. Not many days after, you gave me a little note and asked me to deliver it privately to a Dr. Ryan. I think it was Fitzwilliam Square. ... I went that night and delivered that note and I was in uniform when the doctor opened the door, and I gave it to him. My mind was made up to deliver that note faithfully and all the guns that were previously around the Four Courts would not stop me. I hope I was the means of helping a smiling and brave soldier with such a lot of wounds.

With reference to Chapter XII, the O'Malley and Lynch letters regarding the intended court martial of Ernie O'Malley were later printed in the Republicans' War News paper, PHOBLACHT NA h-EIREANN, with these comments:

Commandant-General Earnan O'Maille . . . had perhaps the greatest individual record during the *[Tan]* war. . . . He is at present in Hospital and unable to stand without assistance, so apparently the Murder Ministry propose to have him carried to face the firing squad, as did the British with James Connolly.

However, all three Dublin papers published extracts from the letters, as did 'The Times' of London and 'The New York Times'; the news was carried by the Press Association, and it is reasonable to suppose that the resultant widespread publicity was a major factor in the indefinite postponement of his trial.

Hospital Wing,
Mountjoy.
3.15 p.m.
9/1/23

1. Today a Free State captain, who subsequently stated that he was to be my prosecuting counsel, informed me that I was to be tried, and wished to know if I required legal assistance. As I had already made up my mind on the matter, I informed him that I did not require legal assistance; that, as a soldier, I had fought and killed the enemies of our nation, and would do so again, so that a trial for the express purpose of passing sentence did not require a defence on my part. The officer, who had been at school with me, tried to induce me to see a solicitor. He stated that he would forward me a summary of evidence.

2. As I do not know the Staff decision on the point of legal advice, I think it desirable to drop you this note. If I do not hear from you, I will refuse to recognize their Court.

3. As I may be removed from here and this may be the last chance I may have of writing to you, I would like to be

remembered to the members of the staff and my comrades.

Another bit of lead won't do me any harm.

EARNAN O'MAILLE

In his reply, the Chief of Staff wrote:

I hope the enemy are not so mad as to execute such a brave and efficient officer as you, especially with your record in the last war against the common enemy. Rest assured that those of us left will see that the established Republic is maintained.

May God save Ireland from such a loss as the taking of your life.

As he relates in Chapter XII, following the news of his intended court martial, Ernie O'Malley began to write down some record of 'what had happened to me' since 1918 when he left home to become a full-time IRA organizer. Those original notes were later typed in a rough draft, and he eventually corrected and amended this. What he wrote in the hospital in Mountjoy was in fact the kernel of what would years later become his book, 'On Another Man's Wound'. The spirit, the flavour and the feeling are already in his short prison notes. While still awaiting the expected trial, he added a brief introduction:

12/1/23

I doubt if I will be able to finish in time. I find it extremely difficult to write; I hate doing it, but Bob *[Barton]* says it is important that I should leave some record.

This diary is not to be in any way utilized; it is for my brothers so that they may know where I have been for the past five years; as well, it may be shown to a few people whom I will name—then it is to be burned.

Previously I told one or two incidents to amplify a tactical theory; when off my guard I once related an incident to Miss O'Rahilly—a rather tame one at that—and she did not credit it. I have glossed over many things, others I have not stressed sufficiently as they concern men who are now fighting for us. I have told the truth; certain facts and traits may have impressed me more than others by reason of my lack of Gaelic tradition and outlook.

I would have liked to develop these notes to show:
(a) the growth of the army generally
(b) the development of units
(c)   ,,   ,,   ,, special services
(d)   ,,   ,,   ,, pure staff work
(e)   ,,   ,,   ,, the people generally
Most of all I would have liked to talk about the rank and
file where I found solace when broken-hearted with the
officers. Perhaps I have expected too much, have become
warped by reason of failures, disappointments, and worse to
my mind, lack of sincerity; anyhow I have always the
impression that I drove too much and did not lead sufficiently
—whatever my intentions to remedy the latter, I have always
been driven back to resort to the former.

                                                    14/1/23
It is a run against time now and I have become rather interested in the work though it is extremely fatiguing: I hope
but doubt that I will be enabled to finish this before the
others finish me. I have received my papers and should be
shot in three days from this.

*The following letter was sent to Liam Lynch by Ernie O'Malley, when
the Irish newspapers published the document which Liam Deasy,
Deputy Chief of Staff, IRA, had signed and agreed to, a few weeks
previously, at the time of his arrest by the Free State forces. The document began: 'I accept and I will aid in immediate and unconditional
surrender of arms and men as required by General Mulcahy. In pur-
suance of this undertaking I am asked to appeal for a similar undertaking and acceptance from . . .', that is from those Republican leaders who
were carrying on the war. O'Malley's letter relates to incidents in
Chapters XII and XIII.*
*(This letter was captured by the Free State authorities towards the end
of March 1923, and copies were made for their Intelligence department
and for the personal files of all those mentioned in the letter.)*

                                                Hospital Wing
To C/S   9 A.M.
   G.H.Q.   10/2/23
Have managed to get hold of yesterday's morning and even-

ing papers; yesterday we went through several kinds of hell here. I'm afraid the ultimate result will tell against us. I think Deasy perfectly honest, but he, a member of the Staff, sets a premium on indiscipline. Like him I too abhor the present nature of the struggle, but I think we should lay more emphasis on the cause than on the effect. There is one point I would like to emphasize—Deasy's command was by far the best armed in Ireland and so, whilst hitting the enemy, according to plan, for the murder of our prisoners, could have also almost made the area untenable militarily for him. I can see an area poor in manpower and in arms doing little else beyond destruction of property but I fail to see why strong areas cannot keep the fight from developing into a vendetta.

I again say prisoners are casualties *and must not be considered*. I may as well warn you that the spirit in some prisons is bad; Barton informed me yesterday that Paddy Fleming had told him that he was afraid a good number in Hare Park would sign the form if given a lead, so it is important that G.H.Q. know who are the officers in Camps so that they may be able to do something to forestall it.

I thought the international situation good and our position strong; now the people will pluck up heart as the Free State correspondence would intimate, to the unthinking, that the situation for them "was well in hand" and so I expect an amount of public opinion will swing round to the side they think may win. This is one result I see—the other is the inclination to ignore G.H.Q., but I am sure the Kanturk surrender will not have much effect. Re Daly of ———; when I was A.A.C.S. there were 27 men from F—— Company who were "on the run", but who were unarmed. Perhaps they were poorly armed when they surrendered; if so I would not blame them too much as I expected them to surrender before I was hit, as I could not understand how unarmed men could stand the strain.

This must have been a stunning blow to you all and you have all our sympathy. The chaplain came to me with the paper yesterday and hinted that I should follow Deasy's example and also that of the Limerick prisoners; I'm glad I managed to contain myself when he was in my cell but when he left I went up in smoke.

I hear that Mick Kilroy is in the basement of "D" wing.
                                        Beannacht De ort
                                        Earnan O Maille

*The next day O'Malley wrote again to Lynch, with further reference to
reactions to the Deasy appeal. The Deputy Governor, O'Keeffe, had
obviously been attempting to persuade the Mountjoy men to sign the
forms of unconditional and complete surrender.*

                                        Hospital Wing
To C/S, G.H.Q.   11/2/23
Michael Kilroy is in "C" Wing and has received a copy of
the summary of evidence; he says he will not consult a
Solicitor. I am telling him to see O'H anyhow as it will come
to the one thing in the long run, but as I will not be able to
get in touch with him for six or seven days it would be well
that you should tell him to see O'H so propaganda may be
got going.

150 new prisoners sent here last night.

Deputy Governor went over to "C" Wing with a bundle of
forms and they were thrown on top of him: morale here, if
one judges the feel by the hospital is excellent. So far I have
not heard that anyone in the Wings has signed the form.
Language in the Hospital on the 10th was anything but
saintly, nevertheless very edifying.

I think things have happened for the best, always we can
rely on the rank and file and I am sure arms will not be
handed in—the result will bring more pressure to bear on
the Staters and enemy government will realize that even if the
leaders go, the rank and file will carry on.

If arms are not handed in, the Staters are down and out
nearly and our morale goes up some. I expect, however, the
Staters will state that arms have been handed in, but they can
be challenged to give names and addresses of men who have
surrendered. For a long time past it has been an "officers"
war, now the rank and file have an opportunity of asserting
themselves.

                                        E. O Maille

*The above letter went through quickly, for on 19 February, Tom
Derrig, then Adjutant-General, was able to reply on Lynch's behalf.*

. . .

2. Note what you say re morale of prisoners. Very glad to
hear this. The very opposite is the case in some prisons, eg.
Limerick, where they were put through it at the revolver
point. Once they showed weakness prisoners there have got
no peace since Deasy's action and are having a deuce of a
time according to themselves. The moral is plain.

3. Things will right themselves very shortly in South. I have
been west and expect big things there very soon. People are
solidly against executions everywhere. Late D/I is i/c there.
All areas very favourable to our men. ... O/C Northern
Command *[Frank Aiken]* is in splendid form. Dublin is doing
fine. Men have been very lax in many areas but we have
plenty manpower. Things were splendid only for Deasy's
unfortunate document. Your own self is the pride of the
country in that respect and I was innundated with questions
about you everywhere.

The next letter, written to Sheila Humphreys, requires a longer ex-
planation. It probably did not reach its destination. The letter as given
below is taken from a Free State copy, which was not perfectly typed.

On 12 March 1923 a note from the Director-General's Office of the
CID forwarded to the Commander-in-Chief, Portobello barracks, a
copy 'of a communication from Ernie O'Malley which was found on the
person of Mrs. Gordon [Winifred (Una) Gordon, later Mrs. Austin
Stack] during a recent raid'.

The reference in the letter to waiting for volleys on the 19th would
imply that those prisoners had been threatened with execution as
reprisals for attacks on Free State officers. However, as with the other
similar threat, described in Chapter XII, those executions were not
to be carried out.

Ernie's letter links Sheila Humphreys and Maire Comerford
together in prison, for those two had been sentenced to solitary confine-
ment because of their defiant attitudes when held in the female hospital
wing of Mountjoy. Accordingly they had been separated from the other
girls, and had been on hunger-strike. A Free State sentry had shot
Maire Comerford in the leg when she was waving to those outside.
The later reference to 'only 14 girls there now' would seem to mean the
number then held in the women's prison.

*The 'Amnesty' was the brief period promised to those who would
accept Deasy's appeal and surrender unconditionally.*

*Although the Free State authorities took the comments seriously,
Ernie was only teasing Sheila about her pride in the Kingdom of Kerry,
her mother's 'native county', when he wrote about Kerry and the West.*

Hospital Wing
21/2/23

Dear Sheila,

I received yours of the 26th Jan on the 19th Feb, my line was
undergoing repairs. As I have now opened a new one I hope
post will be more satisfactory. I was awake on the morning of
the 19th waiting for the volleys which would mean that Mick
Kilroy, Sean Lehane, Tom Daly, Paddy Fleming and some
others have gone over the top and was raging that I was not
fit to go with them. Some hours later I received letters from
you, your Mother and Madge *[Clifford]*, thus changing a very
miserable morning into a happy one. Madge informed me
that all *[blank]* had been circularised re Deasy's proposed
action one week before his letter appeared in the press. I was
in rather bad form the last time I wrote but next morning
realized that the rank and file had always been staunch;
again and again when I was tired of effete senior officers and
went down to the rank and file I was never disappointed, and
now they have fulfilled my expectations. I think it glorious the
manner in which the young lads have faced the firing squads.

Father Mac *[MacMahon]* has not told me about your row in
the hospital and not until I wrote did I know that Maire C
[Comerford] had been wounded. I trust she is now recovered.
Many thanks for information re scrap. I have sufficient
evidence to make them feel small. The Staters are awful
rotters to fire on girls but what else does one expect.

How did Maire find things in Tipp and other places; can
she give me any details of fighting as I am not interested in
destruction of houses, railways, etc. Won't you both now
please write as often as you can.

Guess how many wounds I have. Two went clean through
making a big hole and one came out since. How did you
manage the prison grub? I think it awful and I cannot eat it.
However, the bread is all right and the tea is not too dusty. I

am taking a long time to die, no wonder they call us diehards. I did not get Holy Communion, either, although I got it the morning after I was hit in Portobello, but of course they thought I would die that day, the attitude of the priests is really silly. Paddy Fleming was again removed to the wing; his heart is very weak and he looks wretched yet they will not allow him over to the hospital; indeed the hospital does not represent much, but one is removed from the turmoil of the wings.

Bob Barton and I have a cell each; there is a third cell occupied by [blank] Byrne who is 22 days on hunger-strike. He receives no attention and his cell is locked up at night. There is the ward which contains about 18 beds. Our cells are being whitewashed at present by the "lags". The Governor inserted incandescent gas in my cell, also in Bob's, so the light is less hard on my eyes. Bob B is really awfully good to me, his heart is much too big for his body, he is always trying to make things more comfortable for me, but I would just as soon have things as they are. The spirit in this hospital is good and I always give the lads there whatever news I have. They were delighted on the night of the 19th when I read them Madge's note. Some of them were removed yesterday, I think, to the Curragh and 200 today so they will be able to pull up the spirits of the others. Poor old [Dinny] Lacey is gone, but he was always ready to go and got a soldier's death so what more should one want. The last time I met him in Tipperary Paddy Dalton, Brigade V. Commdt., and [blank] also on the Brigade Staff were with him, and all are now dead. The 2nd Southern always knew how to die, and senior and junior officers have an unbroken record in this from the last scrap. Still their deaths leave an awful gap. I have not got over Sean Treacy's or Paddy O'Brien's death as yet, and now if they execute Kilroy and Sean Lehane and Paddy Fleming I will feel bad. I don't see why they should wait until I am able to stand a trial, sure that's only a farce so what's the use of it. It's too bad to execute the rank and file and leave senior officers untouched. People do not seem to kick up sufficient row about the execution of young lads whose names are unknown to them. What did you guess? I have 12 wounds, there are nine pieces of lead still with me.

We were allowed the papers during the "Amnesty" and they cease today as I expect they are giving us three days grace before they renew the war on the prisoners. I had a note from our Tom *[Derrig]* in which he said to keep my eye on the West, as something big is to be expected there, also he says that the Limerick prisoners were threatened at the revolver point; rather rotten of them to give in when our young lads faced death so gallantly. I expect your beloved Donegal lads have returned to their native county as everything is now all very peaceful there. Is my car still going strong?

I hope you are both all right after the hunger-strike. I have been expecting a note from Miss O'R *[O'Rahilly]* for some time past and indeed if she does not write I will see that the Staters are informed that grenades and revolvers are hidden in front of the house, then the Staters will dig up her "patch"; that's a rather mean revenge though. I had a note from Miss Devaney two days ago; she says there are only 14 girls there now. I am sorry I am not able to write a longer letter at present. Have you any books to read? I am enclosing the sovereign. Please remember me to Mary C. Just think of Joe *[blank]* on the run, isn't it just too lovely for words. I suppose you two are like the other "lags" by this, chewing tobacco, etc. I know you must both hate to have to wear that awful dress but as you never want to wear *[blank]* uniform it won't be too hard. Promise that you won't sign the form and we will be rather relieved. Even if you do you will not lose our respect, as after all you are on the Executive or Staff.

Father Mac has just been back, he says you and Mary C *[?]* are keen on chess; it's a grand old game. B *[Bob]* taught me and I have beaten him in the last two games, and if I beat him in the next it will be something to write home about. Poor old Kerry is rather down and out, but what would you expect. I suppose the West will do Kerry's share of the fight as well as its own. The West is really wonderful. If you had heard David Robinson on Kerry.

The following letter was written on almost his last day in the Hospital Wing of Mountjoy, to Seamus (Jim) O'Donovan, formerly his Director of Chemicals in the Northern and Eastern Command. The third paragraph refers to a matter mentioned briefly in Chapter XIII.

Sean Lehane was then OC of the wing involved, and he regarded O'Malley as the 'Senior Officer' in the prison, competent to deal with such questions.
(This letter to O'Donovan was discovered by the Free State authorities in late July, and copies were made in the usual manner.)

Hospital.
7/4/23

Dear Jim,

Got your note all right. Glad to hear that you are in good form. I have not heard from H.Q. for six weeks, but the C/S seems pleased with the Southern situation. . . . Personally I can see either a complete surrender or an ultimate victory. I would infinitely prefer the former to a compromise. (I blame Sean Hegarty for all this "peace talk".)

Tom Derrig was operated on today. I hear he had lost an eye, and that his condition was rather serious. I had hopes of the best, and of Aiken's area "keeping the ball rolling" with somewhat more energy. I have great faith in the ultimate effectiveness of the Western Divisions. I think it will be difficult to get the 1st and 2nd Southern on their feet again.

I am sorry to see that men are signing the form, more especially those who are awaiting "trial" on a capital charge. I have taken the matter up with Sean Lehane as he has different views on the subject. The enemy will judge such action as a sign of weakness, and will endeavour to bring more pressure to bear.

I hear Mgr. Luzio is all right and I was asked to write him to visit the Joy, but did not. I don't know about the stay on executions, nor care. It seems such an easy matter to us. I think the people outside lay stress on the fact that they are afraid senior officers will be executed. When one realizes that one's life depends on the whim of an I.R.B. clique then the sooner they get rid of us the better. Of course the future is in the hands of God, but "faith without good works is dead".

ERNIE

This letter from Frank Aiken, the IRA Chief of Staff, was smuggled into Mountjoy, but a month later it was discovered either during the course of a routine cell search, or when O'Malley was moved from "A" to "C" Wing. The Free State authorities marked it as 'Document found on Ernie O'Malley, Mountjoy, 25/7/23', and it was to this particular letter that Kevin O'Higgins was to refer when he spoke of reasons for keeping the Republican prisoners in jail and of IRA plans to resume the civil war:

OGLAIGH NA h-EIREANN
(Irish Republican Army)
GENERAL HEADQUARTERS,
DUBLIN.
June 27th, 1923

Dept: C/S
To: E.O'M.

Yours of the 20th June received on 26/6/23.

1. I am sorry to hear that you are still confined to bed. If you were able to move around a little at all you would soon get your strength.

2. It is a splendid idea to start classes. I was never in jail very long myself, but while I was there I was absolutely fed up with the way men used to lounge around.

3. MILITARY ORGANIZATION: Our time is pretty much taken up with our present difficulties so that I have not made a very deep analysis of the real reasons for our failure. I believe your three reasons and the fact that it was a defensive war, and that we always thought the enemy would not go so far, were the principal ones.

4. That question of staff work. There was too much of it done by Division O/C's throughout the country instead of by adjutants, and there wouldn't be call for half as much if the Junior Officers were impressed with the necessity of sending short reports regularly.

With regard to the future; I believe the rifle and revolver is out of date as an offensive weapon, and that rifle men should only be on protection for special corps of engineers. The use of explosives, gas and fire may be concentrated on, also small trench mortars.

ORGANIZATION: Our Organization in the past made for a lot of unnecessary duplication and staff work. You should raise a discussion of this matter and see if it would be better to have County Organization and Battalions, and the present

Divisional Officers merely an Operation and Inspecting Staff. If we have to fight another war with the Staters it will have to be short and sweet, and our units will need to be trained in taking the offensive in large bodies.

NON FIGHTING MEN: I am continually impressing on Divisions the fact that the lack of Civilian organization to back us was chiefly responsible for our present position and that it is their duty to see that our civilian supporters are organized, also that the Fianna are re-organized and trained at once.

Hoping to have an answer from you soon to my circular to members of original Executive of the 23rd inst., and that you will be soon strong again.

Frank Aiken
Chief of Staff

Soon after the death of Jimmy Mooney, told at the end of Chapter XIII, Ernie O'Malley wrote to the dead boy's mother, and his letter appeared in the Republican paper EIRE a few weeks later.

Mountjoy Prison "C" Wing
20/8/23

Dear Mrs. Mooney,

Please accept my deepest sympathy at the death of your son, Jim. I first met him in hospital last January when he was attached to me as orderly. On removal to "A" Wing he insisted on accompanying me, and the Deputy allowed it. Later he was removed with me to "C" Wing. He has been very attentive to me and has helped to nurse me through several illnesses—indeed without him I would have been in a bad plight.

Prior to his last attack he had not complained of any illness, though like most of us here he had not been in such good health since his removal from "A" Wing. On Tuesday last he collapsed in the exercise yard; later had something like an epileptic fit, in the evening he was removed to the prison hospital and later to St. Bricain's. I feel his loss keenly, as do the other lads in the Wing where he was a general favourite. I will forward his belongings to the prison authorities and ask them to have them sent on to you.

Very sincerely yours,
Ernie O'Maille

The Republican bulletin, SINN FEIN, constantly made reference to Ernie O'Malley and his dangerous state of health, from the start to the end of the hunger-strike, and beyond. On 31 October, the front-page gave him special prominence:

Ernie O'Malley T.D.

Ernie O'Malley, one of the bravest soldiers who ever fought for the Independence of Ireland, is now lying at death's door.

Since the declaration of independence was signed at Easter 1916, this man has received no less than 17 wounds in the fight to uphold it. During the war against the Black and Tans, he endeared himself to the people by his great bravery. His famous escape from Kilmainham Jail with Frank Teeling (at the time due for the gallows) and his adventures in a lorry from Kilkenny to Dublin, when he was taken out on the road twice to be hanged, are still spoken of with bated breath. In the six months preceding the Truce, he was mainly responsible for holding the 2nd Southern Division IRA together. He is a man admired and loved even by his enemies. And now lying once more in Kilmainham Jail, with his former comrades for captors, with his wounds opening again from the low state of his health, Ernie O'Malley only says that his body is "crocked" and will always be, and so he is willing to die, especially if by so doing he may save the lives of the other men. This is in keeping with his letter to the late Liam Lynch, Chief of Staff, IRA, when he remarked of his pending execution that "Another bit of lead won't do me any harm." Such bravery surely cannot be defeated even by death.   At the recent Elections in North Dublin constituency, 9785 First Preference votes were cast for the principles for which Ernie O'Malley is now giving his valuable life. It must be obvious to his jailers that should he die, these people have to be reckoned with.

INDEX OF NAMES